ROYAL DUKES

'An excellent book, exciting, wise and ironic . . . Mr. Fulford gives us a series of sober and most intelligent psychological studies of these men. They live in his pages – the foolish but amiable Frederick, Duke of York, the simple and touching William IV, the Duke of Kent, martinet, the detested (but not entirely unpleasing) Duke of Cumberland, Augustus of Sussex and Adolphus Frederick of Cambridge.'

Walpole

The caricature on the cov—— cess of Wales, the Prin—— man, Princess Ch—— Mrs. Carey, the l—— Sussex.
—— Jordan, the Duke of

ROYAL DUKES

THE FATHER
AND UNCLES OF
QUEEN VICTORIA

Roger Fulford

Revised by the author for the 1973 edition

COLLINS

Fontana Books

First published 1933
New and revised edition published by Wm. Collins 1973
First issued in Fontana Books 1973

© Roger Fulford 1933
© in the revised edition, Roger Fulford 1973

Printed in Great Britain
Collins Clear-Type Press
London and Glasgow

TO MY MOTHER

CONTENTS

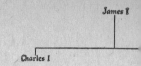
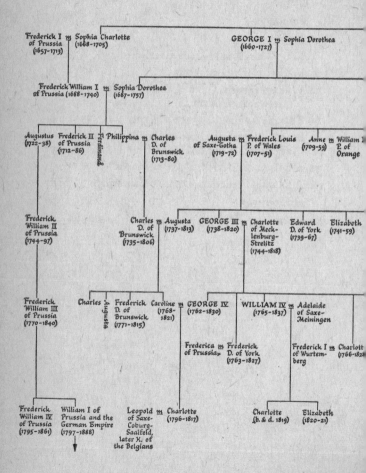

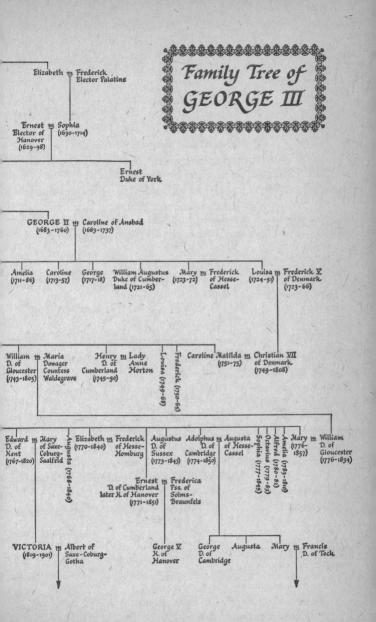

Family Tree of GEORGE III

Elizabeth m Frederick Elector Palatine

Ernest m Sophia
Elector of (1630–1714)
Hanover
(1629–98)

Ernest
Duke of York

GEORGE II m Caroline of Ansbad
(1683–1760)   (1683–1737)

Amelia   Caroline   George   William Augustus   Mary m Frederick   Louisa m Frederick V
(1711–86)   (1713–57) (1717–18) Duke of Cumber-   (1723–72) of Hesse- (1724–51) of Denmark
                                 land (1721–65)   Cassel   (1723–66)

William m Maria   Henry m Lady   Louisa   Frederick   Caroline Matilda m Christian VII
D. of   Dowager   D. of   Anne   (1749–68) (1750–65)   (1751–75)   of Denmark
Gloucester Countess   Cumberland Horton   (1749–1808)
(1743–1805) Waldegrave (1745–90)

Edward m Mary   Elizabeth m Frederick   Augustus   Adolphus m Augusta   Sophia   Alfred   Amelia m William
D. of   of Saxe-   (1770–1840) of Hesse-   D. of   D. of   of Hesse- (1777–1848) (1780–82) (1783–1810) D. of
Kent   Coburg-   Augusta   Homburg   Sussex   Cambridge Cassel   Octavius   Mary   Gloucester
(1767–1820) Saalfeld   (1768–1840)   (1773–1843) (1774–1850)   (1779–83) (1776–   (1776–1834)
                                                                                          1857)
                                                Ernest m Frederica
                                                D. of Cumberland Pss. of
                                                later K. of Hanover Solms-
                                                (1771–1851)   Braunfels

VICTORIA m Albert of   George V   George   Augusta   Mary m Francis
(1819–1901) Saxe-Coburg-   K. of   D. of   D. of Teck
            Gotha   Hanover   Cambridge

ILLUSTRATIONS

Between pages 96 and 97

George III, Queen Charlotte, Princess Caroline of Brunswick and the Prince of Wales by Richard Livesey (*National Trust*)

'Exercising a Hobby from Wales to Hertford!!' – the Regent and Lady Hertford, by Marks, 1819 (*British Museum*)

'The Rival Queans – or a Scene in the Beggars Opera' – the Duke of York, Mrs. Clarke and Mrs. Carey, by Williams, 1809 (*British Museum*)

The Duke of York on the Horse Guards

The Duke of Cambridge, by Thomas Lawrence (*by gracious permission of Her Majesty the Queen*)

The Duke of Cambridge as seen by a French caricaturist, 1803 (*British Museum*)

Between pages 224 and 225

The Duke of Clarence as William IV by Andrew Morton (*Mr. Philip Ziegler*)

'An Illustrious Character' – the Duke of Clarence, by James Gillray, 1802 (*British Museum*)

'A Rejected Trifle from Cumberland to Hanover' – the Duke of Cumberland, by J. Cruickshank, 1814 (*British Museum*)

The Duke of Cumberland, by George Dawe (*National Portrait Gallery*)

The Duke of Kent, by William Beechey (*National Portrait Gallery*)

The Duke of Sussex, by the Reverend Walter Sneyd (*Mr. and Mrs. Robin Bagot*)

'Droits Droits Droits!!!' by J. Cruickshank, 1808 (*British Museum*)

TABLES

FOREWORD

THE father and uncles of Queen Victoria may seem to many people trivial subjects for biography. They are still regarded to-day very much as Peter Pindar (Junior) wrote of them in the second decade of the nineteenth century:

> *Happy as birds, that with each other pair*
> *And warble out their songs devoid of care:*
> *So did these Princes, frolicsome and gay,*
> *Pass free from spleen the jovial hours away.*
>
> *At routs they shone, or blaz'd at grand reviews,*
> *Held levées, talk'd of politics, and news,*
> *But chiefly with the ladies shew'd their parts,*
> *And made sad havoc 'mongst the female hearts.*

The question whether their public lives were quite so trivial, and their private lives quite so scandalous as is generally supposed, must be decided after this book has been read. I only wish to emphasise here one misfortune from which their reputations have suffered.

When Lord Melbourne told Queen Victoria some of the private history of her uncles, her Diary registered no shock, but after she had married Prince Albert in 1840, she completely identified herself with the slightly prudish virtue of her husband's family — the Coburgs — and tried to forget the virile qualities of her father's family. The result was that a heavy curtain of modesty was drawn across the history of their lives. This was unfortunate, as it has given the impression that things were far worse than they actually were. Many writers have peeped behind the curtain and, retailing some tit-bit, have contrived to give the impression that it still conceals a really shocking scene. I have adopted a bolder, more inquisitive and, I think, distinctly fairer attitude by drawing back the curtain and allowing people to judge for themselves.

I have omitted a chapter on George IV partly because his life and character are well known and partly because both appear sufficiently from the lives of his younger brothers. A list of authorities will be found at the end of the book, grouped according to chapters.

I have received a great deal of help with this book. The officials at the London Library, the librarians at the Reform Club and the officials at the British Museum never seem to have minded taking any amount of trouble on my behalf. The librarians at the Foreign Office, the War Office and the Admiralty have given me much valuable advice. My friend, Mr Noel Blakiston of the Record Office, has helped me with the papers from the Lord Chamberlain's Office at the Record Office.

For the Duke of Kent, Colonel Neale, whose grandfather wrote a life of the Duke, allowed me to go through his grandfather's papers.

For the Duke of Sussex, Mr John Gore – whose great-aunt was the Duke's wife – has given me much private information. Lord Leicester has allowed me to see the letters from the Duke to Coke of Norfolk preserved at Holkham. The Librarian to the House of Lords has helped me a great deal over the details of the Duke's first marriage, which are to be found in the case describing Sir Augustus d'Este's claim to the Sussex Peerage.

For the Duke of Cambridge, about whom there was very little printed matter, the British Vice-Consul at Hanover and Herr Broxap of Hanover have helped me with such information as there was at Hanover. Sir Augustus FitzGeorge most kindly supplied me with some family history of the Duke. Mr James and Lady Agnes Durham – personal friends of the Duke's elder daughter – and Lord Hylton gave me further information. Sir Francis Newdigate, G.C.V.O., allowed me to see letters from the Duke to a member of his family. Mr E. N. Adler, and Mr Alfred Rubens gave me particulars of the Duke's friendly interest in the Jews.

My friend Mr Alan Harris read through the typescript and my sister has helped me with the difficult task of indexing.

The frontispiece is reproduced by gracious permission of His Majesty the King, and the portrait of the Duke of Sussex by permission of the Fishmongers Company.

For all this help I acknowledge my deep sense of gratitude.

EXMOUTH,   R. F.
February 1933

PREFACE

❦

READING this book through for the first time since I wrote it forty years ago I have naturally noticed passages which, in maturity, I should express differently and passages which may have seemed light-heartedly amusing when they were written and now seem more laboured. But I have decided not to re-write them; moreover I have thought it best to let the book stand virtually as it was written. A great deal of new material has been published about Regency days and the personalities living then; over the past four decades the period has received much attention from biographers and historians and I have, here and there, used their material to correct things which were wrong. But the book which I wrote was based on the feelings and opinions of contemporaries of the Royal Dukes so far as they were available at that time. Subsequent books have greatly widened and deepened our knowledge of them but their characters and their impact on their own generation have not, in my judgment, been materially changed. The 1933 book therefore stands, as it was written, with a few additions and a few corrections of fact. I have left intact all my rather severe observations about King George IV – though forty years on I totally disagree with them.

During the past thirty-five years, Professor Aspinall, who alas! died as this was being written, has contributed to our knowledge about the Royal Family in the fifty years following 1780 by publishing five important volumes of the correspondence of George III and eleven volumes of the correspondence of George IV. Those who come after will be forever grateful to him for his learning and enviable mastery of the subject. The first chapter of this book has been largely re-written, and by gracious permission of Her Majesty The Queen I have been allowed to quote from the published volumes of these letters.

Reading through the Foreword to the 1933 book I am

conscious that I was ungenerous in two respects. I forgot to thank Mr Harold Lowenstein, who most generously put his knowledge of German at my disposal. Secondly my thanks to Mr Alan Harris were inadequate. He devoted much time to improving the style of the book, and with unflagging charm purged it of many impurities of grammar and some impurities of taste.

I also wish to acknowledge now something which I utterly failed to do at the time – this was the generous praise written about the book by Mr Hugh Walpole. I accepted it with complacency; I remember it now with gratitude and pride. I also offer my belated thanks to Mr Handasyde Buchanan. When *Royal Dukes* was first published he had recently opened a bookshop in Curzon Street, and passing it I noticed that his window was entirely filled with copies of my book. I did not then know him but instead of going inside to thank him I went on my way thinking, 'A very sensible bookseller – he knows what is likely to sell.' I am glad after forty years to confess my vanity and express my true gratitude.

CHAPTER I

KING GEORGE AND QUEEN CHARLOTTE

MECKLENBURG-STRELITZ is a small State in the north of Germany. It is surrounded to the north, east and south by Prussia and to the west by its larger namesake of Mecklenburg-Schwerin. It is rather smaller than the county of Sussex, and, as Horace Walpole tells us, could only be found on the map with the help of a magnifying-glass. In the eighteenth century it was ruled by a ducal family whose members never distinguished themselves, although the second Duke had achieved a little fame from the beautiful dressing-gowns he made. In 1760 the reigning Duke, his three brothers, and two sisters were living, together with the Dowager Duchess, on an income of £15,000, which was a fractional part of the income of an English Duke. Life at Chatsworth or Blenheim must have been on a grander scale than in the palace at Strelitz, where there was study for the boys in the morning, and needlework for the girls, dancing or music in the evening, bed punctually at ten, and best clothes on Sundays. Everything at Strelitz was, in fact, so obscure, so German, and so middle-class that a happier hunting-ground for a Hanoverian Queen of England could not be imagined.

And of the little company of brothers and sisters at Strelitz none was so plain, none so respectable, as the Princess Charlotte. But by a fortunate accident she stood out conspicuously among the lovely obscurities of German Royalty.

In 1760 Frederick the Great, who, in alliance with England, was waging what is now called the Seven Years' War, against Austria and France, soundly defeated the Austrians at Torgau. A close, ungenerous man, he allowed himself no extravagance but the lives of other people, and after every battle his cry went up for more soldiers. It was a cry that had to be answered far outside the boundaries of Prussia. And the Dukes and the Grand Dukes, the Electors and the Serene Highnesses, the Kings and the Prince Bishops, who surrounded Prussia, were bribed and bullied into sending their *quota* of men. Mecklenburg-Strelitz was no exception, and her industries were idle and her fields untilled in order that her sons might be butchered to make the King of Prussia great.

The Princess Charlotte, looking out of the window at Strelitz, saw the misery of the good Mecklenburgers and, laying aside her embroidery, sat down to write to the King of Prussia. She assured him that she knew it was unbecoming one of her sex, in that age of vicious refinement, to lament the horrors of war. 'I am not expert at description,' she wrote, but proceeded to paint a vivid picture of the terrible state of 'my dear country,' and begged him in the name of humanity to spare it any further exactions. Frederick was unmoved. The mills of Prussian policy could not be expected to grind less surely because of the vapourings of a seventeen-year-old girl, and the cause of the Mecklenburgers was not advanced. But it was otherwise with the cause of Charlotte. Her action appealed to the romantic minds of the Prussian Court, steeped in the doctrines of Voltaire. They almost caught, in the stilted phrases, an echo of some classical heroine throwing herself on the mercy of a tyrant. The English Ambassador at Berlin sent a copy of the letter to England. This pleasant story, though believed in former days, is almost certainly apocryphal.

In England the Princess of Wales was at her wits' end. Her father-in-law, King George II, had died, and her son, King George III, was King. Popular, educated, young, handsome, good and, above all, English, he was expected by his mother to restore the monarchy from the depths to which it had been dragged by the vulgarities of those peppery, rather unsuccessful militarists, King George I and King George II. In 1660 Charles II had been restored to the throne of his fathers, and now the Princess of Wales planned that 1760 should see a second Restoration which should put an end to constitutional monarchy. The revolution of 1689 and the accession of George I in 1714 were to be episodes, not foundation-stones, in English history. Everything seemed propitious. Then all at once the Court began to chatter. The King was in love. They had seen him at a Court ball edge his chair nearer and nearer to a teen-age girl and become so engrossed in talking to her that he completely forgot to dismiss the dancers. She was Charles II's great-granddaughter, Lady Sarah Lennox. But his mother knew that George III was not Charles II, and saw the terrible danger ahead. Charles II had been satisfied by many mistresses; his Hanoverian kinsman could only be satisfied with a wife. If he married Lady Sarah, it meant the end of everything – the end of those laborious days poring over Lord Bolingbroke's *Patriot King* and the end of her exhortations, 'George, be a King.' For, to the Princess of Wales, her son might just as well marry a Negress as marry outside the Royal Houses of Europe. It was not for nothing that she had been born a Saxe-Gotha. But she was a clever woman. There were no scenes, no reproaches. She merely waited. Very soon Lady Sarah, anxious to force the King's hand, flirted in front of him with someone else. Within a few months, Princess Charlotte was leaving Strelitz to become the Queen of England.

She set out to marry King George III in September 1761 and had the kind of crossing with which Britannia often hails the consorts of her sovereigns. (Did not Prince Albert tell Queen Victoria that, when he landed at Dover for his wedding, his face looked more like a wax-candle than a human visage?) Twice Princess Charlotte sighted Flamborough Head and twice the yacht, which had been named the *Royal Charlotte*, was blown back almost to Norway. She arrived at St James's Palace in the afternoon of 8th September. Her bridegroom, the King is supposed to have whispered to her later in the day 'never be alone with my mother: she is an artful woman and will try to govern you';[1] they were married on the evening of the day she came, in the Chapel Royal in St James's Palace,

[1] *Lives of the Hanoverian Queens of England* by A. D. Greenwoode, vol. ii, p. 16.

and in the course of the service an anthem was sung, with a solo by the celebrated actor and vocalist, Mr Beard, 'Instead of thy fathers thou shalt have children, whom thou mayst make princes in all lands.'[1] That was a pronouncement which the future was to prove resoundingly true. In the following year, on 12th August, her eldest son was born; on 17th August he was created Prince of Wales and was to be in the future — Prince Regent and George IV. Twenty-two years later, on 7th August, 1783, the youngest child Princess Amelia was born. In a passage in *Nicholas Nickleby* (which is possibly a shade indelicate), Dickens makes a character, who was inordinately proud of one of his children, say that he was certain that this child was to have been 'a closer'. He meant by this that many people commonly believed that on the youngest member of a large family peculiar qualities of grace and character were bestowed by nature. That characteristic benefaction of the youngest of a large family may well have been bestowed on Princess Amelia. But this is incontestable; the strength, the physical robustness and the noisy energy of the older members of the family did not extend to the youngest. Indeed it could be said that the stamina of the family was by then diminished. Princess Amelia was never strong, and the two Princes before her, Alfred and Octavius, died in infancy. Horace Walpole argues that the boys both died from an 'hereditary humour', which was brought into the Royal Family by Princess Augusta of Saxe-Gotha, the 'artful woman' against whom King George III had warned his wife. Hereditary illnesses in royal persons are a fascinating by-way of historical studies, but as Walter Scott remarked of antiquarian researches, they resemble an old lady's knitting which occupies the attention but not the brain. The Princess in question died from a cancer of the breast, the sufferings from which she bore with invincible fortitude, and there is no evidence whatsoever that she passed to her grandchildren any taint, humour or malaise be it scrofulous, scorbutic or phlegmatic. In short the great majority of the family of King

[1] The Annual Register, 1761.

George III was healthy; no morbid symptoms embarrassed their sturdy frames.

More important than speculation about the health of the family is the proven fact of its size. Fifteen princes and princesses could claim no rivals for quantity in the reigning bedchambers of Europe. Some may be tempted to set in competition against King George and Queen Charlotte the great breeding house of Habsburg-Lorraine. It is true that the Empress Maria Theresa had one more child than had Queen Charlotte, but of her 16, eight died between their birth and the age of sixteen. And if we carry the story further – her son the Grand Duke of Tuscany, who was trained for the priesthood, had a family of sixteen children but they were all born before he reigned in Vienna as Emperor. Nor in recorded English history is there anything to set against this prolific family; Edward III, whose numerous sons were to bring tribulation on the Kingdom, had a total of eleven children. King James I's daughter, the Queen of Bohemia, through whom the House of Hanover inherited the Crown of England, had a family of thirteen. Judged therefore by any standard – national or European – the achievement of King George and Queen Charlotte was noticeable, and we are certainly right to remark it and perhaps to excuse it.

II

12th August, 1778, was the sixteenth birthday of the Prince of Wales and there was great excitement at Bulstrode Park where Mrs Delany, a close friend of Queen Charlotte's, was staying with the Dowager Duchess of Portland. The Royal Family were expected to breakfast. They were driving over from Windsor which was about nine miles away and Mrs Delany watched them coming up the drive. The King was driving the Queen in a phaeton and pair. The Prince of Wales and Prince Frederick were trotting behind on horseback. A post chaise and four followed, in which the Princess Royal, who was twelve, was nursing the youngest boy, Prince Adolphus, aged four. In a coach and six came Princess

Augusta, aged ten, Princess Elizabeth, aged eight, Prince William, aged thirteen, and Prince Edward, aged eleven. They all got down and came clattering into the hall. The King asked if he might show the Prince of Wales and Prince Frederick the pictures in the dining-room, and while this was being done the Queen talked to Mrs Delany about *chenille* work in which Mrs Delany used to embroider large, and rather inartistic, flower subjects. The whole family then came and admired the Duchess's china closet, the young ones observing most carefully the curiosities and asking a multitude of questions: the girls skipping along by their father and mother, the boys whistling and trying not to look too interested. They all sat down to breakfast, 'the Royals' – as Mrs Delany calls them – eating abundantly. Before going, the King pressed the Duchess and Mrs Delany to come over to Windsor the following day to see 'all my family.'

When the ladies reached Windsor the next evening, they were welcomed by the Queen and her daughters; in addition to the three who had driven over to Bulstrode, she had with her Princess Mary, who was two, and Princess Sophia, who was one. Punctually at seven the King came in followed by his seven sons. Prince Ernest, aged seven, and Prince Augustus, aged six, were the two who had not been over to Bulstrode. After the Royal Family had strolled on the terrace in order that the people might see them, the rooms were lighted up, music played, and tea was served. The children began to dance together, and in the intervals came up and made themselves pleasant to Mrs Delany. Presently she heard the King say to the Prince of Wales 'that they had better dance no more to that music being composed of *hautbois* and other wind music as he thought it must be painful to them to play any longer but at the Queen's House they should have properer music and dance as long as they liked.'[1]

Here the two eldest Princes danced a minuet, and then the Prince of Wales danced with the Princess Royal, who Mrs Delany thought did not keep very good time. Finally Princess

---

[1] While Windsor Castle was being restored by George III the Royal Family lived in a house in the precincts known as the Queen's House.

Mary and Prince Adolphus took the floor and romped round in a dance of their own composing. Mrs Delany got home by moonlight, charmed with the family and feeling far less tired than she had expected.

The excellence of Queen Charlotte as a wife lay in the fact that she took not the slightest interest in politics, and never had the least political influence, but was content to make a home for her husband who, she realised, was at heart a domestic man and only by force of circumstances a politician. In creating this domestic atmosphere, she was certainly fortunate in living in houses in which privacy was possible and in which the etiquette of Court life could be dropped. George I and George II had lived in St James's Palace and for a country retreat had gone down to Hampton Court or Kensington Palace. While it was unlikely that two Kings, whose chief interests were Hanover and mistresses, would have lived a domestic life anywhere, it was impossible in those particular palaces. It is unthinkable that a large family of young children should scamper through the stately stiffness of Hampton Court or Kensington Palace and still more so that they should knock into ambassadors and Court functionaries inevitably haunting the official centre of the monarchy at St James's. No King, while on the throne, had had a large family to bring up since Charles I, when the palaces of Whitehall, Woodstock, and Oatlands were far more homely than the barren stateliness of Hampton Court and Kensington Palace which the childless William III designed for the Kings of England. As soon as they were married, King George and Queen Charlotte realised the difficulties inevitable to life in St James's Palace: and in 1761 George III bought Buckingham House for the Queen at a cost of £21,000. This had been built by Sheffield, Duke of Buckingham, at the beginning of Queen Anne's reign and was a smallish, red-brick house, similar to the present Marlborough House. It was subsequently known as the Queen's House and in 1775 was settled on Queen Charlotte in exchange for Somerset House. The King and Queen lived here in a minimum of state, partly because the house would not have held a crowd of officials, and the Queen retired here for all her earlier lyings-in. The pomp and circumstance of the Court was reserved for St James's Palace. For country air they would go down to Kew where the Princess of Wales lived and spent her time planning the Gardens with Lord Bute, or – as their enemies whispered – engaged in closer intimacies. After the Princess of Wales's death in 1772 the King and Queen spent much more time at Kew. Finding the house very small, George III decided to pull it down and to build on its site a pseudo-Gothic mansion with the help of Mr Wyatt. This was never finished, but while it was raising its castellated head the Royal Family lived in what was then called the Dutch House and which is the present Kew Palace. After 1775 they lived less and less at the Queen's House in London and divided their time between Kew and Windsor. It was a great step forward in humanising the monarchy when the monarchs left stately palaces for comfortable homes.

In any case it was difficult for the King and Queen not to lead a domestic life with fifteen children and they spent much time and care in arranging the home life of their family. The boys were to work together in groups according to their ages, and each little group had its own house on Kew Green, while the Prince of Wales and Prince Frederick had as well their own suite in the Queen's House in London. Kew was the headquarters of the family life. When the King and Queen were at Kew Palace, the Princes would come up from their houses on the Green to join their parents at breakfast. They would then scatter to work for the morning while the younger children went out into the gardens. On Thursdays, Kew was opened to the public, and the people, flocking into the Gardens or coming up the river with bands of music, would see the Royal Children playing in the distance. The elder Princes might be seen at their model farm which was supervised by Arthur Young, or playing at single wicket cricket, at which game they were said to have no equal. Once a week the King and Queen walked to Richmond Gardens accompanied by the Princes and Princesses in pairs.

Naturally, from their position, there were elements which

were unusual in the lives of English children. For example, at the age of seven months Prince Frederick became a Bishop. The explanation of this being that the see of Osnabrück in Hanover was, alternately with the Emperor, in the gift of the King of England as Elector of Hanover. As there were considerable emoluments attached to the Bishopric, George III was anxious to keep it in his own family when in 1764 the right of appointment fell to him. Until he was created Duke of York, Prince Frederick was always known as the Bishop of Osnabrück and his first set of china, made specially for him by Mr Wedgwood, was stamped with his mitre. The infantile, but Right Reverend, Father in God was admittedly an unusual character to meet in English family life.

Then in 1769 the English nobility had been really rather shocked. They had had to go and make their curtsies and their bows to the Royal Children. At one end of the room there was a dais on which were standing the Prince of Wales, aged seven, in scarlet and gold, wearing the Order of the Garter, the Bishop of Osnabrück, aged six, in blue and gold, wearing the Order of the Bath, while the Princess Royal, aged three, was seated on a sofa between Prince William, aged four, and Prince Edward, aged two, who were 'elegantly dressed in togas according to the Roman custom.' The Press took up the cause of the outraged noblemen, and caricatures soon appeared of the greatest in the land humbling themselves before the Prince of Wales, who was flying a kite, the Bishop, who was astride a hobby horse, and the youngest Princess, who was receiving sustenance from a wet nurse behind a screen.

But such things were the penalties of Royalty, not incidents of family life. There may have been an outcry at the time against the King or the Queen but it very soon died down and was lost in the steady murmur against them on account of the quiet, economical, almost recluse life that they led. Of course this murmur only came from a section of the people, but it was that section of the people who wrote letters and kept diaries and whose voice is most clearly heard to-day. Nor was it unreasonable. Disappointed placemen who only regarded the King as a fountain of honours, and the Queen as a figure off whom should tumble a cascade of posts and pensions, were naturally aggrieved. The lack of fashion and of vice in the head of society shocked the aristocracy. Mr Walpole, with that exact knowledge of domestic science only acquired by bachelors, complained 'the Queen's *friseur* waits on them at table and that only four pounds of beef were allowed for their soup.'

But such criticisms should have died with the critics, and we ought now to be able to look back and appreciate King George and Queen Charlotte at their true worth. It is not easy. For one thing we have to pierce the fog of what may be called the purely ignorant school. A typical specimen of this was that devoted medical friend of Prince Albert and Queen Victoria, the Baron Stockmar, who lived in Coburg. He was consulted as to the education of Queen Victoria's children, and, in one of his long, neat memoranda, explained that having regard to the sons of George III, 'the Royal Children must be given an education at once thoroughly moral and thoroughly English.' The Coburg doctor was no doubt an authority on many things, possibly on morality and, having lived for a few months with Princess Charlotte and Prince Leopold at Claremont, he no doubt regarded himself as an authority on everything English. But the Court life of George III, which was before his time, would appear to have escaped his attention. What could be more moral than a home where no breath of scandal ever touched the parents and where the tutors of the boys were either Bishops or Bishops-to-be? What could be more English than life at Kew with a father who never in his life set foot on foreign soil?

Another difficulty in seeing a clear picture of King George and Queen Charlotte is that we are blinded by what may be called 'the candlelight school.' There are many people who can only picture the eighteenth century as filled with wits and graceful *belles* simpering together at routs, gracing a ballroom and recovering again at Bath, always in a perfect blaze of candlelight. And in this picture of elegant brilliance there could be no place for a King who rose at six o'clock in the morning and, knocking on his children's doors, inquired how each had passed the night, or for a Queen who could say of her magnificent jewellery 'Believe me Miss Burney it is the pleasure of a week – a fortnight at most – and to return no more!' The result has been that the life of the King and Queen has been regarded as something unnatural and quite outside the eighteenth century, as something which explained and justified the character of that Prince Charming of 'the candlelight school,' George IV.

For a true picture of King George and Queen Charlotte it is necessary to remember the background. There are the shadowy figures of George I, completely unintelligible to his subjects, and George II stuffing his yacht with treasure at the time of the '45, really rather glad at the prospect of getting back to Hanover with some pleasant (and valuable) mementoes of his stay in England. From these rather funny, utterly foreign tenants of the throne, liable to notice to quit at any moment, George III stands out as a permanent British figure who never in his life visited Hanover. The acuteness of Queen Charlotte lay in the fact that, although she always spoke English through a suggestion of guttural German, she could yet strip herself of her German upbringing and join her husband in a normal English life. The Princess of Wales was right. 1760 was a Restoration, English life was restored to the monarchy.

And seeing the King and Queen in their proper background, we can look back behind the fashionable world with its masked parties at Vauxhall Gardens, its orgies at Carlton House, its gambling at Brooks's and its elopements to Gretna Green and see the emergence of the middle classes, the manufacturers profiting from the birth of the Industrial Revolution. The mistake made by 'the candlelight school' is that they forget that for every Horace Walpole there were scores of Squire Westons, for each Miss Gunning or Duchess of Devonshire there were hundreds of women quietly busy with their preserves or their embroidery, and for each period house at Bath there were thousands of hovels witnessing the scenes of coarse degradation portrayed for us by Hogarth. As the middle classes awoke to political consciousness it was particularly fortunate that they could see a reflection of themselves in the life of their King and Queen. They were always ready to attack the Bishops, the Peers and the privileged classes but the monarchy they regarded as a part of themselves. A comparison with France may make this more obvious. Louis XVI, by his natural skill and *bourgeois* tastes, would have made an excellent watchmaker, but his wife was regarded as an unsympathetic aristocrat and dragged down the monarchy into the general unpopularity of things privileged. Farmer George alone, therefore, could not have reconciled the middle classes to the monarchy, but the Queen and he achieved it together. Years later, when the King was finally and hopelessly mad, the Queen could write to her eldest son of 'my anxious desire to preserve society upon the respectable footing which it has ever been my own and the King's study to maintain.' To argue that a middle-class King and Queen saved the monarchy is possibly an exaggeration, but it shored it up to withstand the storms ahead. The tragedy of King George's and Queen Charlotte's lives was that, with the possible exception of William IV and the Duke of Cambridge, their sons were anything but middle class.

But the King and Queen are only the background to this book: we are concerned with their sons. And what of the whole family – of the fifteen themselves or, to exclude the two princes dying in infancy, what of the thirteen? The last survivor of the family, Mary Duchess of Gloucester, who died in the 1850's, deep in the reign of Queen Victoria, once tersely remarked: 'There were too many of us.' She was not, we may suspect, voicing here the conventional complaint of members of a large family – too many for privacy, too many for individual enjoyment of things within the home, too many for the particular attention of the parents. Rather we may suppose that she was thinking of those jolts, disagreements, squabbles, which were magnified by numbers and enhanced by the position which they filled. A glaring example of this was the question of the Regency in 1788, when George III went mad, and the elder Princes championed the necessity for a Regent against Pitt and the Government, while the elder princesses were in the opposite camp. What made the position of the Princes difficult, and their lot peculiarly hard, was that there was little enough for them to do. The Prince of Wales had to face the most demoralising of all positions – waiting for an inheritance. The second son, the Duke of York, was a soldier of distinction, but for the rest they passed through life with a star on the breast but few achievements to match their pre-eminence. We can see the contrast at once if we consider the children of Maria Theresa. As the Habsburg sons grew up they became, as is were, satraps of the Habsburg dominions beyond Austria, while the daughters made dynastic marriages or, in one case, assumed the habit and ruled a convent. Such possibilities – either imperial or devoutly celibate – were not available for the Protestant Royal Family and, whatever their matrimonial inclinations may have been, the long-drawn struggle with France barred them from virtually all continental marriages. Consequently the family remained intact to the end of Queen Charlotte's long life in 1818; through youth and maturity to the confines of old age the family life at Windsor remained a force influencing the lives of them all. We can understand though we need not necessarily endorse the remark of one of the Royal Dukes 'Nothing is so terrible in my eyes as a family party.'

For the astonishing fact remains – and it is surely enormously to the credit of the family – that there were no open quarrels, no 'scenes' such as delight chroniclers of the earlier days of the Hanoverian dynasty. It is true that there was a difference between the Duke of York and the Duke of Kent, and it is also true that the Prince of Wales latterly had some disagreements with the Duke of Kent and his younger brothers. But they never cut very deep and they are explained by professional difficulties or the play of politics on family life. It is significant that when the Duke of Kent was mortally ill he sent for his equerry and said 'If I should not survive, if it should please the Almighty to take me, go and give my love to all my brothers and sisters separately.'[1] When the message was given to the Prince Regent he broke down and sobbed without restraint. The Duke of Cumberland, who was certainly not the most feeling of the family, wrote when his

[1] *The Prince And His Lady* by Mollie Gillen, Sedgwick and Jackson, 1970.

eldest sister died whom he had not seen for thirty-one years – she was the Princess Royal and the only one to marry in youth – 'I have hardly a recollection of her: however one can not help feeling deeply when one branch of the old tree drops off.'[1] Although much can be said for and against the eldest of the family – as Prince of Wales, Regent and King – and many biographies of him have been attempted, one point about him is too often overlooked. A large number of letters to him from all his brothers and sisters survive and have been edited, in masterly fashion, by Professor Aspinall.[2] No one could possibly read those letters without being immediately struck in almost every letter by the love and devotion which they show for the oldest of the family. 'G.P.' or Prince of Wales, as he was called within the family, was in a different position from the other twelve; they always called one another by their Christian names.[3] Queen Victoria makes an interesting point here, because even as a girl she had noticed how submissive the Royal Family were to George IV, submission which was in marked contrast to their feelings for William IV.

But over the family 'a shadow lour'd'. The father – the head of the family – was subject from 1788 onwards to periodic fits of madness. A vast literature has developed round King George III so that cocoon-like the outside is too often confused with what is within. This is particularly true of political writers. One example may suffice. Lord Brougham, who was Lord Chancellor under King William IV and who was a writer and speaker of the greatest violence and unpredictability but reflecting the belief and traditions of the Whig Party, tells us that the understanding of the King was narrow and that it was enlarged by no culture, that he had 'a fierce tyrannical disposition' and that the obscuration of his reason

---

[1] *The Daughters of George III* by D. M. Stuart, Macmillan, 1939.
[2] *The Correspondence of George, Prince of Wales* edited by Professor Aspinall, 8 volumes.
[3] I remember seeing a play in the West-end of London many years ago which depicted a scene when the Regent's sisters were entertaining friends at the Brighton Pavilion. One of them said 'Do have some of this – it is George's best champagne'. The phrase jarred at the time, though I had not then realised that the Prince, within the family, was always spoken of formally.

made him extraordinarily suspicious, very unreasonable and dominated by very strong dislikes.[1] Here it can be said that Lord Brougham had no direct knowledge of the King about whom he wrote with such confidence, and probably never even saw him. His sketch of the King, though sharply drawn through his own gifts, was based on what he learned in the inner circles of the Whig Party. Since that time, historians have had no difficulty in erasing the Whig picture and substituting for it something certainly fairer but with the desire to instruct peeping out somewhat too transparently. Therefore if we want to know what the King was really like it is sensible to go back to those who know him and not to those who had or have a political case to argue.

In appearance he was tall, red in the face, well-built but not corpulent. He had a twentieth-century horror of growing fat — possibly encouraged by the spectacle of his uncle, the Duke of Cumberland — the largest prince in Christendom whose charger carried on his back four and twenty stone.[2] George III's determination to keep down his weight was noticed in two ways. He took violent horse-exercise and hunted, during the season, six days a week. When out riding he invariably went at a smart pace so that the gentlemen-in-waiting, accustomed to the comforts of life at court, grumbled at trying to keep up with their master. The other way in which he mastered his weight was by eating and drinking very little. One curious consequence of this was that no one was ever invited to dinner with him. Lord Melbourne told Queen Victoria that owing to the speed and moderation with which he ate it would not have suited him to have company, and that easy-going nobleman added 'that the King would probably not have made it very agreeable for others.'[3] This is not of course to say that the King neglected his public duties — he was available for Ministers, held levées, inspected troops and dockyard establishments. But he was without a private circle of friends, so that the

[1] Lord Brougham 'Political Characters of George III and IV.' *The Edinburgh Review*, October 1838.

[2] Reminiscences of Henry Angelo, i, 33.

[3] Journal of Queen Victoria, vol. ii, p. 94.

family and the Court became his substitutes for friendship.
Many people have thought that this seclusion was encouraged
by his mother. That is incorrect. It was entirely his own doing,
and when he married, he was determined that the Queen
should form no friendship or private circle of her own. No
doubt such was his inclination – but it was in part prompted
by a curious suspicion of the intentions of his fellow-mortals.
Mrs Harcourt, a member of his Court and one of the most
enthusiastic admirers of the King (who kissed him on both
cheeks after his recovery from madness) thought that this
suspicion of people had been planted in him – and carefully
tended – by Lord Bute and that but for this 'he would have
been near perfection.'[1]

There exists an instructive contrast between the character of
King George III and King George IV, which was made by
the third daughter of George III – the Princess Elizabeth.
'My eldest brother' – she wrote – 'was *all heart*. But people
got hold of him, and flattery did more harm in that quarter
than anything. A more generous creature never existed, and
had his talents been properly called out he would have been
very different from what he was . . . My father ever acted on
the finest of feelings and, as an honest man, and with his ideas
of justice would never have done what a man of the world
would have done . . . My brother was always in a dazzle. My
Father was always seeing much further into the danger of
what such and such things would produce.'[2] George III was
cautious, his son was wayward. It is often stated that George
IV disliked his father. This is not the case. Lord Melbourne
told Queen Victoria that he was very fond of his father. Melbourne knew George IV well, and his mother was one of the
inner circle of that King's friends. Many people, gazing at the
great statue of George III in Windsor Park and seeing the
proud words placed on it by George IV *optimus patri* have
smiled, thinking that it reflected what George IV hoped
people would believe rather than what he really felt. In this

---

[1] Mrs Harcourt's Diary of the Court of George III.
[2] D. M. Stuart, *Daughters of George III*, p. 193.

particular he was sincere. But Melbourne adds what is also unquestionably true – 'he was monstrously afraid of him.'[1] In that sentence there certainly lies an indication of the weakness of the son's character but there also lies the explanation for the tragedy of the son's life – his marriage. The importance of this matter in the history of the Royal Family justifies an examination of the point. The future George IV, then Prince of Wales, had been living for several years with Mrs Fitzherbert but he had been made unhappy by Mrs Fitzherbert's atrocious temper and was prepared to embark on what his father would have called 'a more respectable way of life'. The matter was broached between father and son at Weymouth in August 1794, and the son told his father that he wished to marry his first cousin, Princess Caroline of Brunswick, who was niece to the King. The Prince commented thus to his next brother who was campaigning in Holland: 'The King told me I made him quite happy, that it was the only proper alliance, and indeed the one in all respects he should have wished for himself, and the one he should wish to have pointed out to me. I do not say as much for the rest of the family, at least for one person.'[2] The last words are an allusion to his mother, whose niece Princess Louise – in the future to be the heroic Queen of Prussia – was another possible bride. The following letter, written by the Prince to his father, shows at once his expansive nature and perhaps justifies what his enemies used to say that he spoke with his tongue what was not felt by his heart.

Carlton House,
19th Sept., 1794.

Allow me to seize the earliest opportunity after my arrival in London of endeavouring to lay at your feet those feelings of a truly grateful heart and of a truly grateful son, for the gracious and affectionate manner you was pleas'd to express yourself to me as well as to others during my stay at Weymouth respecting my approaching marriage, and which

[1] Queen Victoria's Journal, II, 58.
[2] The corrrespondence of George Prince of Wales, vol. 11, p. 454, edited by Professor Aspinall, Cassell.

at that period really overcame me so entirely that I was not able to give utterance to what passed in my heart.

Believe me, Sir, amongst the many failings to which all men are subject, ingratitude is a vice of which I have not the smallest particle in my composition, and I trust that should my lips and my pen fall short of expressing those sentiments of gratefulness which at this moment occupy my whole mind, the rest of my life will of itself sufficiently bear testimony to the just sense I entertain for Your Majesty's boundless goodness on the present occasion, and which I assure you, Sir, never can be obliterated from my heart. I am too well acquainted how precious your Majesty's time is and how much it is taken up by more essential subjects to trespass any further upon your patience.[1]

Coldly the King replied on the following day 'The thanks you return to me for my expressions on your communicating to me here your desire of marrying my niece the Princess of Brunswick were not necessary; you having done that sufficiently at the time.'[2]

Going back to the Prince's letter we notice that he expresses particular gratification at his choice having met with the King's approval, but as is his wont he wraps up his meaning in language which needs a little explanation. At the end of his letter he refers to the King's expression of pleasure 'at my having myself nominated for my wife the person who was fortunate enough to meet your approbation and in which (i.e. with the King's approval) I wished most ardently to select HER that I hoped would be *most agreeable to you*.'

Now it is obvious that the Prince was influenced – and the present writer would say decisively influenced – by the wish to do what his father wanted or what he knew would please him. That is not of course to the credit of the Prince but it shows the power of the King over the family. He was not only a severe father but, as was perhaps inevitable and correct, he subordinated the instincts of a father to the needs of the nation. He

---

[1] Professor Aspinall, op. cit., vol. ii, p. 459.
[2] Professor Aspinall *The Later Correspondence of George III*, vol. ii, p. 246, Cambridge.

expressed this in words to one of his younger sons 'however much I love my children, that must never make me one instant to lose sight of my duty as Sovereign of this country'.[1]

In addition to this, George III occupied an especial position with his family because of the appalling affliction by which he was visited. If he was a severe father, if his treatment of his family was harsh it had to be endured because to thwart the father might have overset the balance of his reason. We can illustrate the point by one example from our own times. Sir George Sitwell was in the habit of saying to his children in the evening 'I must ask anyone entering the house never to contradict me or differ from me in any way, as it interferes with the functioning of the gastric juices and prevents my sleeping at night.'[2] The respect for the father, strengthened by deference to his position as King was naturally marked in the relations between father and sons. Even the Duke of York, who was the King's favourite in the family, felt it necessary to write in the following terms to tell his father that he was proposing to come to Weymouth 'I beg to return your Majesty my most humble thanks for your gracious permission to pay my duty to your Majesty at Weymouth, and mean to have that honour next Monday.' We should be certainly right in thinking that if the sons of King George III had made their lives and actions conform more nearly to the respect which they showed their father in his presence or in their letters to him the King would have escaped some problems and much sorrow. They certainly did not behave as he would have wished but they felt for him with anguish. And what children of a man thus so afflicted would not have done so? Certainly the insanity of the King, with the problems it created for the Queen and the tragedies for the Princesses, was another strong factor in maintaining the unity of the family.

Rumour has no stronger ally than a royal illness or even a royal indisposition: when the King was taken ill in the autumn of 1788 stories about the unfilial conduct of the elder sons abounded; rumour flew up St James's Street; and as is its

---

[1] Later Correspondence of George III, vol. ii, p. 488.
[2] Sir Osbert Sitwell *Laughter In The Next Room*. Macmillan, 1949. p. 252.

habit it paused at the portals of Brooks's, Boodle's and White's
for a little embellishment. The Princes were supposed to have
told their friends that the King bit anyone who came near him;
and they were also believed to have passed on things which the
King had said such as 'You know I am mopsimus and don't
like French mottoes'. To the Queen one of them was rumoured
to have said 'Madam, I believe that you are nearly as deranged
as the King'. In the Chapter, which follows, on the Duke of
York I have left (page 58) the short passage in which I refer
to the insensitivity of the sons to their father. That was contemporary opinion or gossip and at the time when I was writing, there was nothing else to guide one's opinion. It was
clearly absolutely wrong, as the letters published by Professor
Aspinall now show. When the King was first taken ill and was
still allowed visitors he told the Duke of York, with tears in his
eyes, how happy he had been made by receiving a visit from
the Prince of Wales. To one of their younger brothers the
Prince and the Duke of York sent a joint letter, after the King
had been ill for a few weeks 'We have done everything in our
power to keep it quiet. His complaint is a total loss of all
rationality . . . he is a complete lunatic . . . it is a dreadful
thing indeed.' The third son, the future William IV, who was
serving in the Royal Navy and only heard the news towards
the end of January – 'the shock I first felt was great . . . the best
of Kings and fathers . . . But what are the King's feelings to the
sensations of that dear inestimable woman the Queen'.[1]

The dear, inestimable woman awaits her biographer. In the
meantime we must grope our way towards an understanding of
her strong, unflinching character and quality. As with the
King we should be wise to consider what was thought of the
Queen by those who knew her. Royal persons in those days
were familiar to the small circle of the social and political
aristocracy. Members of the establishment saw them at court
functions and perhaps exchanged civilities. They knew the
surface well enough, but the person below was unperceived.
Many people to-day remember Horace Walpole's assertion
that after the Queen had been in England for some time he

[1] George III's Letters, vol. iii, p. 128.

thought that the bloom of her ugliness was beginning to wear off. Queen Victoria, who of course never knew her, thought that she was 'plain'. Her shortness of stature and a very wide mouth might justify the word, and in old age she certainly became ugly. But as Zoffany's pictures prove she was in youth pleasing and handsome. She was in truth somewhat like the late Queen Mary in miniature. Lord Melbourne told Queen Victoria that she had beautiful hands and a fine figure. Her conversation was set off by a slight foreign accent and, as he told the Queen, she had 'a good manner'.[1] She was severe and a strict moralist; when a lady of tarnished reputation asked the Queen's lady-in-waiting to present her to the Queen the reply was immediate 'tell her that you durst not ask me'. She was a great mistress of the conventions. When she was supervising the wedding-dress of her eldest daughter – in fact the only one of her six daughters to marry in youth – she was heard to say 'As the bride of a widower I know that she ought to be in white and gold: but as the eldest daughter of the King she has a right to white and silver'.[2] The King's family – that is to say his brothers and aunt – seem to have disliked her partly because she was very formal and strict on royal con-ventions. Her eldest sister-in-law complained that for a princess who was by birth a minor Royalty, to give herself airs was something which the King's mother and grandmother, who were also from minor royal houses, had never done.

On the other hand she was obviously very intelligent as we can see from Fanny Burney's diary. Although some may share Charles Greville's view that this particular diary is 'an enorm-ous quantity of trash and twaddle'[3] the trash and the twaddle do not quite disguise the fair picture which she draws of the Queen. She was appreciative of the arts, had a private printing press at Windsor, and wrote several poems; that such tastes were not entirely shallow is suggested from her giving a copy of Lyrical Ballads to a friend soon after it was published.

[1] Queen Victoria's Journal, i, pp. 289, 309, ii, p. 41.
[2] Percy Fitzgerald – Royal Dukes and Princesses of the Family of George III, 1882.
[3] The Greville Memoirs, vol. v., p. 58. 1938.

One thing is abundantly clear. Whatever her appearance may have been and whatever the formality with which she confronted the outside world she was by nature gay and light-hearted. For this there are two pieces of evidence – both conclusive. In her diary Mrs Harcourt tells us that she had often heard from her husband,[1] who went with his father when he fetched the Queen from Mecklenburg-Strelitz, that no character ever had more natural gaiety. The second piece of evidence comes from very much later in life when she was a matriarch who was feared by all her children and disliked by some. The letters written to her by her eldest son show that, old and miserable and battered by circumstances as she was, she still kept her enjoyment of life – her sense of fun. She was much attached to – and greatly amused by Sir Thomas Tyrwhitt, a devoted but diminutive courtier. In royal circles he was variously known as 'our little dwarf' or 'the dear old Saint'. Writing to his mother the Prince Regent said that he had thought of a little *bon mot* of his own to amuse her. 'Why do I call "our little dwarf" the 23rd of June? Because he is the *shortest night*'. Warming to his task he said that he had been tempted to borrow from the Hunterian Museum one of the little embryos (on peutêtre ce que l'on peut appeler aussi *fausse couche* sans se tromper beaucoup de nom): he then intended to adorn it with the appropriate ribands and send it to the Queen as 'a cadeau to have ornamented the mantelpiece of your sitting-room as the perfect resemblance and portraiture of our little hero'. Possibly a little broad for all tastes but certainly not a letter which even a favourite son would write to one who was ruled by the grim decorum of the palace or by manners which were cold and punctilious.

There remains the large question of the relations between the parents of these remarkable children. No doubt to the twentieth-century mind, often languid from a tiring spell on the psychoanalyst's couch, the answer is simple. The King, unable to marry the lady whom he admired (Lady Sarah

---

[1] This is printed in the diary as 'Gen Hanaut', but this is clearly a misreading for Harcourt, whose father was sent by George III to bring the Princess to England.

Lennox), was compelled to marry the Princess (whom he had never had the chance to see) and her severe outlook on life and searching temper drove him mad. That may well be so — indeed there are scraps of evidence for it. At the height of his attack in 1788 he was overheard to say that he was fond of a little dog 'Badine' because it liked him but did not like the Queen. He went on that he had never liked her, that she had a bad temper, and that her children were afraid of her.[1] One of her younger daughters wrote to the Prince Regent in 1812 'It was the object of the dear King's life to keep from the world *all* he *suffered* and *went through* with *her temper*.'[2] That might be thought to dispose of the matter but this, in fairness, must be said. We all know that one of the commonest companions of insanity is a revulsion against those with whom the victim is most closely associated and on whom he or she is most dependent. Greville adds a most pertinent comment in his diary: after recording the sentence about Badine he adds 'Nothing proves him more unlike Himself than this.'

It is also fair to remember one or two points which enable us to judge matters rather more from the Queen's side. Mrs Harcourt points out that when she came to England, the King made it clear that she was to have no society apart from his and no friends apart from him. This was literally carried out, and Mrs Harcourt points out that she never spoke to a soul other than the King, except for half an hour a week, when she sat in a funeral[3] circle with her Ladies of the Bedchamber. She was in fact confined as in a convent. She herself wrote of 'the dear King's great strictness, at my arrival in England, to prevent my making many acquaintances . . . the King's reason was that it was difficult in England to make a society without Party.'[4] Certainly after the King's reason had finally fled, she treated her daughters with severity — savagery might be a better word — but she clearly felt that her daughters had to sacrifice gaiety, independence and private friendship to show

---

[1] *Diaries of R. F. Greville*, edited by F. M. Bladon, 1930.
[2] D. M. Stuart, *op. cit.*, p. 105.
[3] Presumably a mis-reading for formal.
[4] Quoted by Percy Fitzgerald, *op. cit.* Meaning of course party politics.

their feelings for their father's plight. Can we altogether blame her as we remember the position of the family, the compassion felt in those days for madness — compassion which was not made tolerable by kindness of treatment or the hopes of a cure?

To the daughters she seemed a spoiled child, spoiled to avoid a tantrum if she did not have her own way. 'My mother is a spoilt child, for my father spoilt her from the hour she came, and we have continued to do so from the hour of our birth.'[1] So it may have seemed to them but they probably did not realise how she, as a very young woman, had been immured from the world and had sacrificed her true self to the dictates of her husband. And this certainly continued after his final illness in 1810. The Queen and the Princesses were never far away from the mad king: they could hear 'unpleasant laughing' from the part of the Castle where he was: either the Queen or one of her daughters was always in residence at the Castle, although the prospects of improvement or recovery were non-existent.[2]

Affectionate and kind-hearted as the Royal Dukes were, they must have been painfully conscious of the plight of their younger sisters. Each of the sisterhood had a favourite brother except perhaps the eldest who was married and lived in Württemberg. Princess Sophia was much attached to the Duke of York, Princess Mary to the sailor-prince, the Duke of Clarence, and the youngest, Princess Amelia, to her godfather G.P. But all of them loved G.P. Queen Victoria once remarked that all her aunts had high spirits[3]. Those they inherited from their mother. They were coming towards middle life when their father became finally mad and we can see at a glance what their lives became from the following letter written to them by their mother. After explaining that their position was totally different from that of their brothers who, with duties to perform, had to appear in public she continued:

[1] Princess Elizabeth to her eldest brother. D. M. Stuart, *op. cit.*, p. 180.
[2] At the Regent's ball in 1813 it was noticed that two of his sisters were absent: it was explained that the Royal Family had made a rule that there should always be at least one member of the Family at Windsor.
[3] *Queen Victoria's Journal*, ii, p. 3.

'But in your Sex, and under the present Melancholy situation of your father the going to Public Amusements except where Duty calls you would be *the highest mark of indecency possible*. The visits to your brothers I will no further touch upon than to say that you never can be in the House with those that are unmarried without a Lady, and that even that Pleasure, innocent as it is, should be well considered before it is done'.[1] The strictness of nineteenth-century morality evidently began with the Century, not with Queen Victoria. The plight of the four sisters — Princess Amelia had died in 1810 — is well expressed in a letter from the youngest surviving one — Princess Sophia — which was written in December 1811 to the Regent, who had been trying to arrange independent establishments for his sisters. She began by saying that she hoped he had not involved himself in difficulty with the Ministers through his kindness to 'four Old Cats', and she went on 'How good you are to us which however imperfectly expressed I feel most deeply. *Poor old wretches* as we are, a *dead weight* upon you, old lumber to the country, like old clothes, I wonder you don't vote for putting us in a *sack* and drowning us in *The Thames* . . . Ever your unalterably attached Sophy'.[2] The letter is dated from 'The Nunnery, Windsor Castle'.

Now naturally enough romantic-minded mortals, seeing five beautiful and high-spirited Princesses immured in a convent-like existence at Windsor Castle, started to weave stories about their private lives. This was the period of Gothic novels, with changeling children and secret marriages, and what more natural setting for such tales than the mediæval castle by the Thames? The stories flowed more swiftly than the river. Within a decade of Princess Amelia's death a young member of the Bar was writing gleefully to his father that he had met at dinner General Fitzroy who had been the husband of Princess Amelia.[3] It is clear that the Princess fell deeply in love with Charles Fitzroy, but they were never married and

[1] D. M. Stuart, *op. cit.*, p. 101.

[2] D. M. Stuart, *op. cit.*, pp. 286-7.

[3] Charles Fitzroy was the second son of the first Lord Southampton, a General and equerry to the Duke of York, and subsequently to the King.

the Princess had no child born in or out of wedlock. Rumour
has also been busy with the reputation of the next sister,
Princess Sophia. She was supposed to have had a child by
General Thomas Garth, one of her father's equerries. To this
tale there are two objections. If the General had so behaved we
can hardly suppose that he would have kept his position at
Court. The King allowed two of his younger unmarried
daughters to stay with the General in Dorset some years after
the supposed birth and, even if the King did not know of the
birth, it is straining credulity too far to suppose that the Royal
Dukes would have allowed the General to continue on easy
terms with their sister. The other objection was put with
characteristic force by the diarist Charles Greville, a shrewd
man of the world; he said that people doubted if Garth could
be the father 'because he was a hideous old devil with a great
claret mark on his face'.[1] We can only add that there is no
evidence at Windsor that the unmarried Princesses had secret
marriages or 'love' children.

Charles Greville goes on to say – and here he shows himself
in tune with the twentieth century – that 'women fall in love
with anything', and that the Princesses were secluded from
the world 'with their passions boiling over'. If the Princess
Sophia had a child – and it will be remembered that this is
completely unproven – it is possible that General Garth, as a
friend of the Royal Family, assumed responsibility for it. Here
it is important to notice the malign influence of George IV's
wife, Queen Caroline. She was a type, happily rare in the
history of the English Royal Family which gloried in royal
gossip, especially matters emanating from a royal bedroom.
The wife of the Russian Ambassador in London told Prince
Metternich that the Princess of Wales 'gives historical
narratives of the behaviour of each member of the Royal
Family not forgetting the offspring of the unmarried
Princesses.'[2]

In 1857, when the last survivor of the family of George III
died, Harriet Martineau, writing for the *Daily News* from the

[1] *The Greville Memoirs*, 1938, i, pp. 271, 272.
[2] D. M. Stuart, *op. cit.*, p. 142.

fresh, untainted air of Clappersgate in Westmorland, wrote
'All that long series of heart histories has closed. What a
world of misery could this survivor have told of . . . The various
love stories are hidden now in the grave. There let them rest.'
Harriet Martineau was blessed with more than her share of the
optimism of the true Victorian if she thought that the twentieth century would let a hidden love-story rest after the
obsequies of the unhappy mortal were finished.

A further point needs to be made. It was the King's wish
that his daughters should not marry. Queen Victoria told this
to Lord Melbourne, and noticed that he had not known it.[1]
The reason why King George objected was that it was difficult
in those days for a Princess to marry a commoner, and he knew
too well the unhappiness which had befallen his own family
through foreign alliances. His eldest aunt had married the
Prince of Orange whose appearance was so risible that even
the well-bred English courtiers could not hide their laughter at
the nuptial ceremony: a younger aunt, who was a talented and
gentle Princess, married the 'brutal Landgrave' of Hesse-
Cassel who ill-treated her and from whom she was divorced.
His own sister, Caroline Matilda married an imbecile King of
Denmark, and narrowly escaped from that country with her
life. His aunt Amelia endured long years of uncertainty as the
possible bride of Frederick the Great, and was perhaps lucky
to remain single. Of two possible bridegrooms, who were
brothers, for the King's own daughters their own mother said
'the Princesses would reject my sons if they ever saw them'.
And if there were appropriate Princes lingering in the Protestant courts of Europe the long-drawn war with Napoleon
made contact with them virtually impossible. We can certainly
say that the King's treatment of his daughters was severe, but
there were reasons for it. Later on, when possibly he might
have relented, the Queen had forbidden the question to be
raised in case it had the effect of overbalancing his reason. The
Duke of Orleans, the future Louis Philippe, wished in 1808
to marry Princess Elizabeth. She wrote a voluble and moving
letter to her eldest brother and said that she had said to the

Queen 'let me accept it' – but let it never be mentioned while
the King lives. She continued that, however distressing it was
for her and her sisters, they had the consolation 'of considering
my *father* before ourselves'. In conversation with the Queen it
became clear that many suggestions of marriage for the
Princesses had been made but 'rejected without a word *from*
us, and therefore we all felt the sun of our days was set'.[1]
Several years later, when peace had returned to Europe and
the King was given over to incurable insanity, she was allowed
to marry the Landgrave of Hesse-Homburg. Of this Landgrave an Englishman wrote 'an uglier hound with a snout
buried in hair, I never saw'.[2] Sixty years later Queen Victoria
was to refer to this Princess as 'my poor aunt'. The adjective
was not ill-chosen.

All this background is of the first importance in considering
the lives of the Royal Princes of King George III's family.
They lacked the independence from their father and sovereign
which meant that until late middle life they were unable to
strike out on their own and emerge from existence which was
narrow and insular. The point can be best illustrated and more
clearly made by considering what would have happened if the
King had died at the end of a normal eighteenth-century span
of life. Sixty was a fair average age for men at that time so that
it is not unreasonable to suppose that George III might have
died in the late 1790's. The death of the King might or
might not have had important political consequences, but it
would clearly have had important consequences for the
Princes and Princesses. The Princes would have been employed – the Duke of Clarence in the Royal Navy and the
Duke of Kent in the Army – possibly with unfortunate results
for each service. The Duke of Sussex would probably have been
allowed to make a wholly disastrous morganatic marriage with
Lady Augusta Murray, and the Dukes of Cumberland and
Cambridge would have been given important commands in the
Army. The Princesses would have been allowed to marry, and

[1] Aspinall, *Correspondence of George IV*, vol. vi, p. 323-4.
[2] *Memoirs of the Court of England during the Regency by the Duke of
Buckingham and Chandos*, vol. ii, p. 228.

Queen Charlotte would have ended her days amid the swamps and bogs of Frogmore. The compactness of the family, with its subtle restraints and loyalties, would have been broken.

We also have to bear in mind that as the Princes' lives were restricted by lack of money, by having no real occupation and by loyalty to Windsor they were much more prominent in metropolitan life than would have been the case if they had had employment; they were also more segregated from other people than would be true to-day. They were conspicuous with their servants in red liveries, their carriages brilliant with colour and armorial devices; even their secretaries were distinguished by their buttons.[1] They themselves were blazing with a garter-star which, in those sensible times, did not need to be brought out after dark but was very generally worn with day-clothes. They had of course a circle of private friends – especially the Prince of Wales who moved with easy equality among the aristocracy. This was an innovation; his forebears had had friends among the political aristocracy but the Prince's friends were primarily fashionable and secondarily political. His grandfather, Frederick Prince of Wales, had a circle of political friends, and it was probably the recollection and knowledge of this which encouraged George III to believe that it was not possible for someone near the throne to form a circle of private friends without this acquiring some political force. The Prince's friends were a recurring cause of friction between father and son.

One bar erected at that time between royal persons and the rest of mankind was the severity of etiquette. It is wholly mistaken to blame the Royal Family or even the aristocracy for this. Society, in the widest sense, rested in part at that time on men of learning – members of the Bar, the clergy, scholars, and divines. To people of that type we could apply a phrase of Anthony Trollope's – 'their senses were permeated by the sweetness of the aroma of rank'.[2] To give one example. At a dinner-party in his own house a clergyman raised his glass

---

[1] They wore special buttons to show that they were in royal service. *Rival Princes* by Mrs M. A. Clarke, ii, p. 65.

[2] *The Duke's Children*, i, p. 315.

first to one of his guests 'because she was a Baronet's daughter'.[1] This attention to the nice gradations of social life was the frame for the etiquette of court and royal life. And it is also important to notice that King George III and Queen Charlotte were virtually the creators of the Court in Hanoverian times. George I kept his wife under lock and key, and George II's wife was Queen for only ten years and preferred an intellectual circle of friends and the chance of visiting them in their houses – a fancy which was remarked by her husband, George II, in elegant terms 'You do not see me running into every puppy's house to see his new chairs and stools.'[2] It was in the reign of George III that courtiers, by and round the sovereign, were made to stand; levées and drawing-rooms were different from to-day; instead of everyone being presented to the sovereign, the King and Queen moved among the company, picking out the people whom they wished to distinguish by conversation. Spectacles, quizzing glasses or anything of that kind were not allowed at Court. Mankind was instinctively more respectful to members of the Royal Family than it is to-day. We see this when the Prince of Wales, as Regent, attended the dinner of the Royal Academy in 1811. He made a brief but pointed speech expressing his pride as an Englishman when he looked round the walls at the magnificent paintings of contemporary British artists. It is interesting to notice that while he was speaking the whole company, including three of his brothers, remained standing.[3] We can illustrate the point further by descending to the farcical. The extremely foolish Duke of Gloucester, who was nephew to George III, was on a visit to Russia: while he was dancing in St Petersburg the buckle of his shoe became unfastened: he expected his equerry to kneel down and buckle it up again. Moreover in the presence of royalty, curiosity did not drive people forward to gaze and stare: there was still something faintly awe-inspiring about royal persons. Fanny Burney has

[1] *The Bletchley Diary of the Reverend William Cole*, p. 218.
[2] *Lord Hervey's Memoirs* edited by R. R. Sedgwick, 11, p. 502.
[3] *The Farington Diary*, vol. vi, p. 264.

left a masterly description of an occasion when King George
III arrived unexpectedly in a house at Windsor where she was
staying. The scene was not unlike the last moment of Pompeii;
everyone was struck motionless in the posture in which they
happened to be. The King soon brought everyone to life,
because whatever the formality of the Court he was delightfully
easy in company of his own choosing. Indeed it is true to say
that King George III introduced affability into the Hanoverian dynasty. All his sons except possibly the Duke of
Cumberland inherited that affability. Possibly it was a quality
which carried with it certain dangers. The Prince of Wales
had the characteristic markedly and this was partly the
reason why people thought him insincere and apt to say
sometimes rather more than he really felt. Lord Moira, who
knew the Prince intimately and admired him warmly, said
that 'his character was good-natured, quiet, easy of com-
prehension, with an appearance of unsteadiness arising from
people presuming too much upon his affability'.[1] Again that
was broadly true of all his brothers except that the Duke of
Clarence was not quiet and the Duke of Cumberland was not
good-natured. Moreover the whole family, not excluding
King George III, was too often unguarded in what they said
or perhaps unguarded in what they said to people whose dis-
cretion was not tested. When the Prince of Wales as Regent
wished to appoint a friend, William Jackson, to the Bishopric
of Oxford the pious Perceval, the Prime Minister, thought
Jackson a little convivial for the post. All that the Prince
replied was that he hoped when Jackson was Bishop of Oxford
he would often dine at his table and enjoy a bottle of port.
These hasty witticisms were characteristic of the family: they
are dangerous because they lend themselves to repetition.
Princess Charlotte, when a girl in her teens, replied to a gentleman who told her that he thought it wrong for the Duke
(presumably Kent) to live with his mistress in Kensington
Palace 'Oh Lord upon us. What would you have? The Dukes
can not marry, they must love somebody'. That was a retort

[1] *Life of William, Earl of Shelbourne* by Lord Edmond Fitzmaurice, iii,
560.

which, we may be sure, her grandmother Queen Charlotte
would not have liked.[1]

The private and secret histories of the Royal Family which
circulated freely among the aristocracy, were obviously
matters of concern to the Royal Dukes but they had an indirect importance in their lives which was great and has been
often overlooked. Gossip and imagination, when they are combined, create a hot bed, at once rich and receptive, on which
tales about privileged people may enjoy the most luxurious
growth. But at the beginning of the nineteenth century these
tales, so far as the English Royal Family was concerned, rested
on a firm foundation of fact – the King was mad, the Princess
of Wales was bad, the six Princes were wild and the five
Princesses were, in all but habit, nuns. At the same time there
was a great spread of scurrilous and scandalous comment
about the Royal Family, and it is here that the stories about
the Royal Family, recklessly spread but widely believed, had
their indirect influence over the Royal Dukes. The public
respect for them was grievously damaged.

An instance illustrates the point. The following is the gist
of a paragraph published in *The Times* in 1789 when the King
was recovering from his first attack of madness. It started by
saying that the Royal Dukes affected pleasure at the King's
recovery 'But the insincerity of their joy is visible. Their late
unfeeling conduct will forever tell against them'. The writer
went on to praise the behaviour of those who prevented the
Duke of York from rushing into the King's room and 'with
rashness, Germanic severity and insensibility' retarding the
recovery of the King. In this paragraph there was no germ of
truth, and the Editor of *The Times* was very properly clapp'd
into gaol, but what he wrote was widely spread and no doubt
widely believed. Also this kind of attack was something new:
of course kings and princes have been held up to obloquy
ever since the Old Testament was written and long before, but
so far as England was concerned the attacks before 1800
were for the most part, political or dynastic.

We can see this over Swift's celebrated Drapier's Letters.

[1] *Diary of Lady Charlotte Bury*, vol. i.

Belief was general that King George I's mistress, the Duchess of Kendal, was financially interested in the new copper coinage for Ireland, generally known as Wood's Halfpence. On this aspect of the matter Swift is extremely discreet, fearing the possibility of prosecution. He did write a savage epigram about the Duchess which was not published but was found among his papers after his death. It was endorsed in Swift's writing thus 'A wicked treasonable libel. I wish I knew the author that I might hang him.' The danger of retaliation by the Government or the Crown receded by the end of the century; we can point the difference over these attacks on the Royal Family by saying that if George I, who kept his wife a prisoner in Germany, had been treated with the calumny and obloquy with which George IV was treated even the glum Old Pretender would have been back in the land of his fathers. It was not only that the earlier attacks, largely political and always dangerous for those employing them, changed in that they became more personal with ridicule of the Royal Family but they were broadcast by the spread of newspapers and the increasing public which read them.

And those whom the pen did not reach the pencil touched. The crowds which even then sauntered round Piccadilly could see a constant succession of prints on display, ridiculing the Royal Family and drawn by unrivalled masters of the art – Gilray, the Cruikshanks and the Heaths. Examples remind us of the embarrassment which these prints must have caused their victims. When the Duke of Clarence made himself unpopular by the technical, naval questions which he asked during the trial of the Queen, he was at once the subject of a caricature. The print was headed 'Cl – – – ce's Dream'. He is visited by the apparition of Mrs Jordan, whom he was supposed to have rather curtly discarded; waking from his nightmare he puts his foot in the chamber-pot labelled ordan'. Another, a little later, touched the Duke of York, and was headed 'Y – – –K you're wanted or, A R–y–l Miscarriage!!!' In the summer of 1822, while he was attending a levée, the Duke's carriage was seized by bailiffs acting on behalf of an upholsterer. The Duke is shown in a second carriage uttering this sentence 'Damn that upholsterer! he has lost a good customer for I wear out a great quantity of beds, sofas etc. among the Ladies'. In a somewhat different medium for ridicule the Duke of Kent was made to suffer in the memoirs of Mary Anne Clarke – mistress to the Duke of York. In reviewing the book *The Times* referred to it as containing 'such excellent fun . . . it has amused us so much'. In this book the authoress says that she might in the future give an entertaining account of the Duke of Kent's discovery of the St Lawrence, a friendly allusion to the Duke's mistress Madame de St Laurent: later the Duke is described as a good churchman, sober and devoted to his old French lady. Mrs Clarke expressed contrition for giving this exemplary and temperate Prince 'a niche in my work'.[1]

The younger brothers came off more lightly, though when Ernest Duke of Cumberland became influential in opposing the emancipation of the Roman Catholics he is drawn unsparingly in countless caricatures. When he was supposed to have tried to ride down two perfectly respectable ladies on the tow-path of the Thames, the episode was put in a caricature and one of the ladies exclaims 'Oh dear, oh dear I thought it was the *Duke* but its the *Devil* in *Ernest*.'

All these things, however, fade into obscurity against the avalanche of squibs, cuts and caricatures which poured out at the time of the trial of the Queen. 'The Political House That Jack Built', with its spirited attack on George IV. 'This is the MAN – all shaven and shorn, all cover'd with Orders – and all forlorn' – was written by William Hone and illustrated by George Cruikshank. It ran into more than fifty editions.

Nor did this kind of fun – if fun it was – end with the lives of those pilloried. Certainly the caricatures were not easily preserved: they had their day in portfolios on library and drawing-room tables and were then cast out. But some survived – perhaps in folders on library shelves or framed in the up-stairs passages of country houses. A story is recorded of Lady Conyngham – the last favourite of King George IV. She lived to a great age, dying thirty years after the death of

[1] *The Rival Princes* by Mrs M. A. Clark, 1810.

the King; towards the end of her life she was staying in Oxfordshire and complained to her hostess of draughts. A screen, long unused, was brought out, and when it was opened it was found to be blazing with every kind of caricature of the 1820's. Perhaps 'R – L Push-Pin' was among them which depicted the 'lovers' playing the old-fashioned game of push-pin. With a leer Lady Conyngham says to the King 'Try another *push* my love'. He replies 'You rogue, it is of no use, my *pushing* days are over.' Deep into Victorian times these ribald pictures survived, carrying with them hints of Georgian habits – a faint aroma of immorality. Whether what they depicted was true is immaterial: they reminded the Victorians of that world of frivolity and unrestrained sexual appetites from which they themselves had so decorously emerged. Such things maintained the dubious reputation of the Royal Dukes.

There is a further point. During the lives of the Royal Dukes there was an amazing proliferation of diarists and letter writers. Theirs was indeed the golden age of the recorder. The pages of Horace Walpole just catch the elder Princes while Charles Greville has many amusing passages about their younger brothers. Between them and covering the lives of all the brothers are the sparkling pages of Creevey and the great memorialists such as Lady Holland, Joseph Farington, J. W. Croker, Lord Glenbervie, Lord Granville, Princess Lieven and Stockmar together with countless names less familiar but all bringing forward their comments and tales about the Royal Family. Horace Walpole tells us that 'it is very vulgar to be interested about princes and princesses'.[1] That may well be true: but it was a warning which happily for us Walpole himself did not always heed. He meant, we may suppose, that those who really knew members of the Royal Family did not chatter about them: consequently talk about royal persons tended to be carried on by those with just a bowing acquaintance with princes and was therefore merely a surface conversation without knowledge or understanding. An example from Creevey illustrates this point. Although he was occasionally well informed and records personal conversations with George IV

[1] Letter to Lady Upper Ossory. 28th October, 1777.

and the Duke of Kent, he was a great master of tittle-tattle and he is inevitably the source of the information about George IV's figure. Lord Folkestone, shortly to be the head of a distinguished family but a Radical politician of severity and malignancy, wrote to Creevey in 1818 to tell him, 'Prinny has let loose his belly which now reaches to his knees'. This has of course passed into the currency of acceptable quotations. We may accept it without pausing to ask how Lord Folkestone acquired this secret of the royal dressing-room. It is perhaps true that, with advancing years, the Prince did leave off the supports of fashionable youth. Lord Holland puts the point more elegantly when he wrote to Creevey 'They say the Prince has left off his stays, and that Royalty, divested of its usual supports, makes a bad figure.'[1] If the royal figure assumed the deformity recorded by Lord Folkestone it had passed beyond the art of the haberdasher and demanded the knife of Sir Benjamin Brodie – the King's surgeon.

All these influences combined – the attacks in the newspapers, the pictures in the print-shops and the racy stories of diarists and letter-writers – gave the impression that the Royal Family at this time consisted of a company of disreputable Merry-Andrews. So, at any rate, it seemed to the Victorians, and as time advanced further away from the Royal Dukes they seemed more firmly embedded in absurdity and wickedness so that it became difficult to realise that these grigs were the father and uncles of Queen Victoria. Lytton Strachey, in his incomparable biography of Queen Victoria, devoted a few paragraphs to the Royal Dukes, caught up the aura of folly and vice with which each was surrounded and brought them, through the success of his book, to the astonished attention of a wide public. Yet the picture, though it had long endured, was unfair.

Perhaps it would not seem unduly egocentric if I explained how forty and more years ago I became interested in the rather daunting subject of these royal brothers. When I was at Oxford I remember reading some account of the struggle for Catholic Emancipation in the 1820's, and I was struck by the intervention of the Duke of York in the House of Lords who opposed emancipation, proclaimed himself the defender of the Established Church adding 'whatever might be my station in life, so help me God'. The rather unexpected churchmanship of this prince, sandwiched between Kings George and William the Fourth, caught my fancy. Some years later I remember coming out of the London Library (of which I was and am greatly proud to be a member) with a biography of the Duke of York which was written in the year he died by John Watkins. Mr Watkins, a Devonshire man, wrote several books on the Royal Family and he described himself on the title page of his books as Ll.D. (Doctor of Laws), though someone rather cruelly observed 'it does not appear whence he obtained the honour'. His book is certainly not one of the great biographies but I look tenderly on it because emerging from the London Library I met a friend of mine: he was a renowned man of the left with also much knowledge of recent royal history. He looked with some surprise at Mr Watkins's book and then said, 'You really ought to write a book about these risible uncles'. His advice I followed.

CHAPTER II

❧

FREDERICK, DUKE OF YORK

PRINCE FREDERICK was born in 1763. When he was
seventeen he left England to study his profession of the Army
in Germany, which at the close of the eighteenth century was
the military training-centre of Europe. A tall youth with fair
hair, florid complexion, and his father's prominent nose, he
was physically strong and proficient at all games. He was no
scholar, and had no intellectual interests but he had mastered,
without any difficulty, the ordinary schoolboy's curriculum of
his generation. He was inquisitive, enthusiastic and affectionate. A greater contrast between him and his elder brother, the
Prince of Wales, could hardly be imagined, except that they
were both handsome and healthy. The Prince of Wales was
exceptionally intelligent, exceptionally lazy, *blasé* and selfish —
qualities which naturally did not endear him to his family.
Prince Frederick was the type of boy adored by school-
masters and parents. His father and his sisters loved him dearly.

He remained abroad from 1781 to 1787. He lived to be a
comparatively old man, and for the rest of his life he never
enjoyed such importance, such deference or such flattery as
during those six years. He no doubt learned how soldiers
should be trained and manœuvred, and all the rules of the
game as approved by Frederick the Great, but the one lesson
learned abroad, that he never forgot, was that Princes are not
quite as other men are. Everything conspired to show him
this.

He set out from London for Harwich at the end of December 1780, accompanied by a supervisor, Colonel Greville, and
a few servants. There was no excitement. No crowds to cheer
him with a God-speed for the journey. A handful of people at

Colchester to gape at the Royal Arms on the carriage and a small group of the curious at Harwich to watch him embark, and just a mention in the papers the following morning that 'His Royal Highness Prince Frederick, His Majesty's second son, has left for the Continent.' But when he arrived in Hanover he passed through gaily decorated streets, lined with loyal, excited, bawling Hanoverians. They had never seen their Elector since the days of George II, and here at any rate was some proof that he existed. Members of the Government, Ministers of foreign countries, deputations from the citizens, flocked to pay their respects to the Prince-Bishop of Osnabrück. He probably felt that it was better to be a Bishop in Germany than to be a Prince in England.

After spending a few months at Hanover, he went on to Brunswick as the guest of the Duke of Brunswick, who had married a sister of George III. Having married rather above his station, the Duke of Brunswick was anxious to do all he could for an English Prince and, belonging to a famous military family, he spent much of his time expounding to his nephew the mysteries of warfare. Acting on the principle that one good marriage begets another, he did his utmost to entangle Prince Frederick with his daughter Caroline. It might well have succeeded, because the Prince was unused to feminine charms, having had little opportunity of meeting women in England apart from his sisters and his mother's middle-aged ladies-in-waiting. But, as wife of George IV, this wayward and eccentric girl was reserved for an even better marriage, and to make an even more important person unhappy.

From Brunswick his uncle gave him an introduction to Frederick the Great, and every autumn till he returned to England he was present at the Prussian reviews. He also paid several visits to Vienna, but Hanover was his headquarters and it was from there that he made these expeditions to the various Courts of Germany. He was created Duke of York and Albany, and Earl of Ulster in 1784. The King of Prussia seems to have taken a fancy to the young Prince, and a state ball and dinner were always given to mark his visit to Berlin, and at the end of 1785 a review was held in Silesia in his honour. Silesia had been torn from Austria by Frederick forty years before, and the revival of old memories, the excitement and the exposure helped to kill him. Nothing, not even the life of Europe's greatest soldier, was spared to impress on the Duke of York the importance of English Princes. Gratifying as it was, it may be doubted whether the lesson which Frederick the Great had to teach justified the sacrifice. As the old King sat heavily astride his horse, explosively ordering one general to prison and loudly bewailing the incompetence of another, he watched his men marching, drilling and deploying before him and he thought his Army invincible. So they were — against an enemy marching to meet them in the same well-drilled formation. But the enemy that the Duke of York was to meet were the armies of Revolutionary France. Speckless uniforms, perfect time, burnished guns, were useless weapons against enthusiasm. A military system died with Frederick the Great: the weapons of war as he had known them perished with him.

But, despite these opportunities for learning the arts of war, it is clear that the Prince was not looked upon as an entirely satisfactory pupil. Lord Cornwallis who, having been soundly defeated by the American Colonists, regarded himself as Britain's leading soldier, wrote home from Germany about the Prince: '. . . the Royal Person whom I saw does not give much hopes, further than a great deal of good nature and a very good heart. His military ideas are those of a wild boy of the Guards, the uniforms and promotions of that Corps, about which he is vehement to excess. One cannot however help loving him. . . . There is no chance of any good coming but by his being kept abroad, and of the English being kept from him.'

The truth of the matter was that the sudden complete freedom from control, and the example of the German Courts, with their heavy dinners and accompanying variety of wines, their coarse jokes, their public prominence of mistress and bastard, so entirely different from the homely simplicity of the English Court, had undermined his character. While he followed his military career with moderate application, drink and women had become his primary interests. Mirabeau, who was at the Berlin Court during his visits, formed a very unfavourable opinion of him: '*Le Duc d'Yorck puissant chasseur, puissant buveur, rieur infatigable, sans grâce, sans countenance, sans politesse.*'

This freedom to do as he would, and the fêting by Frederick the Great and other German Royalties, naturally all increased his importance in his own eyes. There was, too, another reason for his thinking that whatever the insular English might think of a younger son of their King, and however much they might grumble at having to pay for his keep, a Prince of England was something more than an amiable nonentity. Because, as he passed from Vienna to Berlin and from Berlin to Vienna or back again to Hanover, calling in at Brunswick on the way, he was made the subject of little confidences and treated with far greater importance than was actually due to the younger son of a constitutional monarch. The rulers of Europe could not be expected to appreciate the niceties of the British Constitution: it appeared to them as an obvious fact that they had among them a young man who not only knew the mind, but had the ear of their brother of England. And during these years when the Duke was abroad the attitude of England towards the rest of Europe was of great uncertainty and of great importance. For, after the close of the American War – just as rather more than a hundred years later, after the close of the Boer War – England was in a position of what she proudly called 'splendid isolation,' but which was, more truthfully, unpopular solitude. France and Spain were allied by the Bourbon Family Compact: France and the Empire by the Bourbon-Habsburg Alliance: the Empire and Russia by the alliance of Joseph II and Catherine the Great: while Frederick the Great, on friendly terms with Russia, was supported by the smaller German States. In 1785 Joseph II proposed to annex Bavaria to Austria, compensating the Elector of Bavaria with the Austrian Netherlands. Frederick immediately formed the League of Princes, which was, in effect, composed of Prussia and the smaller German States to oppose Joseph's scheme. The attitude of George III, particularly having regard to Hanover, was awaited with the keenest interest. The first news of Joseph's designs and Frederick's counter-move reached England through the Duke of York and, acting entirely on his son's advice, unknown to his British Ministers, George III joined the League of Princes.

How would a young man of twenty-two, who had been dabbling in European politics, settle down at home to that life of importance without influence which was the fate of younger sons of the King of England? Two years later, in 1787, George III decided that his son must come home. The King had no suspicion that his character had changed, for he had deliberately kept him out of England for so long in order that he might escape the influence of the Prince of Wales. The Duke of York reached Windsor on 2nd August, 1787. As he stepped out of his carriage, the joy of being home again drew out all his old affectionate character and he warmly embraced his parents and his sisters. Princess Amelia, who was four, he had never seen. Prince Alfred had come and gone while he was in Germany. Prince Octavius, who had been a baby when he left, had died three years before, to the terrible grief of his father, who thought he would have died too. These tragedies only made his favourite son seem dearer still, and Miss Burney, from a discreet distance, observed the King's feelings — 'The joy of his excellent father! Oh that there is no describing. It was the glee of the first youth — nay of ardent and innocent infancy — so pure it seemed, so warm, so open, so unmixed . . . Might he but escape the contagion of surrounding example . . .'

But, alas! the news of his return soon spread to Brighton, and 'the contagion' flung itself into its carriage and came bowling up to Windsor. The Prince of Wales bore off his brother to his home at Carlton House, and by the end of the year the Duke of York had ceased to visit Windsor.

II

In the summer of 1788 the King fell ill. It was clearly a

nervous disorder, but the doctors diagnosed it as a touch of biliousness. They advised the waters of Cheltenham, which had been known to work wonders for livery nabobs. In July the King, the Queen and the Princesses drove down to Cheltenham and stayed just outside the town in Lord Falconberg's house. Before they started, a message had come from the Duke of York that he would like to come and stay with them while they were at Cheltenham: but when they got down there they found the house so small that they did not see how they could fit him in. But the King was determined that the Duke should not feel that he had been cold-shouldered out into an inn, and he arranged that a wooden annex should be built on to Falconberg House, and he spent much time supervising the building and furnishing the quarters for his favourite son. The Duke arrived one Saturday and, in spite of all the preparation, casually announced that he would have to return to London the next day (Sunday) for 'military business.'

In the middle of August the King returned to Windsor very much worse, which the doctors brightly attributed to a 'surfeit of Cheltenham waters.' By the middle of October he was clearly on the verge of madness: the Queen described his eyes as looking like 'black currant jelly': the veins on his face were swollen: he was quite unable to stop talking. They could hear his voice ringing through the castle: 'I wish to God I may die because I am going mad.' Like King Lear, the hero of his favourite play, he endured the horrors of knowing that he was going mad:

> O let me not be mad, not mad, sweet heaven!
> Keep me in temper; I would not be mad!

The King was liable to these attacks of madness, of which he had shown the first symptoms as far back as 1765, but there could be no doubt from his ramblings what had precipitated this attack. He knew perfectly well that the 'military business' which had called the Duke of York back from Cheltenham on a Sunday was nothing but the Prince of Wales: as he lay in bed, his hoarse unceasing voice could be heard inveighing against the Prince of Wales, and lamenting that Frederick was following in his footsteps. Just before the floods of madness finally engulfed his mind, they heard him trying to persuade himself that all was well: 'Frederick is my favourite, my friend. Yes, Frederick is my friend.'

It was exactly ten years before that Mrs Delany had written of the delightful relations between the King and his sons and, if anything could have restored them, it should have been this tragedy which had fallen on the father. But, instead of being at Windsor to comfort his mother and sisters and to do what he could, the Duke of York was to be seen night after night drinking and gambling at Brooks's Club, blabbing the secrets of the sickroom and mimicking what his father said and did. Such behaviour in a man of twenty-five was inexcusable, but the only consolation was that, while even his friends were shocked and there was much tittle-tattle flying round Piccadilly and the clubs, there was no public scandal. But that was to come.

By the middle of November the King was unable to transact any business, and even the doctors were obliged to admit that they thought he would die or at the best be permanently mad. It had come too quickly at the end, for him to make any provision for a Regency. How was the country's Government to be carried on?

The Whigs under Fox, who were in Opposition to the Tory administration under Pitt, held that, as there was a void in the Royal authority, it was filled, without further ado, by the heir to the throne and that it was immaterial whether the void was permanent through death, or temporary through incapacity. This view was simple, complete and correct. But in the eyes of Pitt and of all good men and blue it was open to an insuperable objection. Fox, the public and personal enemy of the King, was the bosom friend of the Prince of Wales. The Prince of Wales as Regent would have dismissed Pitt and sent for Fox. Pitt, therefore, claimed that Parliament should nominate a Regent and define his powers. The Prince of Wales, the Duke of York and George III's brothers had some good ground for regarding the Tory proposals as an attack on the monarchy. But their great mistake was in themselves joining in the fray. They should have stood aside while the Whigs fought their battle for them. The Duke of York actually spoke in the House of Lords as the mouthpiece of his brother in support of the Whig view. What disgusted public opinion, and strengthened Pitt's hand, was the spectacle of the Prince of Wales and the Duke of York merely eager to press their personal rights, utterly indifferent to their father's plight and obviously reluctant to recognise that the illness could have anything but a fatal end. It did not need the public statement of the Duke of York in the House of Lords that he had been refused admittance to the King's person to let the world know that the English Royal Family was hopelessly divided.

At the beginning of 1789 the King unexpectedly recovered and the Regency question, over which so much ink had been spilled and so many words bandied, was soon forgotten. But not by the Royal brothers, who felt they had been cheated of their chance of power. They attended the Service of Thanksgiving for the King's recovery on St George's Day, but the Duke of York chattered away to his next-door neighbour throughout the whole service and the Prince of Wales was careful to place his dependants at various points along the route to St Paul's so that the King might hear how much louder were the cheers for 'the ill-used heir' than for his father. It was useless to attempt to hide the differences between the King and his sons.

A month later the King was threatened with a relapse, thanks once more to the behaviour of the Duke of York. Colonel Lennox, cousin to George III's Lady Sarah and afterwards Duke of Richmond, was with some friends when they happened to meet the Prince of Wales. The colonel went up to the Prince and publicly insulted him. It was obviously impossible for the heir to the throne to fight a duel, but the Duke of York, who had overheard the insulting remark, rushed up to the colonel and said 'When I am not on duty I wear a brown coat and I am ready to give you satisfaction whenever you please.'

He never aid a word to his brother but, early one morning at the end of May, crept out from Carlton House in a servant's hat, leaving his own sugar-loaf hat to make his brother think he had never gone out, and drove in a hired post chaise to Wimbledon Common. Here he met the colonel. The ground was measured at twelve paces. The colonel fired first and carried away one of the Duke's curls. The Duke refused to fire, as he said he had merely come out to give satisfaction to Colonel Lennox. After this display of dynastic bravery the Duke became more popular with his fellow-countrymen, but it only made the King redouble his efforts to draw him away from the clutches of Carlton House.

Deplorable as was the Duke of York's conduct throughout these two years after his return from the Continent there is this to be said in his favour. While he had been abroad he had found himself a person of consequence, and he came home to find that he had no official work of any kind, apart from very nominal military duties, and that what he thought or said did not matter a rap except to a handful of rakish friends. Being devoid of intellectual interests, he had nothing to fall back on except pleasure. Satan may delight in finding mischief for idle hands but (perhaps because he is an exiled Prince himself) his task seems far easier when the hands are Royal. The Duke of York may have been an immoral man, he may have been over-fond of the pleasures of the table, but he was not by nature an idle man. Circumstances at this period of his life made him so. The Prince of Wales was by nature a wastrel and, without anything else to occupy his time, it was only natural for the Duke of York to follow in the wake of that great leviathan of pleasure.

But there was one means left to the King by which he hoped to alter the course of his second son. When he had been created Duke of York, the Duke had been given a Parliamentary grant of £12,000 a year; there were some thousands a year in addition from the Bishopric of Osnabrück. (During his minority his father had accumulated the income from the Bishopric and bought an estate in Yorkshire called Allerton Mauleverer for his son.) But an income of £15,000, which was sufficient for his mother and her whole family in Strelitz, could not stand the strain imposed on it by such a reckless and unlucky gambler as the Duke. Greville, who was now a major-general and still looked after the Duke, wrote to a friend: '. . . if he does not soon change neither his constitution nor his pocket can hold out, and we shall be obliged, as the sailors call it, to cut and run for the Continent.' It was obviously impossible, when he was spending all his money on pleasure, for the Duke to maintain an establishment of his own in London, and he was obliged to live either with his parents or at Carlton House. The King very wisely saw that it was hopeless to attempt to drag him away from Carlton House and expect him to live at Windsor or Kew, so he gave him a house for himself in Whitehall. This marked the beginning of the decline in the Prince of Wales's influence over his brother. Two years later, in 1791, the King suggested to the Duke that he should go over to the Continent with a view to marriage.

He went straight to Berlin. He remembered when he was last there a small, round-eyed girl of sixteen, the Princess Frederica, great-niece to Frederick the Great. It was important for the succession that he should marry, because the Prince of Wales was nearly thirty and showed no sign of deserting his 'wife,' Mrs Fitzherbert. Princess Frederica was modest and clever and he really rather admired her, and felt that he might comb the Courts of Germany and do very much worse. They were married in Berlin, and he hurried her home through France at the end of 1791. Passing through Lille, the carriage was surrounded by a revolutionary mob, which, with the real fanatic's delight in the trivial, refused to let them pass unless they removed the Royal Arms from the panels of their carriage. The Duke would have regarded the mob with less contempt if he could have known that these were the enthusiasts who were to revolutionise the warfare he had learned from his wife's uncle and, for the next twenty-four years, were to occupy all his military talents. On reaching England they were re-married at the Queen's House in London, and a grant of £40,000 a year was settled on the Duke.

As a marriage it was a failure. At any rate, judged by ordinary standards. There were no children, the Duke was unfaithful to the Duchess, and for the thirty years of their married life they were more often under different roofs than under the same one. But, judged by the standard of the Royal marriages of the Duke's generation, it was not unsuccessful. Their relations never caused a public scandal or involved them with the law, as happened in the case of the Prince and Princess of Wales. The Queen never refused to receive them at Court, as in the case of the Duke and Duchess of Cumberland. The Duke never locked her in her room on a bread and water diet, as the Duke of Gloucester (Silly Billy) was said to have done to his Duchess. They had married in order to provide for the succession in case the Prince of Wales should have no children and, when it was plain that their marriage was to be childless, the Duke lived independently of the Duchess and she, without complaint or curiosity, was content that he should do so.

Just before his marriage the Duke had sold Allerton Mauleverer and had bought Oatlands Park, near Weybridge. Originally it had been a Royal palace, lived in by Henry VIII and by Charles I, whose son, Henry Duke of Gloucester, was born there. It had then passed into the hands of the Duke of Newcastle, who had largely rebuilt the old palace. The Duke of York had no sooner bought it than a fire swept away all traces of the Royal palace and of the improvements of the Duke of Newcastle. He built on the site of the palace a square, grey house which, on one side, looked over the Thames Valley and, on the other, across to the North Downs. The house stood in a large park, with magnificent trees, and the Duke later added to the grounds by buying the manors of Byfleet and Brooklands. Oatlands was the last link between London and Windsor, and it must have been nearly possible to walk from London to Windsor without leaving the homes of the Royal Family, starting from Kew, through Richmond, Hampton Court, Bushey Park, Oatlands, Virginia Water, to Windsor.

It was here that Frederick the Great's relation spent almost the whole of her life in what was then the depths of the country, the nearest village being Weybridge, which was some three miles away. In many ways she was a negative character, having no desire to figure in London society, no interest in public affairs, and no wish to take sides in the squabbles of the

English Royal Family, but the remarkable thing about her was the ease with which she fitted into English country life. She educated the poor and relieved the destitute. In the summer she stitched away at her work in the garden. Every Sunday she went to church in Weybridge. For miles round Oatlands, she was beloved and worshipped as *Lady Bountiful*. She was not good-looking, with china blue eyes, a pile of flaxen hair, and a face rather marked with small-pox, but she was popular with the people and was much loved by all the Royal Family with the exception of the Prince of Wales. She was untroubled by Court etiquette, and perhaps her greatest pleasure was to drive over to Twickenham to see Mr Walpole's Gothic mansion at Strawberry Hill. The same ritual was always observed: Mr Walpole would lay down a piece of carpet from his front door to the gate and would be waiting to help the Duchess out of her carriage. Inside the house there would be some little surprise for her; on one occasion it was a little couplet written by Mr Walpole, extolling the military fame of the Duke of York, hanging round the neck of a brass eagle he had in the hall. Then he would show her the house, and afterwards there would be chocolate. She always tried to make him sit, but he never would. He explained that as a child his father had taken him to see George I, and there was something about that terrible old gentleman that made him think it impossible to sit in the presence of his descendants.[1] As the years went by she came to London less and less, and, after 1800, she and the Duke really only met when he came down to Oatlands for the week-end.

III

At seven o'clock one morning at the end of February 1793 the King and the Prince of Wales, with an escort of Life Guards, came clattering down the Mall scarcely visible through the foggy half light. The King was on his way to review the three battalions of Guards drawn up on the Horse Guards' Parade under the command of the Duke of York. When the review was over the soldiers, with the Duke riding at their

[1] The Duchess of York was a great-great-granddaughter of George I.

head, marched off to Greenwich: the King, the Queen, the Duke of Clarence and the Princesses drove behind in carriages. When they reached Greenwich, the carriages were drawn up close to the water and as the soldiers embarked they passed by the King and his family. The Princess Sophia, always delicate, fainted away, the Princess Amelia was crying lustily and even the Princess Mary choked as she heard one of the men say as he passed: 'Who would not die for them?' England had begun her struggle with France which was not to end till twenty-two years later.

But in 1793 neither country appeared capable of carrying on war for even twelve months. The English Army, till then never formidable in continental wars, was still suffering from the effects of the disasters of the American War. Since the beginning of 1792 war had been threatening, and Pitt, throughout that critically important year, had done nothing to strengthen the Army except to appoint Dundas – a competent Scottish election agent – as Secretary of State for War. Dundas has been described as 'so profoundly ignorant of war that he was not even conscious of his ignorance.' Pitt no doubt felt that, with Louis XVI in prison, and Girondists struggling with Terrorists, the condition of France was too anarchical, and the position of her Government too precarious to justify any very serious preparation.

And certainly in the history of the world there can have never been a more recklessly impertinent declaration of war than that by France against Holland and England at the beginning of 1793. France was already at war with Austria and Prussia, justifiably regarded as an invincible alliance. Large parts of her country were in revolt against her Government. Sixty-two thousand soldiers had deserted from her Army during the winter of 1792-3. But, despite all these disadvantages, as a result of the campaign of 1792 France was in possession of the Austrian Netherlands and was preparing to attack Holland. The Dutch were incapable of defending themselves. Their Stadtholder, a Prince of the profoundest lethargy and most abysmal stupidity, was so incapacitated by these qualities that his only idea of defending his country was to ask the British to do it for him. For years it had been a cardinal principle of British foreign policy that the mouth of the Rhine should not be in the hands of a strong hostile power, and it was this danger that stirred Pitt to send out a British force to Holland. But if Pitt had been told that both he and Fox would be dead before there came a permanent peace, and that the war would last three times as long as the Seven Years' War, he would have found it as impossible to believe as the information that London would celebrate peace when it did come by illuminating its streets with gas.

George III had insisted that the troops should be commanded by the Duke of York. A young man of twenty-nine, a major-general, he had not only to justify his appointment over the heads of his seniors in age and rank but to reconcile to it the country as a whole which, rather unfairly, assumed that because he was a King's son he must be incompetent. The Duke was quietly confident. He had been to the Continent and thoroughly mastered the art of war: let him meet the French, and he felt he would startle even his rough insular soldiers with the subtlety of his strategy and the deftness of his attacks. He was like a schoolboy who at school acquires a new cricket bat and a thorough knowledge of the cuts and glides of the game and then returns to play for his village team. He waits, with smiling confidence, for his turn to go in, when he is going to do such wonders. But that bumpy unrolled pitch, that swift unerring 'sneak' or that partner who brightly runs him out are disasters with which all his brilliance cannot cope.

So, with the Duke, the difference between the warfare he had learned and the warfare he, in fact, found, was immense. Instead of the rolling plains of Silesia, the broken country of the Netherlands: instead of gentlemanly opponents, men who fought like tigers knowing that defeat meant death from their tyrannical Government: instead of a generous organisation behind him, the Scotch caution of Dundas. And in addition there were two things that made success impossible. One was obvious. To oppose a victorious army with only three battalions of even the finest soldiers is courting disaster. And in this case the soldiers were short of ammunition and shockingly equipped. It was not an expeditionary force, but a Viking raid, that he was asked to lead.

The other was even more fatal to success. The Government had struggled desperately with the King against the Duke's being given the command. His youth, his wildness, the personal risks he ran were all pressed upon the King, and, when he still insisted, they only gave in on the condition that three generals should be attached to the Duke with whom he must always consult. And Dundas was to direct the general plan of campaign from his chair in Whitehall. Thus, while the Duke commanded and was responsible in the eyes of his country, four other men, shielded by him, interfered to divide the command. Dundas's caution was seen at its best in his order that on no account should the troops be more than twenty-four hours' march from their base. But with that good fortune which sometimes attends the foolish they had no sooner landed than the French General Dumouriez had to withdraw his troops to rescue the French Army on his right, which had been routed by the Austrians.

Reinforcements were sent out from England: and Dundas, withdrawing his embargo on their moving from their base, the British were able to join up with the Austrians and together they drove the French out of the Netherlands. So far the British Army had been surprisingly successful, though it must be confessed that it was less owing to their own exertions than to the treachery of Dumouriez. The Allies crossed over into France and settled down to besiege Valenciennes. The Prince of Coburg-Saalfeld, who commanded the Austrians, entrusted the operation of the siege to the Duke of York as a compliment to the English. The Duke acquitted himself, if not brilliantly, at least competently, and after two months the fortress fell. The inhabitants trampled on the *tricolor* and hailed the Duke as King of France. The French Army was demoralised; the road to Paris lay open; for a moment the Duke might have dreamt of Henry V. No such dreams disturbed Dundas's rest. His knowledge of history apparently went no farther back than the reign of Charles II, and remembering that that sovereign had sold Dunkirk to the French he ordered the Duke of York to capture it. The Duke turned north to besiege Dunkirk and by the middle of September, having failed to capture it, he was in full retreat. The failure of the English and Austrian Armies to march on to Paris after the fall of Valenciennes must rank as high in the might-have-beens of history as Bonnie Prince Charlie's failure to march on London from Derby. If they had gone on, the world might never have heard of Napoleon Bonaparte.

Dundas and the British Government were entirely responsible for the decision to attack Dunkirk. Dundas in his laborious way thought that 'the capture of Dunkirk by a Prince of the Blood would give great *éclat* to the commencement of the campaign.' It never seemed to have crossed his mind that there was another foreign word in use in the English language, *finale*, which the capture of Paris would have enabled him to use. The British Government was, it is true, only following the example of her Allies in deciding beforehand what part of France she would annex, and taking steps to see that it was captured. A few years before, Burke had complained that the Age of Chivalry was dead because ten thousand swords did not leap from their scabbards to avenge a look that threatened the Queen of France with insult. The swords were certainly leaping from their scabbards now, not to rescue the Queen of France from the *Conciergerie* prison but to dismember her country.

After this failure to capture Dunkirk the British Army withdrew to the Netherlands. The Duke was severely blamed. His countrymen felt the success of the war was being jeopardised in order to do honour to the King's son. In fact, as the following letter from the Duke to a friend shows, he was in no sense to blame.

Tournai,
Nov. 5th, 1793.

DEAR JACK,

Ten thousand thanks for your very kind letter. You know perfectly well that the attack on Dunkirk was no pro-

ject of mine but that I received the most peremptory orders
from England long before the campaign about it and was
obliged to obey and that I was in a manner found fault with
for having consented to delay my march towards the
coast . . . After stating this I am perfectly willing to add
that then I ordered the march against Dunkirk. I thought
I should have succeeded and am convinced that if it had not
been for every untoward and unlucky circumstance happen-
ing to me I should have succeeded. The Austrians know this
perfectly well and do me full justice . . .

Adieu, my dear Jack, I have not time to add more,
except that I hope to see you soon,

> Believe me ever,
>
> > Yours most sincerely,
> >
> > > FREDERICK.

But the Duke perfectly realised that, at any rate in public, he
must bear the blame for what had happened. Lord Malmesbury, the greatest English diplomatist of the eighteenth
century, who was on a roving commission to try and keep
Prussia faithful to the Coalition, wrote to the Government: 'I
have seen and had a long talk with the Duke of York. I have
always had a good opinion of him which has been enhanced by
his saying that if in the House of Commons any objection were
taken to his military command the Ministers were on no
account to defend him at their own expense.' There was no
danger of an eighteenth-century Tory Government risking
their popularity through any mistaken idea of loyalty to the
general they had appointed and, in the autumn, they pressed
the King to recall the Duke before the next year's campaign
began. The King flatly refused, reminding his Ministers that
the Austrian commanders had repeatedly said that the Duke
had done all that could be expected. The Government were
unconvinced and arranged that for the campaign of 1794 the
Duke, with his 20,000 British soldiers, should form part of the
centre of the main Allied Army under the supreme command
of the Prince of Coburg-Saalfeld. The mistake of this arrangement lay in the temptation it gave to the Austrian commander

to sacrifice the British soldiers in positions of danger and to nurse his own men in safety.

The campaign of 1793 was fought against ill-trained and treacherous troops, but in 1794 these had become a formidable army organised by Carnot and led by Pichegru. However, in the middle of May the Allied Army had advanced to within striking distance of France and the Austrian commander ordered the Duke of York to attack Lille while the Austrian right and left would move out from Menin and Tournai to support him. When the Duke reached Tourcoing, on the borders of France and the Netherlands, he found himself confronted by the main French Army which immediately attacked him. The Austrians had spent the early morning dozing in their quarters, and did not move till mid-day. By that time the English had lost 1,000 men and 19 out of their 25 guns. The Duke himself, conspicuous by the Star of the Garter on his breast, was only saved from capture by the swiftness of his horse. He could have expected little mercy from a Government of which Robespierre was still the head. The Duke was pardonably furious with the Austrians and wrote angrily to the Government. 'I think myself most cruelly and shamefully sacrificed and nothing but the courage and good conduct of the British troops could have saved them from being taken or totally cut to pieces.'

By the end of July the Allies had separated: and the British Army was obliged to fall back on Holland. By October they had crossed behind the Meuse, leaving the southern parts of Holland in the hands of the French. On 3rd October, the King wrote from Windsor to encourage his son.

MY DEAR FREDERICK,

I have not wrote since the reception of yours on having been obliged to cross the Meuse, which though a very unpleasant movement seems to have been necessary.

If I would give vent to my feelings on the supine conduct of the Dutch my pen would never stop . . .

Had not your corps been divided between the two armies and consequently your force reduced to nothing, and the

Austrians by that rendered the superior in both and enabled by that to command every move to be taken, the campaign would not have been fruitless and we would not have the whole to begin again.

Keep up your spirits: remember that difficulties are the time that shows the energy of character and as the rest of Europe seems blind to the evils that await the unprosperous conclusions of this business, it is my duty and that of my country by the greatest exertion to attempt to save Europe and society itself.

> I ever remain, my dear Frederick,
>> Your most affectionate father,
>>> GEORGE R.

But the public needed a scapegoat and Pitt did not hesitate to attribute the failure of the campaign to the inexperience of the Duke. He wrote to the King that unless the Duke was recalled he would be censured by Parliament. The King acidly replied that 'he certainly should not think it safe for his son to continue in the command when everyone seemed to conspire to render his situation hazardous, by either propagating unfounded complaints against him or giving credit to them.' The Duke was recalled at the end of the year and his Army returned to England in 1795. He had in fact showed himself an unlucky but competent general, and we may safely agree with George III that 'to the conduct of the Austrians, the faithlessness of Prussia and the cowardice of the Dutch every failure was easily to be accounted for without laying blame on him who deserved a better fate.' The Government were anxious that Lord Cornwallis should have had the command. If he had, the result would not have been different and the history of the campaigns of 1793 and 1794 would not have needed rewriting.

Five years later the same Government appointed the Duke to command another Army in Holland. We must either believe that the Ministers were incapable of standing up to George III (which we know Pitt was not) or that they had never really believed that the failure of the previous campaign was due to the inexperience of the Duke, and had cheerfully sacrificed him to the prejudices of the mob.

Ever since the war began, Pitt, like some great spider, had been striving to spin an alliance which should entangle the French. In 1799 the Second Coalition, made up of Austria, Russia and England, flapped loosely across Europe. Too loosely, owing to the selfishness of the Allies, to catch Bonaparte. England was always preoccupied with Holland, and insisted that one of the chief objects of the Coalition should be an effort to dislodge the French from Holland, of which they had been in possession ever since 1795. The Duke was therefore appointed to the command of a mixed force of English, Russians and Hanoverians to achieve this object. They landed in that triangle of land between the North Sea and the Zuyder Zee, the apex of which fits on to the mainland of Holland above Amsterdam. It was really impossible to maintain an Army of 50,000 men in this small triangle of land throughout the winter, and it was essential for the Allies to break through to the country south of Amsterdam before the winter set in. They did not land till September. The sandy coast was whipped to fury by the autumnal gales. The Russians were troublesome allies, whose one idea was to blunder forward till they reached the main French Army and then summon the Duke to their rescue. But, despite this, the Duke won three victories, though none of them were sufficiently decisive to enable him to advance. As winter came on, he saw that it was impossible to maintain his Army where it was and on the advice of his generals he concluded a convention with the French by which the Allied Army was to be allowed to leave Holland in exchange for 8,000 French prisoners.

England was appalled. A mob cannot reason, it is only capable of collectively forming the judgment of its least intelligent member. Every half-wit knew that an Army had been despatched under the Duke. A great disaster had followed. The Duke must be to blame. Pamphleteers, caricaturists and lampoonists showered abuse and ridicule on him. People repeated with a titter the utterly unjust lines –

Calm and serene beyond the cannon's reach
He shoots the screaming sea-gull on the beach.

But it must not be imagined that the Duke was a brilliant
general who, in each of his campaigns, was the victim of misfortune. No doubt a Wellington, or a Bonaparte, or the many
officers as capable as they by chance 'forbade to wade through
slaughter to a throne,' would have triumphed despite the
difficulties. The Duke was entirely lacking in any spark of
genius. Like the majority of generals he was in capacity only a
colonel. Brave, obedient, and inspiring confidence in his men,
he would have executed brilliant moves which he was incapable of originating. The caricaturist, Henry Bunbury, who
was one of the Duke's aides-de-camp in the campaign of 1799,
has left on record his opinion of the Duke as a commander. It
is a harsh view which makes no allowances for the crippling
conditions under which the Duke was appointed but it is
representative of military opinion.

Much as I loved the Duke personally, much as I felt
many good and amiable qualities in his character, much as I
owe to him in gratitude for long kindness to myself, I cannot
but acknowledge that he was not qualified to be even the
ostensible head of a great army on arduous service . . . He
was of a cool courage: he would have stood all day to be shot
at: but he had no active bravery. With a very fair understanding he had little quickness of apprehension, still less of
sagacity in penetrating designs or forming large views:
painstaking, yet devoid of resources, and easily dis-
heartened by difficulties. (He could not bring himself to
say no.) To these defects must be added habits of indulgence, and a looseness of talking about individuals after
dinner which made him enemies, and which, in the unfortunate campaign, probably excited the rancour of the
Russian Generals. [1]

[1] In 1949, Lt.-Colonel Burne published a biography of the Duke covering
his military life. This gives a very much more favourable picture of his
capacity in the field, and was published by the Staples Press. The reader is
also referred to an interesting correspondence from the first Lord Anglesey

But if military opinion was hostile to the Duke in the field, it was enthusiastically in favour of his work as commander-in-chief at home. He had seen for himself in his campaigns in Holland that the British Army suffered from shocking organisation and from inefficient officers. Many of the soldiers had been sent out in 1793 in slop clothing, that is a linen jacket and trousers, without waistcoat, drawers or stockings. Money and intrigue were the only channels to promotion. The first task he set himself was to increase the efficiency of the officers, and in 1800 he founded the Royal Military College at Woolwich, and two years later a military school at High Wycombe which was the parent of Sandhurst. Both these places were founded with the idea of giving the officers some chance of learning their profession. Secondly, he was determined to improve the conditions under which the private soldiers had to serve, and he was unceasing in his efforts to make their lives more comfortable. He was very popular with the men, and there were always genuine cheers for 'the brave old Duke of York.'

For more than 120 years the country has recognised the brilliance of the Duke of Wellington but, with the soldiers of 1793 and the military organisation of 1793, Spain could not have been freed from Napoleon, Waterloo could not have been won, Wellesley could not have become Wellington. The Duke of York was the organiser of victory. Almost the last words he spoke were to Peel in 1826, when he said that 'he wished that anyone would compare the troops that had just gone abroad, with the Brigade that landed in Holland in 1793, and that he had determined that no other officer who might command on foreign service should be subjected to the same disadvantages that he had laboured under in 1793.'

IV

By 1800 the Duke's manner of life had changed. Moralists would doubtless say that marriage had sobered him down. In

---

and his brother from Flanders in 1794-5. This was edited by the present Lord Anglesey and published in the *Journal of Army Historical Research*, 1954.

fact it made not the slightest difference, except that he had a rather larger income and a port of call in the country. One of the reasons for the change was that he had work to do. He twice commanded the British troops on the Continent and in 1795 he was appointed commander-in-chief of the Army. The other reason for the change was that after his marriage he ceased to be on such friendly terms with the Prince of Wales. If anything in the Prince of Wales's life could be dignified by the word tragic, it was that, until he was fifty, he lived in a position of great eminence divorced from any kind of responsibility, and the final (and public) quarrel between him and the Duke of York took place in an exchange of letters in which the Duke of York, on behalf of the King, refused to promote the Prince to a higher rank than Colonel of the Tenth Dragoons at the time of the Napoleonic invasion scare. There was never any question with the Prince of Wales of curtailing the carouse in order to be ready for the labours of the day. It was immaterial to him whether the sun went down upon his rest and rose again upon his junketings.

But, with the Duke of York, debauchery had now to take second place to duty. And that was not the whole extent of the change. Of course, a life of pleasure had become a second nature to him which could not possibly be eradicated, but the promiscuous delights of Carlton House were not for a middle-aged man who was liable at any moment to be dragged away on business. It was the manner of his vices as well as the manner of his life that had changed. It was no longer the gay bursts of April but the steady downpour of a later season. It was not a fortune or a property depending on the turn of a dice, but high stakes at whist night after night: not a sudden wild orgy of drinking, but sitting for hours over the port: not a short and sweet romance, but the solid comforts of a double establishment.

When slightly more than foolish forty he set up house in Gloucester Place, off Portman Square, with a lady called Mrs Clarke, who was over thirty and with whom he was completely infatuated. She was a common woman, who had been born in

Bowl and Pin Alley, off Chancery Lane, and had married a stonemason, and had then lived with progressively grander persons till she had now reached the dizzy heights of Royalty. She was good-looking, but her real charms were intellectual, for she was daring, amusing and brilliant. She lived in considerable style in Gloucester Place, with two carriages, eight horses, a butler, coachman, postilion, groom, man cook, gardener and two footmen. The Duke could not bear to be parted from her even for a week-end, and he took a house for her at Weybridge so that she might be near Oatlands. In her gay, light-hearted way she tripped into Weybridge Church one Sunday morning and watched her lover and the Duchess at their prayers. The Duke was embarrassed; the Duchess said nothing, but wrote privately to Mr Pitt, of whom all the sons of George III stood in the greatest awe as he controlled their Parliamentary grants, that such a thing must never occur again. But the Duke was unabashed, and wrote to her soon after: 'How can I sufficiently express to my darling love my thanks for her dear dear letter or the delight which the assurances of her love give me? Oh, my angel, do me justice and be convinced that there never was a woman adored as you are ... Ten thousand thanks, my love, for the handkerchiefs which are delightful: and I need not, I trust, assure you of the pleasure I feel in wearing them, and thinking of the dear hands who made them for me ... Adieu therefore my sweetest, dearest love, till the day after to-morrow and be assured that I shall ever remain yours and yours alone.'

After a few years the passion burned itself out and the good people of Chelsea grew accustomed to seeing the Duke's carriage rolling down the King's Road to visit a house in Fulham, near to Fulham Palace, where a certain Mrs Cary lived. He was really enjoying his work and was reaching a comfortable middle age.

> *Mighty as Mars, as Venus soft in mien,*
> *At our Horse Guards plump Frederick is seen,*
> *To eat, drink, chat and call his Fulham groom,*
> *Promote young boys: bow men from out the room.*

The only thing was that there had been rather a number of these lampoons since he had left that witty Mrs Clarke.

In the autumn of 1808 a carriage, with a lady and two gentlemen inside, might have been seen driving along the south coast. They had told their friends that they were going for the benefit of the sea air after the exhaustion of the London Season. They also hoped that they might see something of these new Martello Towers that everyone was talking about. They came bowing and smiling into Brighton and stayed there for a few days. If the Duke of York had happened to be staying at the Pavilion with the Prince of Wales, and had passed the carriage, he would no doubt have blushed and pretended not to see the occupants.

One of the men in the carriage was Major Dodd, military secretary to Field-Marshal His Royal Highness the Duke of Kent. The Duke of York disliked his brother. For his part the Duke of Kent was too discreet a man to dislike anyone, but he allowed himself to attribute the many disasters that had overtaken his military career to the jealousy and dislike of the Duke of York. Occasionally he even thought that if the Duke had never been born or if something terrible were to happen to him, he would be commander-in-chief instead of him. Now Major Dodd was not so discreet as his master; he was tired of being military secretary to an unemployed Field-Marshal, and he rather fancied himself as military secretary to the commander-in-chief. For a whole year he had been supplying the Press with private details about the Duke of York, and, if the information had in turn been supplied to him by the Duke of Kent, of course no one could have imagined that that Christian Prince would have wished it made public to damage his brother's reputation.

The other man in the carriage was Colonel Wardle, the Member of Parliament for Okehampton. He was a member of the Opposition, needy and ambitious.

The lady was a frail beauty 'with dazzling dark eyes beaming with irresistible archness and captivating intelligence: her skin delicately fair without being of a dead white: a sufficient colour adorning her cheek.' Such was Mrs Clarke, the Duke of

York's former mistress, at the age of thirty-six. She found her companions very agreeable and, if in the middle of surveying a magnificent sweep of downland they introduced his Royal Highness's name, she was glad to talk of him. She always called him 'the Doctor,' and it tickled her bright fancy to tell them of the Doctor's monstrous appetite, of his love of wine and his dear affectionate ways. The Doctor was never very generous and, at the last, his treatment of her had been positively shabby. There could be no harm in telling the gentlemen what she had had to do to make both ends meet. So she tittered on about the Doctor's love-letters, about his kindness to her friends in the Army, and something very ridiculous about a preacher.

On 27th January, 1809, Colonel Wardle, primed with the indiscretions of his little jaunt, rose in his place in the House of Commons to move that 'a Committee be appointed to investigate the conduct of His Royal Highness the Duke of York, in his capacity of Commander-in-Chief, with regard to appointments, promotions, exchanges, the raising of new levies and the general state of the Army.' Encouraged by loud cheers, he said that unless corruption was attacked, and attacked strongly too, the country would soon fall an easy prey to an inveterate enemy. Such a cry was bound to rally all the members of the Opposition.

With the exception of the year 1806, the Whigs had formed the Opposition since 1783. After the terrors of the French Revolution many of them, led by Burke and Windham, decided that it was their duty to support the Tory administration of Pitt, while the remnant under Fox opposed Pitt and the war with France. But when Fox and his supporters became members of the Ministry of All the Talents in 1806 and took their share in prosecuting the war, it was no longer possible for them, on going into opposition again in 1807 after Fox had died, to attack the war. After 1807 it was the management of the war, not its existence, that they attacked. And the members of the Opposition were keeping queer company in those days, with their ears wide open in the hope of discovering some scandal in the administration of the war. For an attack on corruption is the finest political policy in the world. 'Corruption in High Places' is a cry which will never split a party. On the contrary outraged moralists will flock from every quarter to join it. And what better quarry could they desire than the commander-in-chief in an age when Royalty was suspect? Sir Francis Burdett, the mouthpiece of the extreme Radicals, seconded Colonel Wardle's motion.

The Government undertook to defend the Duke. The responsibility mainly fell on Mr Perceval, who was Chancellor of the Exchequer and Leader of the House of Commons in the Duke of Portland's Government. The Government served the Duke of York very badly. Not for them an inquiry by a Committee (which was all the Opposition were asking for) which would have been a businesslike body briefly sifting the evidence more or less behind closed doors. But with the maximum publicity, the maximum delay, and the maximum excitement, the Government demanded that the largest dirty-linen basket imaginable should be dragged before the bar of the House. The Secretary of War, Lord Castlereagh, in his speech airily said: 'I think the greatest possible publicity should be given to this examination, and that every step of it should be in the face of day. I am, therefore, not for leaving it to any select committee, not even to the Twelve Judges, nor to anything short of that full and open examination, which may be had at the bar of the House.' Laudable sentiments enough for an innocent martyr but presumably the Duke of York was not a complete stranger to Lord Castlereagh. Naturally the Opposition was delighted, and it was unanimously decided that the inquiry should take place before the whole House. The proceedings lasted for seven weeks and occupied seven hundred closely printed pages.

It was clearly proved over and over again that Mrs Clarke had taken money to influence promotions in the Army. But the fact that officers thought that if they paid money to Mrs Clarke they would be sure of promotion, proved nothing against the Duke. The point was whether the Duke knew that Mrs Clarke was taking the money, and whether he was influenced by Mrs Clarke in the promotions he made. (It was suggested in the course of the inquiry, but there was not the slightest evidence on the point, that some of the money found its way into the Duke's pocket.) On the really vital question whether the Duke was influenced by Mrs Clarke in the officers he promoted, no evidence was brought except that, after the money had been paid to Mrs Clarke, the promotions had taken place. (There were no doubt many cases where Mrs Clarke had been paid money but where no promotions had taken place which were not of course referred to, as they proved nothing.) But as the Government were able to produce documents from the War Office, and to call officials who had charge of the promotions, to prove that the cases mentioned by the Opposition had all taken place in the ordinary course of events, the Duke must be regarded as innocent on this charge.

But it was nearly as serious for him if it could be proved that he knew that Mrs Clarke was taking the bribes, because to countenance such things was obviously a grave abuse of his public position. On this point the Opposition relied mainly on two cases.

The first concerned an exchange between two colonels – Colonel Brook and Colonel Knight. Colonel Knight's brother paid Mrs Clarke £200, but in his examination before the House of Commons he said that 'Mrs Clarke entreated me to keep it a secret lest it should come to the Duke's ears.' But Mrs Clarke said that she had told the Duke that she had received 'a compliment' from Mr Knight. And Mrs Clarke's butler, at his second examination, said that he had been sent out to change the bill for £200 and had paid the money to Mrs Clarke in the Duke's presence. But when asked why he had not mentioned this at his first examination, he said 'I had a very bad headache: and when I have the headache it affects my memory that I am very forgetful and I did not think of it.' The House of Commons decided that he was too drunk to give any further evidence. Mr Knight had no interest in telling a lie and his statement that Mrs Clarke had entreated him to keep it a secret was undoubtedly the truth.

The second charge concerned operations on the grand scale. A certain Colonel French was raising a levy and, in exchange for Mrs Clarke's assistance in his own promotion, she was to have the patronage of a certain number of officers in the levy for which she issued the following tariff:

	Full Pay Price	Half Pay Price
For a Majority	£2,600	£900
For a Company	£1,500	£700
For a Lieutenancy	£550	£400
For an Ensigncy	£400	£200

The only evidence, apart from Mrs Clarke's, that the Duke knew of this was given by a close friend of Mrs Clarke's called Miss Taylor. She said that she was dining at Gloucester Place with the Duke and Mrs Clarke and that the Duke had said 'Colonel French continually worries me about the levy business and is always wanting something more in his own favour. How does he behave to you, darling?' Mrs Clarke replied, 'Middling!' The Duke answered, 'Master French must mind what he's about or I shall cut him up and his levy too.' But Miss Taylor was not an entirely satisfactory witness. She kept some kind of an establishment for women off the King's Road in Chelsea, and announced that she did not like to give her address before so large an assembly. (Considering the assembly was entirely composed of men she would appear to have missed an excellent opportunity of advertising her establishment.)

The House of Commons cannot have been really impressed by any of the evidence, although no one could help admiring Mrs Clarke for the way in which she had conducted her case. She was examined many times and was caught out in twenty-eight obvious falsehoods but always lived to lie again another day. It was not for nothing that she had known men for twenty years, and her brilliance in dealing with six hundred members of Parliament must have been envied by many 'a rising hope.' Perhaps she was shown at her best when her case would have been compromised if she had been forced to say what a previous witness had told her in the lobby when she was waiting to be cross-examined. The Government speakers pressed her again and again. At last, in answer to Mr Windham, with modest, downcast eyes, she said very softly, 'I cannot tell you because it was indelicate.' Was it surprising that while she was in the House a note was thrust into her hand saying, '300 guineas and supper with me to-night'?

The Opposition would have voted against the Duke whatever the evidence had been, but even the supporters of the Government were prejudiced against him by feeling that, unless he was mad, he must have seen what was going on. There he was, living with a penniless adventuress, to whom he allowed £1,000 a year, but who had a cottage in the country and a large house in London with a retinue of menservants and horses and carriages. He was proved to have known that she had paid £500 (half her income) towards buying a service of plate which had belonged to Louis XVI's nephew, the Duc de Berri. Respectable country gentlemen, carefully watching their expenses in a world of soaring prices, felt that the Duke had been careless to a degree that they could not understand and, despite the weakness of the evidence, felt that Mrs Clarke might have been telling the truth when she said, 'The Duke told me that if I was clever I should never want for money.' Anyone who knew the Duke would have realised that the weakness in this reasoning lay in expecting him to behave like an ordinary prudent householder or even like his father and mother. His attitude to money was that of a mediæval prince living in an age when money was unimportant, and to expect him to understand the value of £1,000 was about as reasonable as expecting him to discover the philosopher's stone. If he ever wanted money himself, his man of business found it for him and if, in doing so, he pulled a long face and tried to explain that it could not be done, the Duke would tell him to go to the King or to Parliament or, more usually, to the money-lenders. Even his tutor said, 'though the Royal Brothers received instruction in Latin and Greek with ease, yet they could never be taught to understand the value of money.' But it was naturally impossible to explain this to an excited House of Commons, and at the close of the evidence the Duke took the sensible step of writing to the Speaker to declare his innocence, which undoubtedly had the effect of rallying the steady Government supporters to his side.

> Horse Guards,
> Feb. 23rd, 1809.

Sir,

. . . I observe with the deepest concern, that in the course of this inquiry my name has been coupled with transactions the most criminal and disgraceful, and I must ever regret and lament that a connection should ever have existed which has thus exposed my character and honour to public animadversion.

With respect to my alleged offence, connected with the discharge of my official duties, I do, in the most solemn manner, upon my honour, as a Prince, distinctly assert my innocence, not only by denying all corrupt participation in any of the infamous transactions which have appeared in evidence at the Bar of the House of Commons, or any connivance at their existence, but also the slightest knowledge or suspicion that they existed at all.

My consciousness of innocence leads me confidently to hope that the House of Commons will not, upon such evidence as they have heard, adopt any proceeding prejudicial to my honour and character; but if, upon such testimony as has been adduced against me, the House of Commons can think my innocence questionable, I claim of their Justice that I shall not be condemned without trial, or be deprived of the benefit and protection which is afforded to every British subject by those sanctions, under which alone evidence is received in the ordinary administration of the law.

> I am, Sir, yours,
> FREDERICK.

When the vote was taken there was a majority of 82 in favour of the Duke – 278 against 196 – but he resigned at once. A hundred and ninety-six members had thought him guilty of 'personal corruption and connivance at the infamous practices disclosed by Mrs Clarke,' and in the face of such a strong minority he could not decently continue in office. And he bore with the greatest dignity, what was far worse than punishment, the indignation of the moral, the sympathy of his friends, and the titters of the vulgar.

His brother, the Prince of Wales, for perhaps the only time in his life, was found in the ranks of morality. Although he could have influenced many of the Whig votes, he never put on his whip in favour of his brother. Fresh from the aristocratic embraces of Lady Hertford, he had been heard to say: 'I have been no party to my brother's irregularities. I have never been connected with the women with whom my brother has been connected. Indeed I dislike such society.'

The other members of his family overwhelmed him with sympathy and very galling were the condolences of the Duke of Kent. His parents and his sisters, who had always been so proud of him and had taken the greatest interest in everything that he did, were not so much shocked by the disclosures as outraged at the treatment of their favourite. Princess Augusta wrote angrily to a friend: 'I have seen many military men and live chiefly in intimacy with men of that profession. All agree that the Army owes everything to the Duke ... I am also miserable to think that the Methodists are doing all the harm to him they can and there are many in this country, they are vile canters, cheating the devil, praying with their mouths but denying in their hearts: and they think it will command popularity to condemn and abuse the Duke of York for what I daresay they do themselves.'

But perhaps worse than anything was the feeling that he had been made ridiculous in the eyes of the world. Six hundred men had sat rocking with laughter while his love-letters to Mrs Clarke were read: they had been distributed by the newspapers to every corner of the country. Mrs Clarke's drunken butlers and abandoned friends had come forward to say how they had seen the Duke and Mrs Clarke together and how it had been 'Darling this' and 'Darling that' between them. He could hear the children in the street, as they tossed up those

heavy Georgian pennies, crying out 'Duke or Darling' instead
of 'Heads or Tails.' The figure of Britannia on the obverse side
was made to do service for Mrs Clarke.

Far away in Paris, Napoleon, who had just rushed back
from Spain, found the English more difficult to understand
than ever. Following the battle of Corunna, which had been
fought on 16th January, 1809, the English Army had been
driven into the sea and its only apparent effect in England was
that the assembly of men, who were ultimately responsible for
the safety of their country, spent weeks in giggling over the
disclosures of a loose woman. Despising Royalty, Napoleon no
doubt thought that it would be better for France that the Duke
of York should be commander-in-chief of the British Army
rather than a more competent commoner, and was therefore
sorry when the news of the Duke's resignation reached him. But
the Duke had formed a totally different picture of himself. He
saw himself as the essential part of the machine which was to
hurl back the thunderbolts of war at France. For a decade he
had sat in the Horse Guards devising an answer to what the
English Royal Family, always rather grandly termed, 'the
insolence of Bonaparte.' On 22nd April, 1809, the first-fruits
of the Duke's toil had landed in Portugal under Sir Arthur
Wellesley, while he, unwept, unhonoured and unsung, had
withdrawn to Oatlands.

But the Duke was not one to be afflicted with self-pity, and
it was in the true Hanoverian spirit that he retired to Oatlands
to lick his wounds. He had been indiscreet and foolish but had
done nothing to deserve such retribution. He never complained.

Public opinion soon changed. At the end of 1809 an upholsterer brought an action against Colonel Wardle for the
cost of furnishing a house for Mrs Clarke on the orders of the
Colonel. It appeared that Mrs Clarke, far from being the
repentant sinner anxious to expose abuses in the public
interest, was heavily bribed by that 'immaculate patriot
Wardle.' Even the Whigs were heartily sick of the whole subject. Like any sensational case, deliberately fanned by irresponsible persons, it exhausted the maximum of popular

interest in one fierce blaze and was then completely forgotten in the ensuing blackness.

Two years later, in 1811, the Duke was re-appointed commander-in-chief. In 1814 the Duke of Wellington appeared in the House of Commons to thank the members for their congratulations, and referred, in warm terms, to the work of the Duke of York, a reference which was loudly cheered by the very men who five years ago had hounded him from the Horse Guards. At the close of the war a vote of thanks to the Duke of York unanimously passed the House of Commons. Many memories must have floated through the Duke's mind as he read what his secretary had written to the Speaker in reply to the vote. 'But it is with peculiar pride I learn, that the favour of the House of Commons has induced them to ascribe to any effort of mine the smallest share in securing these splendid successes.' And it must have been with peculiar pleasure that in his flowing illegible writing he signed the letter 'Frederick Commander-in-Chief.'

v

In November 1810 Princess Amelia was dying of consumption. On the day before her death she took off her ring and asked one of her sisters to give it to her father after her death, telling him 'to remember me.' It is popularly supposed that, on being given the ring, George III went finally and completely mad. It is true that his reason was disturbed by his daughter's death and that at the beginning of 1811 the Prince of Wales was appointed Regent, under certain restrictions which were to expire in February 1812 if the King had not recovered. But, while the King was all the time growing gradually worse, he was not finally mad till the summer of 1811. It was a completely different form of madness from the attack of twenty years earlier, when a cloud had seemed to descend on his reason which it was recognised might at any time lift. In 1811 the King was seventy-three, and, no doubt owing to the previous attacks of insanity, his brain was completely worn out, and there was not the slightest chance of his ever recover-

ing. George IV virtually began to reign in 1810 and the Duke
of York, as eldest brother of George IV, became of far more
importance than as George III's second son.

George IV, both as King and Regent, relied more on the
Duke of York than on any of his other brothers. As young
men they had been devoted friends; the friendship had ended
in a quarrel, and the quarrel had ended in the Duke having the
greatest respect for his elder brother, while the Prince looked
down on the Duke with a certain superior sympathy. But,
during the Regency, there was no other brother who could
have influenced George IV: he disliked the Duke of Kent and
the Duke of Sussex, he regarded the Duke of Clarence as a
genial buffoon, and the Duke of Cumberland and the Duke of
Cambridge were then seldom in England. Consequently the
Duke of York found that men began to listen to what he had to
say, especially on politics, and people even began to whisper
things in his ear, trusting he would pass them on to the proper
quarter.

In February 1812 the Duke was entrusted with a most
delicate negotiation. That month the limitations on the
Regency were to expire and men felt that, at long last, the
exclusion of the Whigs was ended and that the Regent, being
free to choose his own Government, would send for Grenville
and Grey. It was this fear that he would form a Whig Government that had made Pitt insist on the limitations on the
Regent's powers in 1788, but now it was thought the principles of Fox were to triumph, that in death Fox should overcome Pitt, that there was to be something more than 'the
immortal memory.' The Regent wrote a long letter to the Duke
of York, largely occupied with an account of the country's
successes since he had been at the head of affairs, but adding:
'I cannot conclude without expressing the gratification I
should feel if some of those persons with whom the early habits
of my life were formed, would strengthen my hand and con-
stitute a part of my Government.' Coalition with the Tories
was a poor reward for the thirty years' loyalty of the Whigs to
the Prince of Wales! The Duke of York communicated the
contents of his brother's letter to Grenville and Grey, who a

once replied that differences on the Irish and Roman Catholic questions were too wide to admit of any such arrangement. The Duke was hopelessly ignorant of politics; he just saw that his brother wanted Whig support, which was impossible as long as the Tories were already there. Well, the Tories had had a good innings; let them give the Whigs a chance. Reasoning in this fashion, he sent for Grenville and Grey, and said that they had made a complete mistake, and that what his brother had really meant was that they should form a Government of their own. The Whig leaders raised their eyebrows, and politely pointed out that the Regent's letter did not say so. But the Duke insisted — he knew perfectly what his brother meant. The Regent had to disown his go-between, and it was really hardly surprising that when he introduced the Duke to Mr Creevey he said, for all the world to hear: 'He's a damned bad politician, Creevey, but I'll introduce you to him.'

And if he found politics rather much for him, economics were not really very much easier. There was all the distress and unemployment as a result of the new machinery and the return of the soldiers to the labour market after the war. Charity was the only thing he could think of that would do any good. But when he went down to a charity meeting at the London Tavern for the relief of distress and announced, with the rapid way of speaking inherited from his father, 'I will subscribe 300 guineas,' there had been an uproar in the meeting from the unemployed, who had packed it, shouting out that they did not want charity. It was really all most puzzling and, when he could spare the time from the Army, he was glad to bury himself in such diverse questions as religious societies, the relief of children of destitute Yorkshiremen in London, and the public examination of children in the National Schools.

And, by one of those odd turns of fate, the passing years, which had transformed him from a fierce general into a genial, talkative philanthropist, made him more and more important. In 1810, when his brother became Regent, ambitious men had begun to pay him their court, but in 1817 the whole of England wearily turned its eyes to the Duke of York. Princess Charlotte, the Regent's only child, popular with the people because of her youth and spirits, had died in the labour of giving birth to a dead boy. Seven elderly, childless Princes stood in the succession to the throne. What Creevey calls 'the bad life of the Regent' alone stood between the Duke of York and the Regency or the throne. He occupied the same position in the succession that Princess Charlotte had: at George III's death he would be heir presumptive, and it was known that the Regent would neither divorce the Princess of Wales nor, in the event of her death, risk marriage a second time, so that if he outlived the Regent he must be King.

The country was stunned by the Princess's death, and even Byron could write:

> Peasants bring forth in safety . . .
> . . . in the dust
> The fair-haired daughter of the Isles is laid
> The love of millions . . .

And now the millions were expected to transfer their love to the Duke of York. He was never unpopular with the people, but there was more to laugh at, than to love, in him. When the Princess Charlotte died he had lived for fifty-four years, but in that time the world had outstripped him. It had grown older by much more than fifty-four years. He had grown up in the age of powdered hair and knee-breeches: his character was formed when Louis XVI was executed. Then everything had begun to happen. In the next generation, from 1790 to 1815, wars, revolutions and novel doctrines rushed together in an indistinguishable torrent: behind were all the placid reaches of the eighteenth century, with Captain Jenkins's ear, Mr Cowper at tea, and Wesley jogging through the rain to preach, while in front the nineteenth century was opening out in all its ordered, glorious certainty. A person who was born during those eventful years 1790 to 1815, or was very young during them or very adaptable, would have been carried safely through, but the Duke was too old and too fixed in his views. In a different world he remained the same: to nineteenth-century England he appeared as a piece of flotsam swept out of the eighteenth century.

And the eighteenth century was too near for people to admire him as a survival of the past; he merely seemed rather old-fashioned and very comical. His appearance made him seem even funnier. Stockmar describes him as 'tall with immense *embonpoint* and not proportionately strong legs, he holds himself in such a way that one is continually afraid he will tumble over backwards: very bald and not a very intelligent face.'

Nor did his eighteenth-century figure fit very well into nineteenth-century clothes, with their burstingly tight trousers, and people were amused to read in the paper that, while peeping in on his father at Windsor, his spur had caught in the strap of these fashionable pantaloons and he had come crashing to the ground. Then he was seen much more frequently, and at much closer quarters, presiding over those charity meetings, and his audience had to look down the ends of their noses while 'the brave old Duke of York' blushed and faltered for the right word to round off his Royal periods. The public could not feel enthusiastic at the thought of King Frederick.

And, in addition, the life of the Duke and Duchess of York at Oatlands was completely lacking in dignity: it was impossible for the public to picture them at Windsor or Buckingham Palace. The Duke still only came down at the week-end, and the house would then be filled with his friends, gambling, drinking and cracking coarse jokes. The Duke was easily amused by vulgarity, for, as Greville says, 'he had the feelings of an English gentleman.' The company would sit down to dine at eight and would rise from their port at eleven. The Duke then played whist till four in the morning or later, if he could persuade any of his guests to sit up with him, though he always lost, as he could not help betraying the cards he was holding by the expression on his face.

The Duchess fitted comfortably into this life. She had no objection to coarse jokes, so that her husband and his friends could enjoy themselves in her company. While the Duke and his friends were playing for their £5 points at one end of the room, she had her table and played with a few of the quieter gentlemen for 2s. 6d. points. But she grew tired of playing whist long before four in the morning, and she would call her forty dogs, which had been occupying all the best places round the fire, and offending the noses of some of the guests, and stroll out into the grounds, the dogs barking and frisking at her heels. She seldom went to bed at night, but passed the hours in her grotto in the garden. This had been built for the Duke of Newcastle by an Italian and his sons, and had taken twenty years to build: there were four rooms, in one of which was a large bath which Mr Greville was allowed to use, and found the water in it as clear as crystal and as cold as ice. All the rooms were connected with winding passages, and every inch of the inside walls was covered with millions of pieces of spar, and set off by shells and small mirrors. Here the Duchess passed much of the day and some of the night. Outside she had transformed the garden into aviary and menagerie. In the flower garden were eagles, macaws and other exotic birds: a small colony of monkeys was housed on the lawn in front of the windows of her boudoir. Farther away from the house were kangaroos and ostriches. This fondness for wild life explains why Beau Brummell occupied himself, when he was living in exile at Calais, in making a large six-panelled screen for her, on which were pasted all kinds of birds and animals bowered in fruits and flowers. Beau Brummell's biographer, who was Captain Jesse and describes himself on the title-page as 'unattached', calls the screen 'a glorious piece of fiddle-faddle – the trifling industry of a thoroughly idle man.' That may be so. But the thought – for the Duchess did not live to enjoy the screen – shows that the Beau admired her character and charm, and was genuinely grateful for her kindness to him. The dogs were buried outside the grotto, a tombstone marking the place where each lay, with the name inscribed and, in the cases of special favourites, a small memorial verse composed by their Royal mistress. Macaulay visited Oatlands in 1856 and scornfully alluded to the gravestones of sixty-four of her Royal Highness's curs. But some people thought that her Royal Highness was much troubled by presents of dogs from friends and admirers and that some were borne towards the mausoleum with gentle draughts of opium. We can hardly blame the public for thinking that King Frederick and Queen Frederica would have been a difficult pair to honour and obey.

In 1818 Queen Charlotte had died, and the Duke of York had succeeded her as guardian of his father, for which Parliament voted him £10,000. He was often at Windsor, and sometimes watched the blind bearded figure of his father in his gown of royal purple strumming tunelessly on a harpsichord or chattering of ancient troubles. It was as though the mind, like some piece of driverless machinery, was speeding backwards over tracks which it had itself made in the days when sense controlled it. The doctors thought that the death of the brain had lightened the task of living, and that he would live for many years. Then in the cold days of January 1820 they found it difficult to keep him warm and impossible to feed him. On 29th January, in the presence of the Duke, the King ceased to exist. For a few days George IV, who was dangerously ill, was expected to follow his father, and the Duke now felt certain that before long he would be King. It was noticed that 'the Duke of York is all activity and business, and goes about a great deal, and is very popular and becoming more so.'

But there was to be no Queen Frederica. For in August the Duke received an urgent message to go to Oatlands. The Duchess died in his presence, after begging that she might be buried in Weybridge Church, next to her great friend Mrs Bunbury and (though she did not say this) not at Windsor, next to him. After sitting for an hour at the head of the coffin, where it was lying in state in the dining-room at Oatlands, he came out of the house to follow it to the church and was seen to burst into tears. Many women might have cut greater figures in the social world; some might have borne him children; none could have been more considerate to him.

Within a week George IV, who disliked the nearness to the throne of the child of the Duke of Kent, urged him to marry again, and was even ready with the names of eligible brides. But the Duke had no heart to give away because, for the last time, he was desperately in love. There was to be no mistake this time of going to worthless, ill-bred women – society which (it will be remembered) the King disliked. The lady was the Duchess of Rutland. This *grand amour* was first announced to the world by his being seen through the railings of Kensington Gardens walking up and down with the Duchess. So entranced was the lover that he did not notice that the object of his affections was nearly fainting with exhaustion. When at last he noticed this, he rushed off and returned, puffing and blowing, leading a pony, which he insisted on her riding. For two more hours they were seen parading up and down. They were described as 'a pattern of juvenile sentiment.' He wisely felt that, with the Duchess of Rutland enshrined in his heart, a second marriage to a young girl would be rather more than he could comfortably manage.

In the summer of 1821, George IV was crowned. It was a brilliant affair which cost the country more than £400,000. The central figure had been pulled in here and stuffed out there to try and suggest to the crowd something of his youthful beauty. Every available part of his person – his hands, his gloves, his white kid trousers – was flashing with imitation jewellery. But the Duke of York thought it all very lovely, and was heard to exclaim, 'By God! I'll have everything the same at mine.'

It was just as well that he could feel so confident that he would one day be King, in possession of all the emoluments of the Crown, because some of his confidence may have found its way to his creditors and consoled them for the lack of his money. He was faced with literal poverty. The £10,000 a year he had been granted for looking after George III of course ceased with his father's death though, even without that, his income was considerable. But practically the whole of it was absorbed in the interest on his debts, and the sources of credit were long ago dried up. Was it surprising that when, at a dinner, he proposed the health of Mr Coutts as 'my banker for upwards of thirty years,' Mr Coutts was heard to whisper, 'It is your Royal Highness who has done me the honour to keep my money for thirty years'? He was obliged to sell Oatlands, but the purchase money was all absorbed in paying off debts. Princes can be penniless without feeling the pinch of poverty. Tradesmen, though pulling a long face over the lengthening bill, are loath to tear down the Royal Arms from above their doors; servants, though looking a little grim as week succeeds week without wages, are in 'a good place' with plenty of creature comforts; crowds of people can be found who will gladly entertain a Prince; many are even ready to 'lend' a few hundred pounds. So it is not surprising that, with his complete ignorance of money and nothing to bring poverty home to him, the Duke, although he was virtually penniless, decided on building a new house in Stable Yard, in St James's Palace. It was to be quite small. Then it struck him that it might not be finished before he was King and, in any event, he would not have been there long before he would have to turn out for Carlton House or Buckingham Palace, whichever he should decide to live in when he became King. So he thought it would be very much more sensible, and much more economical in the long run, to build a palace, and then there would be no need to move when he came to the throne. Wyatt was called in to design it, and all the plans were first submitted to the Duchess of Rutland. Disraeli tells us in *Lothair* that the land round the house was diverted from one of the royal parks, and that the resulting house was not unworthy of Vicenza in its best days. Naturally, long before building had begun, it was heavily mortgaged, and by the time the Duchess of Rutland had laid the foundation-stone the mortgagees were threatening to foreclose. So serious was the situation that the Government were obliged to advance money on the property themselves so that the mortgagees should not foreclose and put up speculative houses cheek by jowl with St James's Palace, which they were threatening to do. Neither the Duke of York nor the Duchess of Rutland lived to see it finished, but it was thanks to them (and, perhaps, to the Government) that nineteenth-century society could delight in the stately gracefulness of Stafford House, which is now called Lancaster House and was the home of the London Museum. And now all the world may see the style of grandeur designed for a penniless, sixty-year-old widower.

While the palace was building the Duke lived in South

Audley Street, and from here he would drive over to the Horse Guards, or to his headquarters in the King's Road where, under his own eye, were housed so many of the dependants of those who had fallen in the wars. He was always a welcome visitor to Windsor, either to the Castle or to Frogmore, where his sister, the Princess Augusta lived. He often went down to the Duke of Rutland's house at Cheveley, near Newmarket. The years were slipping by quietly and peacefully.

Then in 1825 the country was thrown into a ferment by the Roman Catholic question. As a young man, the Duke had become a Whig, but there was no danger of his siding with the Whigs on this question. It was the Whigs in their wild, irresponsible moments of being 'agin the Government' at all costs, that had appealed to him as a young man in the twenties in revolt against his father. He had never absorbed the solid, sober principles of Whiggery. He had never understood politics, and, like all people in that baffling position, found his steps wandering, with surprising steadiness, towards the right. But for all that he still had one principle which was now nearly 140 years old – the British Constitution. It cannot strictly be called a political principle, because it was, in the nineteenth century, common to all political parties. He interpreted it as meaning a limited monarchy dependent on suppression of the Roman Catholics. These were what he called 'the sacred principles on which the House of Brunswick holds the throne.' The desire of liberal-minded persons, by no means confined to the Whig party, to give freedom of worship to the Roman Catholics – to allow them the same benefits as were now enjoyed by the other religious bodies outside the Established Church – clashed with the Duke's principle: and with a man of the Duke's mentality, principle should never yield to 'subtle reasoning.'

Of course, it would be a mistake to rank the Duke of York and George IV, who shared the Duke's view, or even George III, who had made it a condition of ministerial office that the Roman Catholic question should never be mentioned to him, with the numerous fanatics who still believed every Roman

Catholic to be a potential Grand Inquisitor. With the Royal Family it was not a religious but a constitutional question. They felt they owed their throne to the Protestants, and that the Coronation Oath would be broken if they agreed to freedom of worship for the Roman Catholics.

Early in 1825, Sir Francis Burdett had introduced a Bill, which gave relief to the Roman Catholics and which had passed the House of Commons by 248 votes to 227 votes. When the House of Lords met on 25th April, the Duke of York was observed standing in his place and holding in his hand a petition from the Dean and Chapter of the Collegiate Church of Windsor. It was a petition that no concessions should be made to the Roman Catholics. The Duke spoke in support of the petition, and wound up his speech by saying: 'I feel very strongly on the whole subject: I cannot forget the deep interest which was taken upon it by one now no more: and the long and unhappy illness in which . . . [His Royal Highness was too affected to finish the sentence.] I have been brought up from my early years in these principles: and from the time when I began to reason for myself, I have entertained them from conviction: and in every situation in which I may be placed, I will maintain them: [Then solemnly striking his breast with his right hand] so help me God.'

Once more, as in 1809, the scurrilous printing-presses of London groaned and clanked under a weight of abuse and ridicule of the Duke of York. For, after his speech, Whigs, Radicals and the Irish saw that as long as he lived there was no hope of a Bill for the Emancipation of Roman Catholics becoming law. As heir to the throne he had sufficient influence with his brother to keep him true to the Protestant cause, and as King he would have unhesitatingly vetoed any such Bill. The massive shade of Royalty had indeed fallen across the sunshine of their hopes. They were not merciful opponents. His name was cursed throughout the length and breadth of Southern Ireland. Mr Brougham, the Radical gadfly not yet confined out of harm's way in the House of Lords, savagely ridiculed the Duke in a speech in the House of Commons when he said '. . . all hope of recalling them from their errors

— so help them God [cheers and loud laughter] — was but visionary.'

But in 1809, during the Mrs Clarke scandals, the Duke had found no defender except a dutiful Government; public opinion had been solidly against him: now, however, while he was as fiercely attacked, he was equally stoutly defended both in Parliament and in pamphlets by a large section of the public. Votes of thanks for his speech poured in from all over England. Protestant societies, representing all degrees of fanaticism, brayed out their gratitude. Evangelical ladies worked little pictures of the Duke on samplers and carefully stitched underneath:

> *Long may the Duke of York and veteran laws*
> *Form the strong bulwark of our cause.*

The Duke was cheered in the streets, and, remembering 1809, smiled to himself when he saw chalked up by the urchins, 'Damn the King, the Duke of York for ever.'

The street arabs did rough justice. For the King had let it be known that he agreed with every word of the Duke's speech, though he told his friends that he thought the 'So help me God' at the end was unnecessary. But there was some method in their scribbling. All the world knew that the King would never willingly give way on the Roman Catholic question, but it was felt that if a Roman Catholic Emancipation Bill passed Parliament the King might yield to the bullying and fawning of his Ministers as, in a burst of passionate sobbing, he actually did in 1829. But with the Duke of York it was seen to be different. The invocation to God, the broken sentences about his father, the fervent striking of the breast, showed that he was deliberately encasing himself in that dynastic obstinacy against which the arrows of justice and reason had so often shivered themselves to no purpose. Many years later Lord Melbourne told Queen Victoria, 'Your uncle the Duke of York declared many times that he would have gone to the scaffold sooner than give way about the Roman Catholics.'

In these gay, hectic days of 1825 he may have even pictured

George III and Queen Charlotte receiving Princess Caroline of
Brunswick, with the Prince of Wales standing in the background,
by Richard Livesey

'Exercising a Hobby from Wales to Hertford!!'–
the Regent and Lady Hertford, *by Marks,* 1819

'The Rival Queans–or a Scene in the Beggars Opera'–
the Duke of York, Mrs Clarke and Mrs Carey, *by Williams,* 1809

The Duke of York on the Horse Guards'

The Duke of Cambridge,
by Thomas Lawrence

The Duke of Cambridge as seen by a French caricaturist, 1803

himself mounting the steps of the scaffold, while afterwards Protestants gathered throughout England to thank God for the example of Frederick, King and Martyr, and some Protestant bards sang of another 'memorable scene' and another 'comely head.'

But at the beginning of 1826 all the enjoyment in his hard-won popularity was removed by the news of the death of the Duchess of Rutland. It was round this lady, who was nearer to fifty than forty, that his life had revolved for the last seven years. He toiled up to Belvoir Castle from Brighton through the snow to attend the funeral. On getting back to London, he slaved away at Army and Protestant business, but the zest for it all was gone.

The one bright spot was his little niece Victoria. He gave her a donkey to ride, and she used often to call and chatter away to him, which gave him great pleasure, as he was really too broken to go out much into society. He thought she would be rather dull with her old uncle, so he used to arrange a Punch and Judy show for her in the garden. She was very fond of him, but thought him 'a very shy man.' In the summer of 1826 he went down to Brighton for his health and she wrote to him on his birthday:

Tunbridge Wells,
10th August, 1826.

My Dear Uncle,

I offer you many affectionate congratulations on your birthday – very many with my best love – for all your kindness to me – and it has been a great pleasure to me, to be able to write this year to my Uncle, the King, and to you.

We hope to hear that Brighton does you a great deal of good.

Believe me, my dear Uncle, your very affectionate niece –

Victoria.

But his was a case for which Brighton could do nothing, except to recall the memories of the old days at the Pavilion when he had not had to be so careful as to what he should eat and what he should drink. A few days after he received this letter from his niece, his secretary was telling him 'although great confidence is felt in the extraordinary resources of your constitution your complaint has now assumed a more serious character, but yet there is more to hope than to fear.' It was heart trouble, aggravated by dropsy. He was rushed up to London in five and a half hours to undergo the operation of tapping. He felt unable to face the loneliness of South Audley Street so he was driven to the Duke of Rutland's house in Arlington Street, and he sent at once for the Bishop of London to administer the Sacrament, while he was still in full possession of his faculties. He said to the Bishop: 'I have in the course of my life faced death in various shapes and I am now doomed to view its approach in a slow and lingering form. I do not deny that I shall resign my existence with regret though I feel no alarm. I admit that my life has not been pure and there has been much in my course that I wish had been otherwise.'

The operation was successful, and twelve pints of water were drawn off, but the doctors were obliged to tell him that he could not expect to live for more than a few weeks. It was not at all the death he had pictured. In so far as he had thought about death, he must have seen himself as a popular, good-natured King passing over to the music of his people's grief or, if things had gone very wrong over the Roman Catholic question, finding death as Charles I and Louis XVI had found it. The martyr's crown he had never seriously thought of, but the earthly crown had always seemed to him absolutely certain. Instead, the brother he was to have succeeded, rheumatic and gross but still able to move, came painfully to see him and persuaded him to take a little gruel. It was no comfort to know that he should never have counted on outliving his brother — especially as he was only a year younger and had not been able to lie down in bed for many years owing to his heart. He had to face as best he could the end of his hopes.

It was not only the power and importance that had made him look forward to the crown but, with its revenues, his own affairs were to be straightened out and his debts paid off. As soon as it was known that he was dying, his creditors flocked

to Arlington Street like vultures to a battlefield. The public
felt sorry for him and, little knowing how ill he was, argued
that recovery was impossible as long as he was tormented by
debts. Peel wrote to Lord Liverpool, who was then Prime
Minister, urging that the Government and the King should
co-operate to relieve the most pressing of the debts. But
George IV, with £500,000 a year at Windsor Castle, was a
very different person from George, Prince of Wales, with
£100,000 at Carlton House: he had grown careful when it
was no longer necessary, and nothing was done. So with his
creditors banging on the door and the noise of the building of
his palace ringing in his ears, the Duke of York prepared for
death. He was dying, as *The Times* acidly remarked, 'with
neither house, nor furniture, nor horses, nor tangible property
of any kind incidental to the condition of a gentleman.'

Many a man would have cursed the fates which had kept
him waiting on the threshold of a throne, only to hurl him
back with the stigma of having robbed people in a less enviable
position than his own. But with all his faults there was nothing
mealy-mouthed about the Duke of York and, when confronted with death, he showed the traditional fortitude of his
race and, in addition, an unsuspected streak of philosophical
sense. There were to be no moanings over his death, no elaborate death-bed scenes. He liked his favourite sister, the Princess
Sophia, to come in and say a few prayers with him. Then he
would settle down for the day's work. Right up to the end, the
officials came over from the War Office to consult with him
about the English troops that were to be sent to Portugal, and
the general business of the Army. He sat most of the day in an
easy chair, while his secretaries did such writing as was
necessary, and at night he changed into a larger chair with a
foot-rest so that he could get some sleep.

But even when he had transacted several hours' business for
the Army there was still the Roman Catholic question to
haunt his mind. Were the sacred principles of the House of
Brunswick safe in the hands of George IV? He felt doubtful,
and decided from his death-bed to issue one last challenge to
the Church of Rome. In the middle of November his last con-

fession of political faith was embodied in a memorial to Lord Liverpool. He thought that the country was on the 'Brink of the Precipice and wished to God that the task of warning his countrymen had fallen into other hands than his.' His solution for drawing the country back to safety was to form a Government on an exclusively Protestant basis, by which he meant one that was pledged to combat what he called 'Catholic Ascendency.' It was known after his death that he had submitted a memorial to Lord Liverpool, though the contents were kept secret, and it was suggested by one pamphleteer that the policy he had advocated for Ireland was 'Enrich her! Give her the Bible! Laugh at her demagogues.' Such a policy, which was at least novel, could not have been less effective than his age-old suggestion of reforming her through an aggressively Protestant Government. Lord Liverpool sent the memorial to the King with the comment that, if the Duke's suggestion was adopted, it must sooner or later lead to the formation of a Government on an exclusively pro-Roman Catholic basis.

But after this the Duke grew gradually weaker, and by the New Year he was unconscious. On 7th January, 1827, he died. Mr Greville wrote in his diary that evening: 'I am just come back from taking my last look at the poor Duke. He was set exactly as at the moment he died, in his great armchair, dressed in his grey dressing-gown, his head inclined against the side of the chair, his hands lying before him and looking as if he was in a deep and quiet sleep.'

The country was genuinely grieved. They had lost a Prince who was manly, gentle, unintellectual – three qualities which were truly English – and whose weaknesses – extravagance, drunkenness and lustfulness – were, no doubt, wrong but not unattractive in the great of the earth. He was contrasted favourably with George IV, fondling an unpopular mistress, hoarding every garment he had ever worn, clearing the streets before he went out for a drive that no one might see how the years had ravaged his appearance. Crowds flocked to pay their last respects to the Duke as he lay in state in St James's Palace: so great was the press of people that women were dragged from the crowd, their shoes and bonnets gone, their gowns torn from their backs. The funeral procession set out for Windsor through packed streets, the houses shuttered and draped in black, with an occasional streamer on which was written 'The Soldier's Friend.' Staunch Protestants bought prints of him, with cherubs' wings sprouting below his Field-Marshal's hat.

Seven years later the Duke of York's column was raised to commemorate his work for the Army. He rises up to heaven from the *débris* of Carlton House and looks away from the scene of his revels across to the Horse Guard's Parade. And if the spirit of the Duke of York should ever hover above that stern, Roman toga'd figure, with the lightning conductor darting from the bald head, he might learn what a life of misfortune, what the French Revolution, what even Mrs Clarke, had failed to teach him. He would see the crowds below, crawling up the steps on their way to business or their pleasures, ignorant that the massive column was to perpetuate the memory of one who did much for the English Army, of whom Mr Croker said 'Most kind and best natured of princes,' ignorant even of their grandfather's joke that the lightning conductor was the file for his unpaid bills. He would see that, after all, even Princes of England were only human and shared the common fate of man, whose trace cannot be found after he has passed.

CHAPTER III

❖

WILLIAM HENRY,
DUKE OF CLARENCE

IT was a glorious day in the middle of June 1779, and the *Prince George*, Admiral Digby's flagship of 98 guns, was lying in Portsmouth Harbour waiting the arrival of a new midshipman. Presently the ship's boat was seen cutting its way across the water and the sailors hurried forward, curious to see what their new shipmate was like. A small boy between thirteen and fourteen, rather short for his age, with a pointed head and a very red face, clambered on board.

For a whole month the boy had been looking forward to this moment. It was a month before, that his father had told him that he intended to make a sailor of him, and he had heard the news with such obvious pleasure that his father had written to a friend: 'The boy has behaved with that spirit on this occasion that makes me flatter myself that he will turn out well.' For a whole month he had enjoyed the rarest human pleasure – the hero-worship of his brothers and sisters. The last night at home, his father had given a dinner-party in his honour and had drawn him aside afterwards to give him a Bible, hoping that he would read it and would not allow his companions to ridicule him out of his pious habits. It added to the boy's pleasure to remember that his two elder brothers were still to stay at home. For about Prince William Henry, King George's third son, there was an independence, a boisterousness of spirit and an anxiety to excel that justified the King in thinking that the sea was the proper place for him.

But the first plunge rather dashed his spirit. It was such a complete change: instead of the firm green spaces of Kew, the gently heaving deck; instead of the large respectful crowds, tersely explanatory officers; instead of those abandoned games of cricket with his brothers, the Prince of Wales and the Bishop of Osnabrück, a group of strange, inquisitive midshipmen.

Away from home, a boy's one desire is to be just the same as his fellows and on no account to look conspicuous. Was not Paul Dombey more crushed by knowing that he was thought old-fashioned than by all his ill health? But it was impossible for the Prince to pass unnoticed. For, apart altogether from being the King's son, he was cruelly distinguished from his fellows. What must have been their amusement to hear that the new midshipman was to be attended on board by Midshipman the Reverend Henry Majendie? The explanation of this doubly professional gentleman was that George III, after bombarding various admirals with a series of questions on uniforms, geometry and dry bedding and indeed everything that his son could possibly need, decided, on his own account, that the really important thing for the boy was a classical tutor. After some years of toil, Mr Majendie had won a pass degree in the University of Cambridge. His college rewarded him with a Fellowship, for which it was necessary for him to be ordained. The King no doubt felt that, in matters of scholarship, a Cambridge college could not err, and he decided that the Reverend Henry Majendie was the very man to teach his son the classics. He was made an honorary midshipman and later became a Bishop. It is impossible to help feeling that honours came rather easily to Mr Majendie.

But not even the classical tutor could postpone for ever that awful moment when the new boy is left face to face with his fellows. Every schoolboy knows it. Treacherous parents have left, the last link with home is gone. To his imagination it appears that the boys have been banded together for years for the express purpose of getting to know everything that is to be known about their surroundings and about the rules by which their lives are bounded. His shipmates crowded round the Prince. Each longed to show that he was familiar with every plank, every rope, every bell and every breeze that ever blew. But they could not show their knowledge as they did not know

how to address their new shipmate. At last one, bolder than
the rest, asked by what name he was rated on the ship's books.
The prince piped up: 'I am entered as Prince William-Henry
but my father's name is Guelph and therefore if, you please,
you may call me William Guelph for I am nothing more than a
sailor like yourselves.' (The voice was the voice of the Prince
but the words were surely the words of George III.)

After this his popularity was certain and, within a few days,
he was stealing from his berth at midnight to cut down the
hammock of one of his closer friends. Life on board presented
many chances for those fierce practical jokes so loved by the
Hanoverian dynasty. Before long he had his first fight – with
a Marine – and astounded friend and foe by saying to his
opponent after it was over, 'You are a brave fellow though
you are a Marine.' This rough tactlessness was rather becoming to a sailor in his teens.

But fights and even practical jokes had soon to be forgotten
in sterner business. France and Spain, seeing that England was
absorbed in trying to subdue her American colonists, had
declared war on England in 1778. In the summer of 1779 the
enemy planned that a joint Franco-Spanish Fleet should sweep
westwards along the Channel, like a great broom, driving
before it every English ship. Then behind the Allied Fleet, in
the waters they had cleared, a French Army was to be rushed
across the Channel to Portsmouth. The British public was
thoroughly alarmed. For forty years they had bawled those
brave, redundant lines about Britannia ruling the waves, and
now it seemed that they must unlearn them.

The British Admiralty did their utmost to allay anxiety by
complete inactivity, and absorbed themselves in court-
martialling an admiral and a vice-admiral. George III was not
the man to allow his servants to exceed him in any display of
indifference towards foreigners and, to any croakers who
thought that because the British Fleet was outnumbered by
two to one it must be destroyed, he could prove his own confidence in the British Fleet by pointing to the small figure of
his son in white trousers, short coat and billycock hat pacing
the deck of the *Prince George*.

The Admiralty and the King might pooh-pooh the danger, but nothing but good fortune saved the British Fleet and possibly, the prince's life. All through August the *Prince George* and the main British Fleet were retreating westwards before the Allied Fleet. The Prince's first experience of a British ship in action was to see how she should be handled in order to avoid the enemy. But just as the success of the enemy's plan seemed certain, they were obliged to put back to the French ports owing to a severe outbreak of illness among their sailors.

In the winter, the *Prince George* sailed, with a part of the Fleet under Rodney, to convoy provision ships to the Gibraltar garrison which was in the throes of its three years' siege. On the way they fell in with some Spanish ships off Cape St Vincent and Prince William had his first experience of victory when all the enemy ships were either sunk or disabled. After touching at Gibraltar the *Prince George* returned to Plymouth, Prince William being ordered to London to hand over to his father the captured Spanish flags.

A full Court was held in his honour on 9th March, 1780, and the Prince was solemnly introduced to his father by the First Lord of the Admiralty, and, after presenting the flags he gave his father a plan of the Gibraltar garrison, explaining carefully the position of the new English batteries which he had seen. The public was wild with enthusiasm, following its anxiety of the previous year. Rodney and Prince William were on all men's lips: patriots as they lifted their glasses toasted 'the intrepid boy': the Poet Laureate (Mr Pye) ground out an ode in which he compared the Prince to 'a budding rose beneath the morning dew.'

The King and Queen took their little hero to Drury Lane to see *The Tempest*. He sat in a box with the Prince of Wales and the Bishop of Osnabrück, facing his father and mother. As he stepped to the front of the box, the pit broke into tumultuous cheering, handkerchiefs fluttered, hats were flung into the air, the theatre rang with huzzahs. People outside, hearing the commotion, poured into the pit, and for a quarter of an hour the cheering and excitement made it impossible for the curtain to go up and show the first act of *The Tempest* with, suitably enough, a ship at sea rolling in the middle of a thunderstorm.

The Prince himself, as he sat looking down on this enthusiastic scene, or across at the proud smiles of his parents, or beside him at (let us hope) the admiring glances of his elder brothers, might well have pictured a splendid and important future opening before him, himself commanding great ships forging their way through brilliant seas or belching broadsides at an immeasurably stronger foe, while from time to time the famous Naval Prince returned to the cheers of his free and prosperous countrymen.

And for the next few years everything conspired to make him feel that he was a very important person. After eighteen months in English waters the *Prince George* sailed for America and reached New York harbour in September 1781. Prince William was the first English Prince – and the last – to see New York while it owned allegiance to the English King. In 1781 New York was the last stronghold of loyalist America and the citizens felt that King George III like the owner of the vineyard in the Bible, had sent his son to soften the hearts of the rebels. He was given an uproarious welcome and it was freely believed that his presence would end the war.

He spent the winter in New York itself. But the rebels were unfortunately like the wicked husbandmen and, instead of forgetting their grievances, they put their heads together to take the Prince. They were encamped across the River Hudson in New Jersey and planned to steal across the river at night and surprise the Prince in his sleeping-quarters, which were known to be lightly guarded. Washington himself wrote to the officer who had originated the scheme to congratulate him on 'the spirit of enterprise so conspicuous in your plan for carrying off the Prince William Henry.'

The Prince was quite unconscious that the rebels, who claimed to set so little store by Princes, should waste their time in capturing one. He sauntered through the streets of New York and, when the winter came on, spent much time on a frozen lake outside the city. He could not skate and felt that the indignities of learning ill became a Prince, so he had a special chair made for himself; his friends pushed him over the ice, themselves skating behind and shouting, 'Huzzah! Huzzah! for the Prince William.' Had the rebels but known, this uncontrollable chair would have seemed to offer far more possibilities than any lightly guarded sleeping-quarters. As a matter of fact their plans leaked out and, from thenceforward, the Prince was more carefully guarded.

But the King was not entirely satisfied with the reports of his son and, after he had taken part with Rodney in the defeat of de Grasse on 12th April, 1782, he was transferred to the *Barfleur* under the command of Sir Samuel Hood. The King wrote to Hood and begged him to keep a strict eye on the youth, adding that 'William was ever violent when controlled. I had hoped that by this time he would have been conscious of his own levity.'

At the end of November 1782 the *Barfleur* sailed into Port Royal in Jamaica where the Prince was really treated like a King. A body of cavalry, formed from the planters, was raised to attend him whenever he landed in the island and there was a steady stream of balls and fêtes in his honour. The Governor's wife wrote rapturously home. 'He is a handsome likeness of both the King and Queen with the most animated, interesting countenance I ever saw. He has an amazing flow of spirits and great good humour . . .' But alas! the war that gave him his importance and his popularity, could not be expected to last for ever and, in the spring of 1783, news reached Port Royal that the preliminaries of Peace had been signed, which was speedily followed by orders for the ships to return to England. At the end of June, Prince William landed at Spithead.

Much was made of the Prince on his return. The King seemed to forget his complaints of his son's character in the pleasure, enjoyed by most insular persons, of listening to the tale of other people's travels. The Prince for his part was modest and determined to please. He even went down one day to call on an unattractive, rather lonely, completely masculine great-aunt, George II's only surviving daughter, the Princess Amelia, who lived at Gunnersbury Park. She happened to mention that Mr Horace Walpole was coming to

have dinner with her that evening, and the Prince at once
asked if he might come too, in order to meet him. The Princess
was agreeable and Mr Walpole, when he heard, was delighted
with the attention. He was presented to the Prince and, at the
risk of tumbling on his nose, hurried forward to kneel and
kiss his hand. Prince William would not allow such deference.
[It was from some points of view a pity as Mr Walpole had
kissed hands with George I, and his mouth would have been a
curious link between the first Hanoverian King and the last.]
Mr Walpole was entranced: adjectives were exhausted in
praising the Prince: he was charming, lively, cheerful, talkative, manly, well-bred, sensible and exceedingly proper in
his replies: and what really delighted Mr Walpole who, as a
good Whig, was not over fond of George III, was that the
Prince had preferred 'the company of us old women' to that of
his parents at Windsor.

The next two years were spent by Prince William, with the
Duke of York, travelling in Germany, and in June 1785 he
returned to England to join the frigate *Hebe* as third lieutenant.
He made a complete tour of the coast of England, landing at
various points, and in October the *Hebe* returned to Portsmouth for the winter. There was very little to do and Portsmouth was dull. Very dull after the gay German cities with all
their attractions for a bright young Prince. The naval commissioner, Sir Henry Martin, had some lovely daughters.
Prince William used to spend many of the long winter evenings
there and, as the new year broke with its suggestion of lengthening days and additional duties, he asked Miss Sarah Martin
to marry him. She was devoted to him and gladly accepted.
But her father, with one eye on the King, despatched Miss
Sarah to an aunt in London. The intentions of sailors are
generally honourable and the Prince made a dash for Windsor
to try and persuade his parents to consent to the marriage. The
King was out hunting and the Prince poured out his passion
into the unromantic ears of Queen Charlotte. She told the
King, as soon as he got back, who wrote off to Lord Howe.
'On returning from hunting this evening the Queen desired to
speak to me before I went to dinner. It was to communicate to

me the arrival of William. I find it indispensably necessary to remove him from the Commissioner's House at Portsmouth. And therefore desire that either the *Hebe* may be removed to the Plymouth station, or William placed on board the 32-Gun frigate that is there. I merely throw out what occurs to me on a very unpleasant and unexpected event.'

So ended the first of the many attempts made by the Prince to get married, and the following day he was gloomily covering the road between Windsor and Plymouth, where he was going to join the frigate *Pegasus* of which, in April, 1786, he was appointed captain.

In the summer, the *Pegasus* was ordered to sail for Halifax and it was on this voyage that the Prince celebrated his twenty-first birthday. The officers entertained him to luncheon and he was just able to stagger to the deck afterwards, in an effort to reach his cabin, when the sailors, who were quite drunk, seized him and carried him shoulder-high round the deck at considerable danger to his head from the beams. The care of the ship was left to the midshipmen during the prostration of their elders and one of them wrote in his journal: 'It was altogether a strange scene, one that would have astonished the members of a temperance society.'

From Halifax the Prince sailed south to the West Indies and put in for the winter at the English harbour in Antigua. The senior officer on this station was Captain Nelson. The Prince had first met him when serving in the *Barfleur*. Although he had been rather tickled by Nelson's appearance, with a pig-tail of extraordinary length and an old-fashioned uniform, he had taken to him from the first on account of his enthusiasm on professional topics, and, above all, because 'he was warmly attached to my father and was singularly humane.' The Prince was Nelson's best man at his wedding to Mrs Nisbet, which was to turn out so unhappily, and he certainly showed some power of observation when he said to Nelson, 'I never saw a lover so easy . . . it is not what is vulgarly called love.'

For his part Nelson certainly had the highest opinion of the Prince. So much so, that when the Prince wrote, on hearing of the death of an officer 'Collingwood, poor fellow, is no more: I have cried for him,' Nelson wrote to the dead man's brother, afterwards Lord Collingwood, and, telling him what the Prince had written, added, 'A testimony of regard so honourable is more to be coveted than anything this world could have afforded.'

But the friendship of the King's son was an important thing for an ambitious officer without influence, like Captain Nelson. And when he wrote home: 'Prince William is under my command ... he has his foibles, as well as private men; but they are far overbalanced by his virtues. In his professional line he is superior to nearly two thirds, I am sure, of the list: and in attention to orders and respect to his superior officers I hardly know his equal. This is what I have found him' – it was probably Prince William rather than Captain William Guelph that Nelson admired. It is always difficult to hold a middle view and it would be easy to agree with Nelson that the Prince was a heaven-born seaman, or to take the purely perverse line, which is a form of inverted snobbery, and is the peculiar province of Whig historians, of belittling all his achievements because he was the son of a King. But against Nelson's view there is the opinion of one of the officers on board the *Pegasus* that 'the Prince was deficient in almost all the qualities necessary for a person in high command ... and it was therefore better he should be on shore than on sea.' Both this statement and Nelson's are wide of the mark. The Prince had a natural aptitude for a sailor's life. He was suited for it in character because he was quick without being clever and being both physically and mentally insensitive, he was capable of whole-hearted enthusiasm for his work. The discipline he maintained on the *Pegasus*, and his anxiety that it should be the best ship on the station were proofs of this. He had that careless good-nature which made him exceedingly popular with the sailors. His constitution was excellent. But against this must be put the fact that he was unreliable and, if he thought his superiors lacking in deference, he would simply not obey them. He was on excellent terms with Nelson, who was his superior officer in the West Indies, and they worked very well together. But when Nelson was recalled in the autumn of 1787 the Prince took exception to his successor, and withdrew his ship from Antigua and sailed away to Halifax. The Government then ordered him to spend the winter in Quebec as a punishment for gross disobedience. This naturally only roused him still further, and, disregarding the dangers of the Atlantic in mid-winter, he sailed for England. It was not for nothing that George III had written to Lord Hood: 'William was ever violent when controlled.' Not that the Prince was entirely to blame for a certain intolerance towards his superior officers, when the flattery of his fellows and his popularity with the public made him feel far more important than he really was. It was only a hundred years since James II and Rupert of the Rhine had commanded English Fleets on no other naval training than the Army of France in James II's case, and spectacular cavalry charges in Prince Rupert's. The Prince was justified in feeling that his was a gruelling training compared with that of earlier sailor Princes, and that a Prince of England could not for ever be expected to obey orders from these captains in the West Indies.

When he reached Plymouth, his father sent an urgent message that he was on no account to leave, but to regard himself as in disgrace down there. The Prince of Wales and the Duke of York only saw in this a splendid means of mocking their father, and set out from Carlton House for Plymouth at the beginning of January 1788. Instead of the prison which the King had designed that Plymouth should be, it was at once transformed into a city *en fête*; it was a centre of gaiety. The three brothers strolled arm in arm through the streets, all affability to the cheering inhabitants, while the Fleet fired Royal salutes whenever they approached the dock, and, every evening, there were dinners and balls. After his brothers had gone back to London, it was naturally very dull, but Naval dockyards seemed to have the effect of rousing the Prince's passions and he fell violently in love with Miss Wynne, a merchant's daughter. News of this reached the King and the Prince was immediately ordered to leave Plymouth and was appointed to the command of the frigate *Andromeda*. He was once again a free man. He would have seemed to have found a new meaning for the old adage that 'Love laughs at locksmiths.' After cruising in the Channel the *Andromeda* passed over to Halifax and wintered in Jamaica.

II

In January 1789 the *Andromeda* sailed up to Halifax, and the Prince learned there of the madness of the King and of the quarrels over the Regency. But he was not recalled to England till after his father had recovered. He reached Spithead on 29th April, 1789. He made the journey from Halifax in the remarkably fast time of three weeks, but it was not the wish 'to be in England now that April's here' that made him urge the sailors to cram on every inch of sail. And as he rattled over the road between Portsmouth and Windsor, he probably never noticed 'whether the brushwood was in tiny leaf' nor 'whether the chaffinch was singing on the orchard bough,' for his mind was occupied with other matters.

Private information had reached him from his friends, while he was at Halifax, of the divisions in the Royal Family, and he had to make up his mind whether he should throw in his lot with his father or his brothers. The question of taking neither side, but of trying to keep on good terms with both, did not arise. There was nothing neutral about Prince William.

He was very fond of his father. He told Fanny Burney when he reached Windsor: 'I am very sorry for His Majesty: no man loves the King better: for every sailor loves his King.' Apart however from this sailor's love, by which he seemed to set such store, he was devoted to him as a son. When he saw his father, whom at one time he must have thought never to see again, he had to confess that he was so overcome by emotion as to be scarcely able to stand.

But affection pulled strongly in the other direction. He could not forget that, when he had been in disgrace at Plymouth, his brothers had stood nobly by him. And pique inclined him to side with his brothers. In the discussions over the Regency, his name had been suggested for the Council of

Regency but the Queen had (almost contemptuously) refused to have him – him the darling of the Navy, the hero of the Jamaican sugar planters! It rankled very much. But the scale was turned in favour of his brothers by the fact that he was, in his twenty-fourth year, without a Dukedom. His brother Frederick had been created Duke of York at twenty-one. Why should he still be waiting at twenty-three? As a Prince he was dependent on his father's bounty, but as a Duke he would be in receipt of a Parliamentary grant. He calculated that, if his father had consented to his being made a Duke at the same age as the Duke of York, he would have been £30,000 richer than he was, because for three years he would have been drawing at least £12,000 a year.

Within a week of his return, it was announced in the newspapers that Prince William had decided to offer himself for election to the House of Commons and would stand for Totnes, in Devonshire, as a protest against the delay in granting him his Dukedom. It was an effective threat and, as the King signed the patent creating his son Duke of Clarence and St Andrews and Earl of Munster, he was heard to say: 'I well know that it is another vote added to the Opposition.'

It was even more than that: it was another Royal Duke added to Carlton House. On 1st June the new Duke gave a party at Willis's Subscription Rooms, to celebrate his Dukedom and to compliment his brothers. As the guests wandered through the various rooms, they were allowed to look through an open door into a room where were seated their host and the Prince of Wales and the Duke of York with a handful of privileged guests. The Royal brothers were sitting against the wall and above each Royal head was a transparency of their arms, and underneath was written in huge letters 'UNITED FOR EVER.' (It might well have been added – 'Less in brotherly love than in fatherly hate.') Thus, tastefully, the Duke of Clarence announced to all the world that the popular sailor Prince was supporting his brothers against the King.

But while politically and publicly the Duke of Clarence was ranged against the King, he remained, in private, on good terms with his relations at Windsor. His interests had demanded that he should side with his brothers, but he managed to do it without showing their insolent contempt for his father. The resentful bitterness of the Prince of Wales was entirely lacking in his character. He was all pleasantness at Windsor, affectionate to his father and respectful to his mother, and very gay with the King's strongest partisans – the six Princesses. On first seeing the Princess Mary, he pretended not to recognise her, because she was so much grown, and jokingly asked if she was one of the Queen's ladies-in-waiting. He cheered up the Princess Sophia by treating her to a show of gallantry in what he called 'my old style . . . my mad frolics . . . upon my word I am almost ashamed.' And after chatting to the Princess Augusta, he said: 'She looks as if she knows more than she would say. I like that character.' A strange remark from one who all his life was famous for saying a great deal more than he knew.

But when once the Dukedom was safely his, the ties that bound him to Carlton House were very thin. The politicians that surrounded the Prince of Wales, like Fox, Sheridan, and Lord Minto, found much to titter at in the bluff ignorance of this sailor Prince. Before long even the gaieties of Carlton House began to pall. With the Prince of Wales the cultivation of wild oats was a life's work, and when the Prince was sixty, Lord Byron, in the strangely becoming rôle of moralist, could inquire 'when George IV would learn the decencies of good three-score?' But at twenty-three the Duke of Clarence had learned something of decency and began to pine for a more domestic immorality. Marriage was out of the question, as a slight contempt for foreigners (noticeable in sailors) made him reluctant to marry one of the many eligible German Princesses. The Royal Marriage Act made it impossible for him to marry a commoner and the only English person he could have married was his first cousin, the Princess Sophia-Matilda of Gloucester, who was not then seventeen.

In the autumn of 1789 he was quite tired of Carlton House and took a house down at Richmond, bringing with him a certain Miss Polly Finch. His house was within walking distance of Strawberry Hill, and Mr Walpole gleefully described the shock to the 'pious matrons *à la ronde*.' But what his reputation lost on Miss Finch, the Duke did his best to make up in other ways. He paid his bills regularly. He only drank four glasses of wine at dinner. Every night he locked the doors himself, that his servants should not stay out late and give his establishment a bad name.

These small sacrifices were not without their effect on Richmond society, and when, having bought Petersham Lodge, in Richmond Park, he began to entertain on a large scale everything was forgiven. Old eyes winked, younger ones sparkled, and Mr Walpole called. The Duke returned the call, and was then shown the printing press which, before his eyes, ran off the following poem:

THE PRESS AT STRAWBERRY HILL TO H.R.H. THE DUKE OF CLARENCE

Sir,

> *When you condescend to grace*
> *   An ancient Printer's Dwelling,*
> *He such a Moment must embrace*
> *   Your virtues to be spelling.*

> *Your Naval Talents, Spirit, Zeal,*
> *   Shall other Types record;*
> *He but one Sentiment can feel,*
> *   And Gratitude's the Word.*

> *Condemn not, Sir, the Truths he speaks,*
> *   Tho' homely his Address:*
> *A Prince of Brunswick never checks*
> *   The 'Freedom of the Press.'*

But if in Richmond there were only four glasses of wine, trips to London made greater indulgences possible. There was, for instance, the evening of a Court ball in 1790, when Miss Burney and Mrs Schwellenberg – the fierce but devoted servant of the Queen – were discussing a little fruit with two gentlemen friends and the Duke rushed in, ordered champagne and, leaning back in his chair announced: 'I will drink the

King's health if I die for it: yes, I have done pretty well already: so has the King I promise you. I believe his Majesty was never taken such good care of before: I should have done more still but for the ball and Mary — I have promised to dance with Mary. I keep sober for Mary.' At last Mrs Schwellenberg, seeing that her gentlemen were becoming hopelessly drunk under the torrent of toasts the Duke was forcing them to drink, said hoarsely to him, 'Your Royal Highness, I am afraid for the Ball.' The Duke, perhaps remembering his sister Mary, rushed from the room, saying to Mrs Schwellenberg as he went, 'Hold you your potatoe jaw, my dear.' Meanwhile Mr Walpole was scratching away to his correspondents, to tell them how well-bred and how sober the Duke was.

III

Miss Finch was soon sacrificed to the scruples of suburban society. But Miss Finch — or a succession of Miss Finches — was not what the Duke wanted. Sailors, obliged to wander in professional life, generally desire something more constant in love, and the Duke of Clarence at the age of twenty-six wanted a home and a wife. He would have made an excellent husband, faithful, considerate and useful about the house. But marriage was impossible, and what he sought in default was a home rather than an establishment, and a matron rather than a mistress.

It was, I think, in this frame of mind that he courted Mrs Jordan. The popular view, expressed by many writers with a wealth of ridiculously romantic language, is that 'the jolly tar' dropped in one evening to the theatre at Richmond and fell suddenly (and violently) in love with 'the brilliant and beautiful actress Mrs Jordan.' The weakness of this lies in the fact that, ever since 1785, Mrs Jordan had been a favourite with the London public, and was on friendly terms with the Prince of Wales and other members of the Royal Family. The Duke must have seen her scores of times before 1791, both on and off the stage.

And there was very little about Mrs Jordan to inspire love at first sight. She was thirty, stout, with coarse manners and several children by several fathers. The charms of Mrs Jordan, which were not physical, were ill-suited to a mistress but well became a wife. She was a woman of great maternal affection rather than a great lover. Hazlitt wrote of her: 'The child of nature whose voice was a cordial to the heart . . . to hear whose laugh was to drink nectar . . . whose singing was like the twang of Cupid's bow . . . she was all exuberance and grace.' Such qualities would have been an ornament to any home.

It was at the end of July 1791 that the newspapers announced that the Duke of Clarence had fallen in love with Mrs Jordan, but she kept him at bay for three months, because there was some chance of her last 'friend' marrying her and thereby making some of her children legitimate. At the end of October 1791, realising that marriage was hopeless, she went to live with the Duke at Petersham.

No doubt they were very foolish. Together they strolled through the fashionable parts of London, 'Her Grace bearing her new dignities with becoming indifference.' They drove up together to Drury Lane from Petersham, and on one occasion the Duke was seen through a crack in the curtain talking and joking with her on the stage. They went to see a play together, and their antics drew the attention of the whole audience to their box. It was after this flouting of public opinion that the storm broke. The newspapers were full of the scandal. Mrs Jordan was hissed: the King was angry. Peter Pindar asked a question which everyone was asking:

> *As Jordan's high and mighty squire*
> * Her playhouse profits deigns to skim;*
> *Some folks audaciously inquire*
> * If he keeps her or she keeps him.*

But they learned their lesson and, burying themselves at Petersham, were soon forgotten.

Unfortunately, Government, too, forgot the Duke of Clarence. At the end of 1792, war with France was threatening and the Duke, in the course of a debate in the House of Lords on the state of the nation, said: 'I have already in private made an offer of my professional services to my country, and I am glad of an opportunity of expressing the same sentiments in public.' He was obviously absolutely confident that he was offering something which would be eagerly accepted, and that after ten years of the drudgery of a sailor's life he was to be rewarded by high command. But the offer was never accepted. For a generation England was to use all her resources in an effort to overcome France but, even in the most critical days, the sailor Prince was not destined to be dragged from Mrs Jordan. Far from the brilliant picture he had imagined of himself in the van of a great victorious fleet, he was to sit at home, an ageing country gentleman, the acknowledged leader of that grumbling army of retired admirals and disappointed half-pay captains who could never understand what the Government was thinking of, nor why on earth Nelson did that and did not do this.

This rejection of his offered services by the Government was a glorious opportunity for those countless people who delight to collect every trickle of gossip that filters through from the servants of Royalty. One had heard that it was because the Duke had been associated with the Opposition — so very wrong for sailors to be politicians, so wicked for a King's son to mix with Whigs. Another knew for certain that it was because he was friendly with the Prince of Wales, and that the King had absolutely refused to consent to his command. A third was equally certain that it was Mrs Jordan who had refused to sleep in a hammock on board ship, and that the Duke would not leave her. So malicious improbability was piled on malicious improbability, and the authors were not the least abashed when the Duke of York, a member of the Opposition, a friend of the Prince of Wales and a keeper of mistresses (each of which reasons had been suggested for the Duke of Clarence's neglect) was appointed to command British troops in the Netherlands.

The reason no doubt was, that the Duke of Clarence could no longer go to sea as a mere captain. His training days were done. He must have gone, if not as an admiral of the Fleet, at least as an admiral in command of a squadron. Several admirals 'to advise him,' on the principle of the Duke of York's generals, were out of the question. Naval warfare did not lend itself to councils of admirals debating what was to be done, while the wind and the tide swept the opportunity past them. And, as the Admiralty authorities turned back the pages of the Duke's record and saw how he had sailed away from the West Indies without leave, and then home from Halifax also without leave, they could not feel that he was suited to have the control of even a squadron of ships in such critical days.

To a certain extent, the Duke had no one but himself to thank. But it was a severe punishment. It was not only a professional blow, but his early life had not fitted him to spend his days as an idle leader of the fashionable world. While his elder brothers had been learning the French for this and that, he had been learning Naval swear words; while they had been learning how to point a toe and turn a leg, he had been climbing the rigging; while they had simpered to lovely ladies, he had been grinning at Jamaican Negresses. Sea legs, in their proper place, are no doubt desirable but, condemned to roll and swagger on the polished floors of London, they are apt to be funny. But, where smaller-minded people would have stormed and raged at the shattering of their careers, he was uncomplaining, at any rate in public, and settled down to make the best of a bad job.

His friendship with Nelson enabled him to hear direct the latest news of the ships on active service, and he was able to write and tell Nelson: 'Whenever I am, where I ought to be, namely at the Head of the Navy, it will be both my duty and inclination to distinguish you.' There were only two gaps in this correspondence – when Nelson lost his arm at Tenerife and when his letters were captured after the Battle of the Nile. So hurt did the Duke feel at this last silence, without of course knowing the cause, that he had almost decided not to speak in the House of Lords on the motion congratulating Nelson and, when he realised the true cause of the silence, he wrote an

enthusiastic letter praising his friend's strategy and the disposition of his ships and ending with a passage, characteristic
of the Hanoverian attitude of regarding the Almighty as their
own peculiar property: 'I admire and approve exceedingly of
your lordship's having in so public a manner returned thanks
to the Almighty for His gracious assistance afforded to His
Majesty's Arms: I have frequently been surprised it has not
been practised in our fleets oftener and I trust every successful
Admiral will in future follow your Lordship's good example . . .'

For twenty years the two sailors were close friends, and
when, on that dreary day in November 1805, the Duke
passed into St Paul's for the memorial service to his friend,
through the lines of the sailors from the *Victory*, he was seen
to be unrestrainedly sobbing. And it was no affectation that
the foremast of the *Victory*, against which Nelson received his
fatal wound, was prominently displayed in the Duke's dining-
room, surmounted by a bust of his dead friend.

He was also able to occupy himself, during this period of
neglect, by speaking in the House of Lords on the political
questions of the day. The Prince of Wales, the Duke of York
and the Duke of Clarence had all been associated with the
Whig Opposition, but none of them can truly be described
as Whigs. It was the Whigs as an Opposition, not Whig
principles, that attracted the Royal brothers. As a matter of
fact, they all had that rather garish patriotism which dis-
tinguishes people of Conservative tendencies, and the Prince
of Wales and the Duke of York, though Whig by name, were
Tory by conviction. But it would be unfair to rank the Duke
of Clarence with his Tory brothers, masquerading as honest
'blue and orange' men. He was no Whig but, equally, he was
no Tory. Without any guiding principle in politics, he decided each question on its merits, like an inexperienced rider
to hounds who has no fixed rule when to shirk a hedge and
seek a gate, or when to soar over or skim a fence, but somehow manages to clamber over each obstruction as it presents
itself. And it was surprising how often, especially in later life,
the Duke of Clarence landed on the Whig side.

But while the Duke's political views were often sound, and sometimes important, they were almost always accompanied by a flow of oratory which was more alarming to his supporters than to his opponents. He regarded himself, when speaking, as a man-o'-war thundering against the enemy, and any stray little thought that wandered through his mind, while he was on his feet, had to be made the most of and hurled against the foe. For instance, on one occasion he was speaking against the abolition of slavery and, as he had seen slavery in the West Indies, his views on the subject were always listened to with respect; but, glancing at the smugly sentimental Whig Peers around him, he thought he would give them a bit of a knock and he rapped out: 'The business of this sort of freedom was begun by a Mr Ramsay, who was one of the most tyrannical men that ever governed a plantation in the West Indies but who, philosophised by these new fangled principles of liberty, which have deluged Europe with blood, became now as great a tyrant to order and good government as he was before to justice, moderation and true liberty.' Mr Ramsay was in fact a clergyman who had devoted his life to the religious instruction of Negroes, but the Duke went on: 'I assert that the promoters of the abolition are either fanatics or hypocrites and in one of these classes I rank Mr Wilberforce.' Even Whig Lords woke up to cry: 'Withdraw! withdraw!'

His entire lack of self-consciousness and tact is shown by his speech on the Bill for the more Effectual Prevention of the Crime of Adultery in 1800. He spoke against the Bill, which sought to make it impossible for the guilty parties to a divorce to marry. He began by remarking that not even the Bishops were stronger opponents of adultery than he. The Bishops, remembering that he was fresh from the arms of Mrs Jordan, may well have thought his remark a little personal. He continued his speech unabashed, and his knowledge of the subject was so intimate and his views so humane that it was generally believed that Mrs Jordan had written the speech for him. When the Bill was debated a month later, the Duke delivered another speech. He traced the position of an adulteress under the Mosaic Law, and under the laws of Greece and

Rome, and devoted his peroration to 'that sex, who are the sources of all endearing comforts of life. Let us not assemble here,' he thundered, 'to forge the galling chains of prostitution and degrade the English fair sex. But let us rather adopt the Christian charity of a right reverend prelate towards a fallen female sinner.' Here the illustrious Duke read a long extract from a sermon preached by the Bishop of Rochester at the Magdalen Hospital.

But, apart from his correspondence with Nelson and his speeches in the House of Lords, the twenty years he spent with Mrs Jordan were years of retirement, and, till 1797, were spent at Petersham, and, after he was made Ranger of Bushey Park in 1797, at Bushey. He was an affectionate father, and was absorbed by the cares and anxieties of bringing up his ten children, who were all, except one, named after the sons and daughters of George III.[1] His brothers always came to dinner at Bushey on his birthday. In 1807 it was an especially grand function. Mrs Jordan had put the servants into new liveries and the dining-room was lighted by some new patent lamps. The Prince of Wales led Mrs Jordan in to dinner and sat on her right. The Duke of Kent and the Duke of York brought their bands with them, which were concealed in the shrubberies outside the window. The King's health was drunk in a solemn manner, while some cannon on the lawn blazed off a few rounds. When the Duke of York's health was given, his band struck up his famous march outside the window. After dinner the Duke of Kent's band was playing through some of the choruses from Haydn's *Oratorio of the Creation*, while the youngest FitzClarence was brought down to be admired by his uncles. The great Radical of the day, Mr Cobbett, was so outraged by the choice of music which ushered in the little bastard that he savagely attacked the Duke in his paper *Cobbett's Weekly Political Register*.

But such publicity was rare till, in 1811, the whole scandal blazed up once more. In the summer of that year Mrs Jordan, who had never completely left the stage, was fulfilling a short provincial engagement and, on the last night of the tour, was

[1] See page 160 for a list of the Duke's children by Mrs Jordan.

at Cheltenham playing the part of Nell in *The Devil to Pay*. Nothing wrong was noticed till the lines in the play where Nell is told that she has been made laughing drunk when, to the amazement of the man acting with her, instead of the famous Jordan laugh, 'the most enlivening thing in nature equally beyond praise and description,' she burst into tears. That evening the whole company knew that the Duke had asked her to meet him at Maidenhead with a view to a final separation.

No one knew what happened at this interview except that the Duke made it clear that the parting was for ever. Afterwards Mrs Jordan wrote to a friend: 'Could you believe or the world believe that we never had for twenty years the *semblance* of a *quarrel*. But this is so well known in our domestic circle that the astonishment is the greater. Money, money, my good friend, or the *want* of it, I am convinced made HIM at the moment the most wretched of men, but having done wrong he does not like to retract. But with all his excellent qualities, his domestic *virtues*, his love for his *lovely* children, what must he not at this moment suffer?'

Certainly money was one of the reasons. When he was created Duke of Clarence, he was given an annual grant of £18,000, and, in addition, £2,500 a year from Treasury grants. This was, of course, plenty to keep up his apartments in St James's Palace and the large house at Bushey and to provide for even ten children, but the Duke was careless and extravagant, and a large slice of his income was absorbed in interest on his debts. If he married he could expect, apart from what his wife was granted, that his own income would be increased to £40,000, as in the case of the Duke of York. At present he had all the expenses of marriage without its emoluments.

But money was not the whole story. The Duke had begun to feel rather restive. Matters of State seemed very remote at Bushey, but in London there was no escaping these speculations about the succession. The King was finally insane, and only three lives stood between the Duke of Clarence and the throne – the Prince Regent, the Princess Charlotte and the Duke of York. In a sense two of them did not count, because he had always said that, thanks to his more regular habits, he would outlive both the Prince of Wales and the Duke of York, so that if anything were to happen to the Princess Charlotte he would be King, and in any event King of Hanover. And, even if the Princess became Queen, there was Queen Elizabeth, who had never married, the two Queen Marys, who had been childless, and even Queens might die in childbed. If England was not to know him as King William the Fourth, there was an excellent chance of his legitimate children ascending the throne. And from this rosy picture he must have turned with something of a shudder to Mrs Jordan. He saw, as he came nearer the throne and 'the fierce light which beats upon it,' that Mrs Jordan, plump, motherly and coarse, would look increasingly unsuitable. At any rate, she made it impossible for him to marry. So, I think, he reasoned. In 1791 he had wanted a matron and a home; now, in 1811, he wanted, if not a Queen, at least a Duchess.

He offered Mrs Jordan £4,400 a year and the care of their daughters, but the daughters and part of the annual payment were to revert to the Duke if she went back to the stage. She soon went back and, by 1816, all her money was absorbed by the troublesome children of an earlier connection, and she fled to France to escape her creditors. One July day in 1816 she sat in squalid lodgings at St Cloud, sighing from morning to night, and fell back dead on being told that there were no letters from England.

From 1811 to 1816 the newspapers were full of bitter attacks against the Duke for his cruel treatment of Mrs Jordan. He was held up to public odium for having lived on Mrs Jordan's earnings and having flung her aside to fend for herself when she became an encumbrance to him. There can be no doubt that he lived on Mrs Jordan's money, because there is a letter from him to his banker, Mr Coutts, in which he says '. . . to her [Mrs Jordan] I owe very much and lately she has insisted on my accepting four and twenty hundred which I am to repay as I think proper.' But Mrs Jordan herself never allowed the Duke to be attacked and, in writing to her friend Sir Jonah Barrington, said, '. . . And now my dear friend do not hear the Duke of C. unfairly abused. He has done *wrong* and he is suffering for it. But as far as he has left it in his own power he is doing everything KIND and NOBLE, even to the distressing HIMSELF.' Years later, when the Duke was King, he commissioned Chantrey to execute a bust of Mrs Jordan and told him that he had been much blamed for his treatment of Mrs Jordan but that, after they parted, he had regularly paid her £2,000 a year.

It was really rather absurd of the public to blame the Duke for sending Mrs Jordan away poorer than when she came to him. The sin remains the same even if it stands on a solid foundation of gold. As a general rule in these cases, the more there is to pay the less there has been to love. And Mrs Jordan, at the end, was not ungenerously treated and, during the twenty years she lived with the Duke, there were compensations for the lack of money in the shape of Royal favour and domestic bliss.

For twenty years they lived the quietest and most *bourgeois* of lives in the charming surroundings of Bushey, or occasionally in the Duke's apartments at St James's, which Mrs Jordan had made a riot of colour with blue sarsnet hangings relieved by crimson panels. And, only the Christmas before they parted, Mrs Jordan wrote: 'My two beloved boys are now at home . . . we shall have a full and merry house at Christmas: 'tis what the dear Duke delights in: – a happier set when altogether I believe never existed.'

But the public was not allowed to believe in the domestic happiness of the Duke and Mrs Jordan, and *The Times*, in one of its fortunately rare flights of fancy, described Mrs Jordan as 'a woman who . . . had been admitted into the secrets of harems and palaces, seen their full exhibition of nude beauty and costly dissoluteness, the whole interior pomp of Royal pleasure, the tribes of mutes and idiots, sultans and eunuchs, slavish passion and lordly debility.' Let us hope the readers of *The Times* remembered that it was a far cry from the Sultan's harem in Constantinople to Bushey Park.

IV

Now that the Duke was free from Mrs Jordan, his proposals of marriage flew through England, which certainly suggests that this anxiety for a wife was the chief reason for his parting from his mistress. His first attempt was with an heiress called Miss Tilney Long. He wrote to her, asking her to marry him and, on being refused, went down to Ramsgate, where she lived, and asked her again four times, but she still would not have him. He returned to London and sent her one last proposal, adding 'the Queen sends her best wishes and regards,' to whom as a matter of fact he had not said one word on the subject. The country was mildly amused and wags were heard to say:

> Man wants but little here below
> But wants that little Long.

After the sixth refusal from Miss Long, he wrote to Lord Keith, proposing for his daughter Miss Elphinstone and, on receiving a stern refusal, turned his attention to Lady Berkeley. At last, he heard of an heiress in Brighton called Miss Wykeham and, hurrying down, he told her that he had not a single farthing but that, if she would care to be Duchess of Clarence and perhaps Queen of England, he would be happy to convey the honours. She accepted. Ripples of laughter carried the good tidings up to Carlton House, but the Regent buried his head in his hands and groaned. He sent for his brother and told him that he would never consent to the marriage and that he was making himself ridiculous.

Disappointed, the Duke turned to the Continent. The Princess Anne of Denmark was suggested but would have none of him, and then there was an agonising period while the Czar's sister considered his proposal. The excitements and the uncertainty of this marriage, so much grander than anything his family had yet attempted, drove him nearly mad. One day he was down at the Pavilion at Brighton with the Regent when the Russian Ambassador's wife – the Princess Lieven –

happened to be a guest at dinner. When she was leaving, he went down to see her off and, just as she was driving off, knocked the footman aside and leapt into the carriage. He was hatless and rather drunk. 'Are you cold, Madam?' he asked. 'No, Monseigneur,' the Princess answered. 'Are you hot, Madam?' 'No, Monseigneur.' 'May I hold your hand?'

The Princess was beautiful, she knew something of Royal Dukes and could only imagine that a most terrible assault was about to be committed in her carriage. Actually the Duke, a trifle confused with anxiety and drink, only wished to find out what were the chances of his marriage to the Czar's sister. It is hardly surprising if the Princess wrote home to say that the Duke was imbecile. At any rate that marriage came to nothing.

These frantic efforts to get married occupied the Duke from 1811 till 1813, when he decided to go over to Holland to watch the efforts of the English to dislodge the French from Antwerp. He was rather an anxiety to the English general as, elated with the disasters that were everywhere overtaking the French, he was of the opinion that it was the duty of a sailor Prince to drive the French from Antwerp single-handed. The Government had to restrain him. But in 1814 the Allied Armies were in France and there was peace. Peace brought, if not honour, at least recognition.

He had been created Admiral of the Fleet or Commander-in-chief of the Navy in 1811, and in 1814 he was given his first employment and hoisted his flag in the frigate *Jason*, which was to escort the Bourbons back to France. Louis XVIII, plump and shrewd, accompanied by the Duchesse d'Angoulême, angular and melancholy, the only surviving child of Louis XVI, boarded the *Royal Sovereign* at Dover. As the ships stood out to sea, the Bourbons looked back to England which had sheltered them for twenty years, and they could see at the extreme end of the pier the solitary, ageing figure of the Prince Regent, bowing again and again to his cousin of France. At Calais the Duke of Clarence led the English ships, with their yards manned and all their sailors cheering, past the *Royal Sovereign* while all the guns in Calais fired a *feu de joie*. England had been at war for a generation and the Duke of Clarence must have thought rather bitterly that, in all that time, his only experience of the enemy's gunpowder was this noisy welcome to the Bourbons.

Then, in the summer of 1814, he was allowed to hoist his flag as Admiral of the Fleet in the *Impregnable*, from which the Emperor of Russia, the King of Prussia and the Prince Regent were to witness a grand review of the Navy. As the Duke came on board with the distinguished visitors, he fancied he saw something amiss with the top-gallant yard, so, putting his hand to his mouth, he shouted out a stream of oaths to the sailors up there. A little ignorant of Naval life, the Emperor and the King of Prussia began to think that this was part of the entertainment, but the Prince Regent, ever one to cover an awkward moment, quietly remarked: 'What an excellent officer William is.'

After this, the Duke lived in complete retirement with his children at Bushey, until the death of the Princess Charlotte in 1817 once again brought up the question of marriage. Even if he died before the Prince of Wales and the Duke of York, which he never thought faintly possible, it was practically certain that they would never now have heirs and that any child of his must wear the crown. His mother had heard of the amiable qualities of the Princess Adelaide of Saxe-Meiningen, who was twenty-six and had been very carefully brought up by a widowed mother. The Duke was agreeable, but he explained to the Prime Minister, Lord Liverpool, that the country demanded he should give them an heir, and the country would have to pay. The Government therefore proposed on 13th April, 1818, that an extra £7,000 per annum should be granted to the Duke of Clarence, and £3,000 per annum to his wife. No doubt the Government made a great error in tactics in presenting the marriage as a purely business arrangement, for there is nothing like a little romance for softening the sentimental heart of the Radical. Canning said: 'Into this alliance His Royal Highness entered, not for his own private desire and gratification, but because it was pressed on him for the purpose of providing for the succession to the throne.' (Loud derisive laughter.) The Radicals' amendment, that the grant to the Duke of Clarence should be increased by only £6,000 (£3,000 for himself and £3,000 for his wife), was carried by nine votes.

The Duke's income at the time of this debate was about £20,000-£18,000 Parliamentary grant, £2,500 Treasury grant, £1,100 Admiral's pay; and he certainly expected that it would be brought up somewhere near the £40,000 granted to the Duke of York at the time of his marriage in 1791, or the £50,000 given to Princess Charlotte's widower, Prince Leopold. He was so angry at the beggarly £6,000 offered by Parliament that he sent down a message by Lord Castlereagh to the House of Commons, that he certainly should not accept the £6,000 and that the proposed marriage might be regarded as at an end.

But in the summer of 1818 the newspapers came out with the news that 'The Duke of Clarence is to be married after all,' and, at the beginning of July, the Princess Adelaide arrived at Grillon's Hotel in Albemarle Street. After the shortest acquaintance they were married in Queen Charlotte's presence at Kew. As he had refused the £6,000 offered by Parliament, they went to live in Hanover, where the cost of living was much lower than in England.

The Princess Adelaide, either as Duchess of Clarence or as Queen of England, was never popular. She was plain, evangelical, an excellent wife and an equally good daughter. Her mind was much occupied with 'the end,' and, though a child of the eighteenth century, she was the first of the Victorians. The Duke's life with her showed that he had never been a wicked man by choice, but only by force of circumstances. He was essentially a faithful husband, whose morality had been sacrificed on the altar of the Royal Marriage Act. There can be few men who, after accustoming themselves to the brilliant gaieties of Mrs Jordan, could settle down to faithful married life surrounded by the drab virtuousness of a Queen Adelaide.

In March 1819, within a few days of the birth of the second Duke of Cambridge, a daughter was born to the Duchess of

Clarence who only lived a few hours. But in the following August the Duke's suspicions were aroused and, too modest to ask the Duchess herself, he wrote off at once to the Prime Minister, Lord Liverpool:

Lichenstein,
August 2nd, 1819.

MY DEAR LORD,

Though it is with real satisfaction yet it is also with an anxious mind I now address your Lordship to request you to inform the Regent that there is every reason to believe the Dutchess once more with child: it is now a fortnight since Halliday and myself had our suspicions; but within the last three days the symptoms that attended the Dutchess in her last pregnancy have so fully appeared that Halliday thinks it is his duty to write by to-morrow's post to Sir Henry Halford on this most interesting event: things being thus I should be uneasy if I did not address these lines to your Lordship for the information of the Regent: my anxiety to see the Dutchess safe landed in England must be and is very great: I lament we cannot leave this place till the Fifteenth instant and with the two visits I cannot put off to my two sisters and with the week I have promised the Dutchess to spend with her sister at Ghent it will not be in our power to reach Calais before the Fifth or Sixth of September. I trust and hope to arrive with this excellent and admirable Princess at St James's on the Tenth of that month. I make no doubt the yacht will be on the Fourth at Calais: Your Lordship can easily imagine the feelings I must have on the interesting state of the Dutchess and the anxiety I shall undergo till the happy moment arrives which I trust in God will make her a mother: having every wish to comply with the desires of this superior minded Princess I shall be most happy when these three necessary visits have been paid and to see the Dutchess at St James's under the able care of Sir Henry Halford which will also relieve the mind of Dr Halliday.

I shall of course write occasionally till my arrival in

England and trust I shall have nothing but what is favourable to communicate. Adieu and ever believe me,

Mv dear Lord,

Yours sincerely,

WILLIAM.

Unluckily the round of visits was too much, and there was a miscarriage at Calais. However, in December of the following year, the Princess Elizabeth Georgiana Adelaide was safely born, but only to die in March 1821. In 1822, on account of the Duchess's health, they decided to accept the £6,000, with all arrears, and live quietly at Bushey. From here, where it had seemed so simple to produce those healthy FitzClarences, the Duke was excitedly writing in March 1822: 'in all human probability the Dutchess is six weeks gone with child, she is thank God particularly rude and has enjoyed perfect health since she resided at this place.' But nothing came of it. The public continued to spread reports that a child was expected, right up to the end of the Duke's life. Even when he was King, he was heard to mutter, rather bitterly, when reading a newspaper report that the Queen was with child, 'Damned stuff.'

The Duke and Duchess lived very quietly down at Bushey, till the death of the Duke of York in 1827 stimulated public interest in the Duke of Clarence as heir presumptive to the throne. In the spring of that year, it was decided to bring him out of his retirement and to revive the office of Lord High Admiral of England for him. The last Lord High Admiral had been Queen Anne's husband, Prince George of Denmark, who had died in 1708. Historically it was an office of very great power and importance: the Lord High Admiral being not only in command of the Navy but at the head of Naval administration at Whitehall with a seat in the Cabinet. The Government decided that, in the nineteenth century, such powers were too much for even a Royal Duke and it was arranged that the Duke should not have a seat in the Cabinet, and that the majority of his powers should only be exercised through a Council, drawn from the officials at the Admiralty.

As is generally the case with any organisation after a particularly triumphant period, the Admiralty, in 1827, was content to rest on its laurels. Fresh suggestions were all met with the formidable argument that the old way had been good enough for Nelson, or that, thanks to the old arrangements, they had been able to drive the French off the seas. Placid, smiling self-satisfaction seemed fixed on the faces of the civil servants at Whitehall.

For fifteen years the whole machinery of Naval administration in Whitehall had been under the control of Viscount Melville who, since 1812, had been First Lord of the Admiralty. He was an extreme Tory, whose father had been impeached for speculating with public money, but whose moral susceptibilities were now outraged at being asked to serve under Canning, whose mother had once been an actress. His resignation made the Duke's appointment possible.

But though Melville went, the spirit of Toryism lived on in the Admiralty. In particular there was an obscurantist knight called Sir George Cockburn who, after a series of little triumphs against the French, had crowned his career by escorting Napoleon to St Helena. Cockburn was unfortunately appointed to be one of the Lord High Admiral's Council. The Secretary of the Admiralty was no less a Tory than John Wilson Croker, the Rigby of Disraeli's novel *Coningsby*. Croker, having rebuked Lord Macaulay for his 'brilliant imagination which tickles the ear and amuses the fancy without satisfying the reasons,' was described by that Christian nobleman as 'a bad, a very bad man: a scandal to literature and politics.' Thanks, therefore, to Lord Macaulay and Disraeli, Croker is now regarded as something positively loathsome. He was in fact a very respectable, exceedingly able Member of Parliament, who treated everyone with cold reserve unless they were extreme Tories. Though as Secretary of the Admiralty he was not especially powerful within its walls, in Parliament and in Apsley House, the headquarters of Toryism and the home of the Duke of Wellington, he spoke as one with authority. It was obvious that he would do his utmost to see that the rude blasts of progress did not ruffle him as he worked in the Admiralty. Into these reactionary surroundings leapt the bright and bustling figure of the Duke of Clarence. Every morning he would hurry round to the Admiralty with a volley of questions on matters that had been forgotten since the Battle of Trafalgar. He would preside over his Board, brushing aside the mild protests of the Cockburns and the Crokers, and in the evening he would give a large dinner in the First Lord's house, announcing to his guests: 'I delight in hospitality and mean to practise it here.' Then in the summer he would sail away to Portsmouth or Plymouth to inspect the dockyards, despatching the Duchess, who was not a good sailor, overland. It gave the greatest pleasure in Portsmouth and Plymouth to see this elderly gentleman poking round the docks quite unattended and chattering away to all and sundry, and then for some of them to see him in the evening in all his glory of uniform and orders giving a ball on board his yacht the *Royal Sovereign*.

A hater of shams and humbug and officialdom, the Duke delighted in unorthodoxy. He wrote, for instance, to the Marquess of Anglesey telling him of his son's appointment to the *Royal Charlotte* yacht in the following terms.

> Admiralty,
> Nov. 6th, 1827.
>
> DEAR MARQUESS,
>
> As Lady William Paget is far advanced in her state of pregnancy and your lordship is a man of gallantry I am sure you, my excellent and old friend, will approve of my having this day signed the Commission appointing Lord William Paget to the command of the *Royal Charlotte* yacht which his Lordship will join in a few days.
>
> Ever believe me, my dear Lord,
> Yours most truly,
> WILLIAM.

Nor was he likely to endear himself to the officials at the Admiralty by shouting out, at a public dinner, to an officer who had obeyed his orders in preference to written orders from the Admiralty: 'You did quite right, sir, and I would not give a damn for any officer who did not know when the good of the Service required his disobeying written orders.'

But it could not last. The Crokers and Cockburns had expected a new broom, but not one which they could only feel betrayed most of the properties of a witch's broomstick. There was continual friction between the Duke and his Council, and in the summer of 1828 he thought of a scheme for outwitting them. It had been arranged by the terms of his appointment that he was to be always subject to his Council, except when he was on board ship flying his flag as Lord High Admiral. His yacht, the *Royal Sovereign*, was lying in the Thames, so he hoisted his flag as Lord High Admiral and issued a number of orders from there without any reference to his Council. Sir George Cockburn strongly protested, and the Duke wrote to Wellington, who had become Prime Minister in January 1828, that unless Cockburn was removed he would resign. After consulting with Croker, the Duke of Wellington wrote to the King, taking sides against the Lord High Admiral. The letter reached the King late at night and he replied:

Friday night 12 o'clock 11th July, 1828.
My Dear Friend,

I have this moment received your box, with your long most interesting and important letter, and other annexations, concerning which at this late hour I will say nothing, but reserve my sentiments (which bye-the-bye are entirely in unison with *your* representations) for a personal interview, when I shall fully enter with you into every part of the present matter, so (as I hope) not only to settle this *immediate* question, but to put the extinguisher upon *all* and *every* future attempt which might otherwise and at some most unexpected moment hereafter arise or rather recur if not *now* and *immediately*, (but with good humour and firmness) stopped *in limine* . . .

Believe me always your most sincere friend,

G. R.

Three days later, with less obscurity, the King wrote to the Lord High Admiral: 'You are in error from the beginning to

the end . . . I love you most truly . . . but you must give way.'
The Lord High Admiral bowed to his brother's wishes but
absolutely refused to see Cockburn alone, or to give him any
orders unless he was always accompanied by another member
of the Council.

The next month the Duke was at Plymouth. It was beautiful
weather and there was a squadron of ships waiting the arrival
of a vice-admiral to go to sea for manœuvres. The Duke decided that they really need not wait for the vice-admiral and,
hoisting his flag in the *Royal Sovereign*, led the squadron out
to sea. For several days everyone, including the vice-admiral,
was in complete ignorance as to the whereabouts of the ships.
Wellington complained at once to the King, and to the Duke
of Clarence. The Duke offered to resign. The King wrote to
Wellington: 'I love my brother William, I have always done
so to my heart's core: and I will leave him the example of
what the inherent duty of a King of this country really is. The
Lord High Admiral shall strictly obey the laws enacted by
Parliament . . . or I desire immediately to receive his resignation.'

The Duke of Wellington showed this letter to the Duke of
Clarence, who regarded it as an acceptance of his resignation.
The King sent for his brother and told him that the letter he
had written to the Prime Minister was not meant as an acceptance of his resignation, but the Duke blurted out that he must
resign if Cockburn was to remain. After many letters, and a
two-hour walk in Kensington Gardens, Croker had persuaded Wellington to resign himself rather than agree to the
dismissal of Cockburn. The King, therefore, had no alternative
but to accept his brother's resignation.

The Duke's resignation was unquestionably a misfortune
for the Navy. It is easy to make the mistake of believing that
his administration of the Navy was wholly farcical, because
he was sometimes funny. After fifteen years of Lord Melville
cooped up in Whitehall, it was excellent to have the Duke
going round the Naval stations; for, as he said, 'The eye of the
Lord High Admiral does infinite good.' He initiated the
system of half-yearly reports from each ship in the Navy on the

state of preparation for battle, and he put into commission the first steamship. He also introduced milder punishments, abolishing the cat except in the case of mutiny. Even that extreme Tory the Duke of Cumberland had to acknowledge that, since his brother had been Lord High Admiral, 'he had heard officers of all ranks and of different political feelings . . . say he perfectly understood his business and had done a great deal of good since he had been at their head.'

But it was a misfortune of his character that when he found his enthusiasm checked by the stonewalling attitude of the Admiralty officials, he had no idea of worming his way through with subtlety and flattery, but simply rushed full tilt against it. George III was right when, years before, he had said: 'William was ever violent when controlled.'

Exhausted by all this excitement, the Duke went to bed for a week and asked for nothing better than to be left alone to the soothing influence of the Duchess and of Bushey. But early in 1829, he was dragged from his retirement by the Roman Catholic question. George IV, after threatening to retire to Hanover and leave the Duke of Clarence to deal with English politicians, had consented to the introduction of a Roman Catholic Relief Bill as a Government measure. When the measure, which had passed the Commons by large majorities, came up to the Lords, the Duke made a sensible speech, insisting that it was not a concession but merely an act of justice, and enlivened the debate with one of his naval touches. The shades of 'the venerable Duncan, Earl Saint Vincent and one more dear to me than any other officer in the service' were marshalled before a startled house, 'their heads lifted in admiration of this measure of justice.' Observing the single eye of his brother the Duke of Cumberland, the most formidable of the opponents of the Roman Catholic claims, contemptuously staring at him, he was visited by one of those unfortunate inspirations which came to him from time to time, and said: 'The opponents of this measure have unjustly and infamously attacked the Duke of Wellington's Government.' The Duke of Cumberland rose as soon as the Duke of Clarence had finished speaking, and incisively and acidly complained of the personal attack made on him by his illustrious relative. The Duke of Clarence, thoroughly roused, replied: 'My illustrious relative has been so long abroad that he has almost forgotten what is due to the freedom of debate in this country.'

This speech very much added to the Duke of Clarence's popularity. It was not, of course, so important as the Duke of York's speech on the same subject in 1825, because George IV had consented to the introduction of the Bill and therefore whether his successor was favourable or hostile to the measure did not very much matter. But it was important because it showed people that the Duke of Clarence in politics was not a reactionary Tory, and that when he became King the long exile of the Whigs from Royal favour might well be ended.

For in the spring of 1830 all the world knew that George IV was dying. At the end of May, he sent for the Duke of Clarence and said to him: 'God's will be done. I have injured no man. It will all rest on you then.' For many years now the Duke had never for a single moment doubted that 'it would all rest on him.' Nor had anything been left to chance. His physician assures us that every morning he gargled two gallons of water to ward off any unsuspected germs. On wet days the windows of his study at Bushey were flung wide open and, puffing and blowing, he marched up and down for hours, to keep properly fit against the day when affairs of State would make exercise impossible. He was a laborious letter-writer but, as he frankly admitted, it was useful to keep his wrists and fingers supple for the unending stream of 'William R.s' that he knew must one day be his task to add to official documents. Above all, the dangers of a sudden chill, which had proved fatal to the poor Duke of Kent, were warded off by a magnificent pair of goloshes.

v

Very early in the morning of 26th June, 1830, Sir Henry Halford, physician to George IV, rode quickly through the chestnut avenue of Bushey Park, up to the Duke of Clarence's house. He was the first to greet the Duke as King, and told him that at two o'clock that morning, after asking that the windows should be flung wide, King George had fallen back in his chair crying, 'O God, this is death.' Queen Adelaide, who was present, gave Sir Henry a prayer-book to mark the occasion. Before long the people of Putney and Chelsea were surprised to see an elderly gentleman, with a long piece of black crape flowing from the crown of his white hat, whirling through their streets in his carriage, grinning and bowing to all and sundry as he passed. Few of them knew that George IV had died, and still fewer of them had any idea what William IV looked like, but the new King was determined to be on good terms with his subjects. A small crowd had gathered outside St James's Palace on hearing of the King's death, and a faint cheer was raised as the new King drove into the palace, at which the grins and bows were redoubled.

He had driven up for the swearing in of his Privy Council. The Privy Councillors were all assembled in St James's Palace in a fever of curiosity as to what their new King would be like. He had lived in such retirement that very few of them knew anything about him. He had the reputation of being kind, good-natured, free and easy, a trifle peppery and very outspoken. At any rate, they knew they must no longer expect the solemn, distant dignity to which George IV had accustomed them. They were standing in groups, black and solemn, talking quietly together, wondering how much grief would be shown for their late master. Suddenly the doors were flung open and a short, red-faced figure bustled in and, without acknowledging anyone, walked up to the table and, seizing a pen, signed with a bold splutter 'William R.' The whole room heard him say: 'This is a damned bad pen you have given me.' Then one by one the Privy Councillors knelt to kiss his hand. As the Chancellor of the Exchequer knelt, he said to him: 'D'ye know that I am grown so near sighted that I can't make out who you are. You must tell me your name if you please.' The proceedings ended by his reminding them of the country's loss and, in softer tones, of his own grief at the death of 'the best and most affectionate of brothers.' The

Privy Councillors scattered to their homes, a little startled, but agreeably impressed by the speech at the end.

The funeral service for George IV took place at night on 15th July, 1830. There was much solemnity but little grief. Behind the coffin, which weighed two tons, walked King William, in a long purple cloak, as chief mourner. His train was carried by his nephew, Prince George of Cumberland, and the purple was only relieved by the melancholy brilliance of the Star of the Order of the Garter. The congregation were trying to recall the virtues of their late sovereign when they were astonished to see the chief mourner dart up to Lord Strathavon, who was sitting in one of the stalls, and greet him with a hearty handshake. The ponderous coffin moved slowly on, but to everyone's embarrassment the chief mourner was seen to be gaily nodding to right and left as he recognised friends in the congregation. Lord Ellenborough observed that a Coronation could hardly be gayer.

Five days later the King made his first public appearance and reviewed the Guards. He had never before worn military uniform and, with a pair of gold spurs half-way up his legs, he was observed to look like a fighting-cock. (He could not ride a horse that day as the gout stones in his fingers prevented him from holding the reins.) It was very pleasant, after it was all over, to change back into ordinary clothes, and he thought he would just take a turn down St James's Street. He met his friend, Mr Watson Taylor, and slipping his arm through his, they strolled along together. A few minutes later a handful of members of White's Club, drowsily surveying the street below them, were astounded to hear a noisily enthusiastic crowd coming down St James's Street, and to see in the centre of it the new King, who, as he was swept past the window, was kissed on the cheek by a street-walker. The clubmen rushed down and, forming a solid phalanx, managed to escort the King, who all the time was holding on to Watson Taylor, into St James's Palace. He was perfectly unconcerned and, as he turned round to thank them, said: 'Oh, never mind all this: when I have walked about a few times they will get used to it, and will take no notice.'

With these flourishes of genial eccentricity the King opened his reign. Mr Creevey, when he heard of all these doings, feared a strait-waistcoat, and Mr Greville wrote in his diary: '[The King] is a mountebank bidding fair to be a maniac.' These worthies had only lived under two English Kings – George III, who was mad, and George IV, who in the seclusion of Windsor firmly believed that he had led the British Army to victory at Waterloo – and it had become natural for them to regard madness as almost a part of the kingly office. What they mistook for madness in King William was a complete lack of any sense of situation. By nature one of the friendliest and most cordial of men, the King never understood that there were occasions when these bursts of bonhomie were hopelessly out of place. He never realised how narrow was the division between affability and lack of dignity.

But, however much Mr Creevey and the polite world might giggle, King William brought to the monarchy something of which it stood in vital need. All Kings are human beings, but King William IV was one of the few to realise it. For three years George IV had never been seen by his loyal subjects but, when they saw King William driving about London in an open *calèche*, and heard that he had said to his brother-in-law the King of Würtemberg – 'Let me drop you at Grillon's Hotel' – they knew that, instead of something remote, distant, awful, the old gentleman with the pineapple head, which was frequently bared in answer to their cheers, was someone very like themselves. There can be no doubt that the King was thoroughly happy.

But all the summer the political atmosphere was oppressive. Look where one would – abroad, or at the noisy meetings in the manufacturing towns or the scenes of disorder in the country districts – it was impossible to avoid feeling that the storm was gathering. It was a storm from which no shelter could have been found in the fastness of Windsor or the heavily shuttered carriage in which George IV drove from Windsor to Virginia Water; the new King, with a cheery smile, went out to face it with his people.

At the end of July he dissolved Parliament, as a new

Parliament had then to be elected after the sovereign's death. The Tory Government, under the Duke of Wellington, realised that they were fighting the stiffest battle since the peace. Money, corruption and ale were poured out in equal strength by Tories and Whigs. But the Tories were handicapped from the start by the apathy of their right wing, which had never forgiven Wellington and Peel for introducing Catholic Emancipation in 1829. Suddenly, in the middle of the election, there was no news from France for four days. Gradually rumours of disturbances in Paris filtered through, and then it was known that the King of France and his family were tossing in a small boat off the Isle of Wight, and that Louis-Philippe was King of the French. That boatload of proud, seasick Bourbons was a more striking advertisement for Reform than any number of posters. Where France led the way, England should not lag behind. The Whigs won fifty seats from the Tories and, although the Duke of Wellington's Government had a small majority, it was a totally different House of Commons from that which for fifteen years had seemingly only existed 'to hunt and vote and raise the price of corn.'

But the country as a whole was disappointed with the election. All their discontents had been crystallised in the cry of 'Parliamentary Reform,' and they did not see that they were any nearer their goal so long as the Tory Government could continue in office. All over England organisations were springing up to intimidate Parliament and to agitate the people. But, as the Tory members sped along the isolated roads to their far-flung constituencies, and noted the obsequiousness of the hostlers as they changed their horses, they thought 'the accounts grossly exaggerated.' With this feeling of security, the Duke of Wellington, at the beginning of November 1830, made his pronouncement that 'the present system [of elections] possessed the full and entire confidence of the country and that no better system could be devised by the wit of man.' It was the last straw, and disorders broke out all over the country which the new police found difficult to control. The Lord Mayor of London wrote to Wellington that if he came to the Lord

Mayor's banquet in the City on 9th November he would advise his coming strongly guarded. The King had already announced that he and the Queen would attend the banquet.

The King was very busy. There were 48,000 papers, which had accumulated during the illness and inactivity of George IV, waiting for his signature. The chalk stones in his fingers, which had made it impossible for him to hold the reins of a horse, made it equally difficult to hold a pen. But he toiled away. Every evening he settled down to his task of signing, the Queen sitting near him with a basin of warm water to bathe his fingers at intervals. After a long evening he confided to her: 'It is cruel suffering, but, thank God, 'tis only cramp: my health was never better.' And although the events in France had made him a little nervous, it had been some reward for all his labour to drive through the streets and find that he was cheered just as loudly as ever. And then, suddenly, on 7th November, the Duke of Wellington had come to say that it would be most unwise for him and the Queen to go to the banquet in the City, and that, if they went, the Government could not be held responsible for their safety.

It was naturally impossible for them to go after this, although the streets were already gaily decorated in preparation for their visit. When it was known that the King dare not face the City of London there was panic, and Consols slumped. The disorderly element had won a bloodless triumph. 9th November passed off fairly quietly: a panicky middle-class mayor and the Iron Duke had together contrived what was called at the time 'one of the boldest acts of cowardice.' The King, who had been made to look ridiculous, was angry. Surely even the Whigs would treat him better than that.

Eight days later, thanks to the defections of the extreme Tories, the Duke of Wellington's Government was defeated, and tendered their resignations to the King. As the King took leave of the Duke he asked him: 'What kind of a man is Lord Grey?' and the Duke replied: 'An ill-tempered, violent man.' The King was in an agony of nervousness and indecision, both of which were aggravated by the Duke's parthian shot. But he made up his mind to send for the 'ill-tempered, violent' noble-man to form a Whig administration.

It must not be supposed that the King sent for Lord Grey to form the first Whig administration for half a century in the same sort of irresponsible way that he had taken Mr Watson Taylor's arm in St James's. His Tory Ministers had done their best to assure him that he was placing himself in the hands of dangerous demagogues, and he felt that he was opening the flood-gates to a mass of things of which he disapproved, and that quite probably he would be swept away in the confusion. Whatever his own thoughts may have been, he could not shut his ears to the words of Queen Adelaide as she sat netting a purse after dinner at Windsor. She thought the French Revolution was going to be enacted in England. She could not, alas! make an attractive Marie Antoinette, but she was heard to mutter that 'please God she would prove a courageous one.'

But about the second Earl Grey there was nothing 'ill-tempered and violent': nothing suggestive of Revolutionary France. In 1830 he was sixty-six, of great personal charm and distinction, preferring country life in Northumberland to the hurly-burly of Westminster. With Lord Lansdowne and Lord Holland he represented those Whigs who had always remained faithful to Fox while he lived, and now sought political inspiration from his 'immortal memory.' He was the type of politician essential to the cohesion and efficiency of any progressive Government. With his progressive beliefs on a firm, intellectual basis, he could hold the balance between Whigs like Palmerston and the Duke of Richmond, whose progressive principles withered with their generous youth, and dangerous gentlemen like Brougham and Durham, whose reforming enthusiasm was fanned to a dangerous heat by every breeze of popular excitement. The King felt that he could trust Grey.

For the first few weeks of the new Government things jogged along pleasantly enough. Grey was charmed with the King, and the King assured Grey that 'he had complete confidence in his integrity, judgment, decision and experience.'

The King and his Ministers were seemingly absorbed in the Irish question and the King's Civil List. But the King and his Ministers knew that these matters had about as much relation to the purpose for which the Government was formed as the weather which the nervous lover eagerly discusses before making his proposal of marriage.

In January 1831, when the King was at the Pavilion at Brighton, Lord Grey, in writing, made an allusion to Reform, and the King answered that the letter was particularly interesting to him because of the direct reference to 'the perilous question of Parliamentary Reform.' Two days later the King wrote to Grey to say that some of his objections to Reform would be removed if he could be given an assurance that no increase would be made in the number of Members of Parliament, and that the period for which Parliament was to be elected was not lengthened. In this mood of sweet reasonableness the King prepared to learn what his Ministers proposed on 'the perilous question of Reform.'

On the last Sunday in January, Grey journeyed down to Brighton to explain the outlines of the Bill. Whig circles were buzzing with excitement, and Mr Creevey gaily wrote to his niece: 'My eye, what a crisis!' That morning the King listened to his chaplain reading the special prayer appointed for the service: '. . . who in Thy heavy displeasure didst suffer the life of our late gracious Sovereign King Charles the First to be this day taken away by the hands of cruel and bloody men . . .' It was 30th January.

As soon as Grey arrived in Brighton he was told that the King was ready to see him at the Pavilion, and on the afternoon of 30th January the King listened carefully to everything that Grey said to him, and asked a number of questions to make sure that he perfectly understood the proposals. Grey afterwards said to Creevey: 'The King's conduct was *perfect*.' After Grey left, the King wrote a long letter which was to be read to the Cabinet. He would never consent to universal suffrage or election by ballot, which he dubbed 'wild projects springing from revolutionary speculations.' He outlined his general objections to Reform, the chief of which was 'his dread . . . of the introduction into the House of Commons of such measures of Reform as would be likely to be rejected by the House of Lords whence must arise a quarrel between the two branches of the Legislature . . . upon a matter affecting a main feature of the Constitution of the country . . . he had not lightly or inconsiderately given his support to the measure but he was determined to afford them his utmost countenance and support . . . It must convince them that he is dealing fairly by them.'

It was, therefore, very unfortunate that, having secured this important undertaking from the King, Grey had almost at once to try and cajole him into exercising the Royal prerogative on behalf of the Government in the shape of granting them a dissolution. It was obviously impossible for them to carry a contentious measure like the Reform Bill in a House of Commons in which there was still a Tory majority. The King resolutely held out against a dissolution, and nothing that Grey could say shook him from the view that the King was not justified in dissolving Parliament unless he had good reason to suppose that the House of Commons no longer represented the views of the country. As he pointed out, in spite of the noisiness of the Reformers there was no reason to suppose that the views of the electorate had materially changed in the six months since the election.

But when on 1st March, 1831, Lord John Russell unfolded the outlines of the Bill, he had no stronger ally than the folly of the Tory Party. The Tory members listened to the proposals of the Bill with horror, relieved by bursts of mocking laughter. The Bill could not have survived an immediate division. But the Tory leaders decided to let it pass its first reading unchallenged, and that it should be killed on the second reading by the pungent ridicule of Croker and Sir Charles Wetherell. However in the debate on the second reading the sober arguments of the Government speakers had their effect on the Tory country gentlemen, who were prepared to admit that some measure of Reform was necessary. The Bill passed its second reading by one vote on 21st March, 1831.

Where all Grey's arguments with the King in favour of a dissolution had failed, the blunder of the Tories in not immediately killing the Bill converted him, and this unexpected victory entirely altered his attitude. Here was clear proof that the opinion of the country had changed since the General Election in the summer of 1830, and when in April the Government was defeated in Committee, the King agreed to dissolve Parliament. The Tories were never tired of blaming the King for truckling to the Whigs on the question of a dissolution. The Duke of Wellington, with a wealth of historical references to Charles I, said that the King had given the monarchy a shake from which it would never recover. But it was the bad tactics of the Tories in not defeating the Bill when they had the chance at the beginning of March that made a dissolution possible.

And the Tories passed from stupid blunder to stupid blunder. It was as though they were determined to show the world that the King was firmly behind the Whigs. The Tory Peers learned that the King was going to dissolve Parliament by commission, and they decided to keep his commissioners waiting while they passed an address to the King protesting against the dissolution. (The King's commissioners might not interrupt a debate in progress in the House of Lords, though of course any debate was closed by the arrival of the King.) The Whig Government only heard of the decision of the Tory Peers on the morning of the dissolution and, at 11.30, Brougham the Lord Chancellor, and Grey hurried to St James's to beg the King to go down in person, because if this address had passed the House of Lords it would have been of great electoral value to the Tory Party.

The King was naturally furious at what he rightly regarded as an attempt by the Tory Peers to dictate to him on the exercise of the Royal Prerogative. Court officials told him that it would be quite impossible for him to go down to Westminster at such short notice: there would be no time for the Guards to line the streets: it would be quite impossible to plait the manes of the horses for the state coach. The King listened gravely, and then, turning to Grey, said: 'My Lord, I'll go if I go in a hackney coach' and with a hearty guffaw 'I always ride at single anchor.'

Early that afternoon the Tory Peers had begun to debate their address to the Crown against a dissolution, when their triumphant voices were checked by the sound of firing, which announced that the King had left St James's on his way to Westminster. Lord Londonderry snarled out a torrent of abuse at the Duke of Richmond, raising his cane in his hand as he spoke. Many of the Peers seemed to be scuffling.

The King had reached the robing-room, and turned rather pale on hearing this noise but, placing the crown crooked on his head, he marched into the Chamber. He quickly recovered his composure, bowed gravely to the right and left, and asked Brougham to be sure and point out Cobbett to him when the Commons came to the Bar, as he did not know him by sight; and then, when the Commons assembled, he read his speech in a loud voice. He returned to the palace through wildly enthusiastic crowds. 'Well done, old boy,' they yelled. 'Served 'em right. Well done, old boy!'

The result of the General Election which followed the dissolution in the summer of 1831 was a comfortable majority for Reform. Except in the rotten boroughs, the Tories had been swept away before the tempestuous cry: 'The Bill, the whole Bill and nothing but the Bill.' And when, on 8th July, the Bill passed its second reading in the House of Commons by a majority of 136, the Tories realised that they were indeed undone. But while the country boiled so that they could almost hear the hiss of escaping steam from the large industrial towns like Birmingham, Manchester and Glasgow, the Tories deliberately prolonged the suspense by a series of brilliantly obstructionist tactics. Party feeling in England never ran so high as in the summer of 1831 and, as Whig and Tory wrestled and tussled, they could feel underneath the seething of public excitement, and each felt that the other was completely indifferent whether there was an upheaval in which everything they cherished would be destroyed, or not.

In September there was a momentary lull in political feeling on account of the Coronation. The King had been opposed to any Coronation at all, on the grounds that it was a 'useless and ill-timed expense,' and that it was important to avoid any excuse for 'popular effervescence.' He consulted high legal opinion as to the possibility of doing without the Coronation, but it was held that some such ceremony was essential for swearing the oath before Lords and Commons. The King's brother, the Duke of Cumberland, demanded the Coronation in its entirety as some compensation for the King's support to the Bill in its entirety. But the King would not hear of the flashing jewellery, the white kid knickers lined with white satin, the gorgeous banquet (for Peers only) at the public expense, which had marked George IV's coronation. His brother's Coronation had cost £400,000; his should only cost one tenth of that sum. When the Tory Peers heard of these curtailments they threatened to boycott the Coronation. The King merely observed: 'I anticipate from that greater convenience of room and less heat.' For a long time he stood out against being kissed by the Bishops, but on this he had to give way. Macaulay, who was in the Abbey, thought that the King behaved awkwardly and added, rather unkindly, that the bearing of the King made the foolish parts of the ritual appear monstrously ridiculous.

He set out from St James's Palace on 9th September punctually at 10.30 for Westminster Abbey. Wild enthusiasm greeted him and, if there had ever been a lull in the cheering, he might have caught the oaths, shrieks and catcalls which greeted his brother of Cumberland, who drove just in front of him, lying well back in his coach trying to avoid recognition. For the King and Queen it was an ovation the whole way, and as Mr Greville sat writing up his diary he was disturbed by 'the great acclamations.'

After the ceremony the King gave a large private banquet at St James's. He asked his guests to join him in a toast, 'The land we live in.' With one eye on the Duke of Cumberland, he said: 'I think the Coronation has been unnecessary but — [thumping the table] — I am quite as anxious as before the ceremony to watch over the liberties of my people.' After the ladies had withdrawn he made another speech, rambling on about nothing in particular and ending with a really coarse toast, adding 'Honi soit qui mal y pense.' Prince Talleyrand, the French Ambassador, with his corpse-like, wrinkled face, murmured: 'C'est bien remarquable.'

But though the King may have been quite as anxious as ever to watch over the liberties of his people, he was now not so anxious to watch over the safety of his Whig Government.

Apart from the disorders in the manufacturing towns, which were redoubled at the delay in the passing of the Bill and of which the King was of course officially informed, it was forcibly brought home to him that in the temper of his people the monarchy could not hope to escape attack. He had listened in St James's Palace to a howling mob, brandishing sticks, which had surrounded the Queen's carriage on her return from a visit, and had held up the carriage while the people nearest to it pressed their faces against the glass and shouted out insults. And when he was returning from the theatre a stone had been flung through the glass of his carriage which had hit Prince George of Cumberland. He saw, too, that a conflict between the House of Lords and the House of Commons – which had from the very first made him nervous of Reform – was now inevitable, and that while this was being fought out, with all its excitements and the animosities it would raise against the privileged classes, there might well be a revolution. He almost begged Grey to modify the principles of the Bill so as to reconcile a sufficient number of the Tory Peers to ensure the passage of the Bill through the Lords. He reminded him that he had sacrificed his own prejudices and scruples, and that he now expected some sacrifice from his Government.

But, with some justification, the Government felt that the country now demanded the whole Bill, and that modifications of it would not lessen but increase the popular excitement. The Bill, practically unchanged, reached the House of Lords on 9th October. Despite an impassioned speech from Brougham, which ended from his knees, apparently more in liquor than in prayer (he had been supported in the course of it by frequent sips of mulled claret) the Bill was rejected by forty-one votes.

The King agreed to a short prorogation of Parliament while Grey was to try his hand at winning over some of the moderate Tories, and the King was to play on the loyalty of the Bishops. But neither made much headway, and once more, in January (1832), Grey journeyed down to Brighton to wring a concession from his master. He explained the dangers of a second rejection of the Bill by the Lords, emphasising to the King the disordered state of the country which had culminated at the end of 1831 in the Bristol Riots, and that he had really no alternative but to ask the King to make a partial addition to the House of Lords. The object of the Whig Government was to persuade the King to make a small creation of Peers at once, with the idea of showing the Tories that the King was behind the Government and that further opposition was futile, as they could always count on swamping the Tory Peers by new creations. The King absolutely refused to do this, as he felt that he was delegating the Royal Prerogative to his Ministers, that there was no guarantee that the small creation of Peers to be made at once would intimidate the Tories into withdrawing their opposition, and that he would never consent, after this small creation, to any 'second edition.' On 15th January the King wrote an important letter to Grey, which was laid before the Cabinet, saying that if 'the dreaded necessity arose he would not deny to his Ministers the power of acting up to the full exigency of the case.' Although the King thus agreed to a creation which was to be unconditional as to numbers it was to be subject to the condition that there should be no permanent addition to the Peerage, which was to be avoided by drawing only on the eldest sons of Peers, the collateral heirs of childless Peers, and Irish and Scotch Peers. All through the spring of 1832 the King was repeating his promise, and wrote to Grey in March: 'Your Lordship will not find the King fail you in the hour of need, being satisfied that every attempt will have been made to avert the necessity of the dreaded alternative.'

On 14th April the Bill came up to the House of Lords and was passed by a majority of nine votes. A month later the Government was defeated in the Lords on the committee stage of the Bill. Grey wrote to the King that, unless he could consent to an unlimited creation of Peers, the Whig Government would resign. Regretfully, in fact in tears, the King accepted the resignations of his first Whig Ministry. After fruitless efforts to form another administration, the King had to give way, recall the Whig Ministry, and humiliate himself by consenting to their demands. Knowing that further opposition was useless, the Tory Peers mostly absented themselves from the division and the Bill at long last passed the House of Lords. It was given the Royal Assent on 7th June, 1832.

The King has been much blamed for 'not keeping his promise to Grey' on the question of the creation of Peers. The public had always believed that the King and the Whigs were fighting the battle for the Bill against the Tories, and when at the most critical moment the King slunk off to fight for the enemy, their indignation knew no bounds. After accepting the resignations of the Whig Government, the King drove up to St James's from Windsor: the streets into London were lined by crowds, howling and yelling and flinging clods of dirt at the carriage as it dashed by in the middle of a strong escort of cavalry. Mr Creevey wrote: 'Our beloved Billy cuts a damnable figure in this business,' and the last survivor of the great tradition that English history is history by Whigs, of Whigs, for Whigs, can comment: 'If therefore the King had not in May gone back on his written promise of 15th January there would have been no national crisis.'[1]

It is utterly unjust to suggest that the King broke his word to Grey on this question, though it would be a mistake to blame Creevey and the mob for seizing the most pungent lie they could easily manufacture to beat one whom they could only regard as a traitor. For there is nothing in the King's character, not even the necessary subtlety, to suggest that he would promise something in January which he had never the least intention of performing in May. The true facts are that he promised in January to create an unlimited number of Peers, though Grey assured him that twenty-one would be the

[1] Professor Trevelyan in *Grey of the Reform Bill*.

maximum, and, when Grey's maximum enlarged itself to fifty or sixty, the King, with many grumbles, said that his promise held good. But the promise was always subject to the condition that there should be no permanent addition to the Peerage. And when Grey needed fifty or sixty new Peers he could only find forty from the three classes defined by the King. Many of the Whig Peers objected, on the grounds of expense, to their sons being elevated to the dignity in their own lifetime. Many of the Scotch and Irish Peers were not such as Grey felt justified in recommending to the King. No doubt in all three classes there were many who would not support the Bill. And when the Government was defeated in May, what Grey was asking the King to do, and what the King refused, was to make a permanent addition to the Peerage by drawing on other commoners as well as the three classes limited by the King. Lord Grey told the King that both 'he and Lord Brougham agreed that His Majesty had never encouraged them to expect that he would consent to so extreme a creation.'

The difficulties which confronted the King during the struggles over the Reform Bill, and the skill with which he met them, can be fairly estimated by imagining what would have happened if either of his next surviving brothers had been King. The Duke of Cumberland, as King Ernest the First, might possibly have allowed Grey to form an administration in November 1830, but when the Whig Government was defeated in April 1831 he would never have granted a dissolution, and would have relied on an extreme Tory Government to stamp out the enthusiasm for Reform. He would have been driven off the throne in six months. The Duke of Sussex, as King Augustus the First, would have gone the whole way with the Whigs and would have put the Royal Prerogative at the disposal of the Whig Ministry in 1832, to make what additions to the Peerage they thought fit. As a result of this, many of the moderate Whigs would have been transformed into embittered opponents of Reform; there must have been a wholesale creation of new Peers, and the Bill could only have been passed by the greatest display of arbitrary sovereignty since the days of the Stuarts.

The conduct of the King during the political crisis of 1830 to 1832 showed considerable wisdom, and is deserving of much praise. His sending for Lord Grey and the Whigs in November 1830, which George IV would never have done because of his dislike for Grey, made the introduction of the Bill possible. His consent to a dissolution in the spring of 1831, which gave the Whigs a large majority, made the passage of the Bill inevitable. His attitude over the creation of Peers was straightforward, and in keeping with his conception of a constitutional sovereign as one who acts as an umpire rather than a player in the political struggle he sees going on all round him.

But his conduct in the second political crisis of his reign showed less wisdom, and has been much misunderstood. The result of the General Election of the summer of 1832, the first to be held under the reformed franchise, was to give the Whigs a substantial, but not overwhelming, majority. During the next two years the King was growing increasingly restive under the activities of his Whig Ministers, particularly when they came to deal with the Irish Church. When Lord Grey resigned the premiership in the summer of 1834, it was confidently expected that the King would take the opportunity of dismissing the Government and sending for a Tory administration; but, acting on Lord Grey's advice, he sent for Lord Melbourne. The Whigs seemed unshakably in office, and Sir Robert Peel set out for Italy.

At the same time Lord Chancellor Brougham, a Scotsman born and bred, set out for Scotland. The Chancellor's native air seemed to have an electric effect on him. No such flamboyant figure had been seen in Scotland since Prince Charlie in the '45. He moved from town to town receiving complimentary addresses, preaching the most Radical policies, and taking to himself the credit for everything that the Whig Government had done. He apparently only once remembered that he was the servant of the King, and then announced that he would write by that evening's post to tell His Majesty how popular he was with the citizens of Inverness. Staying with the Duchess of Bedford, 'The Liberator of Scotland,' as he styled himself, was discovered playing hunt-the-thimble with the young ladies of the house, the Great Seal playing the part of the thimble.

Exaggerated reports of these antics reached the King. *The Times* described him as 'travelling about like a quack doctor,' but the King took a graver and saner view and thought the Chancellor out of his mind.

Brougham's 'progress' in Scotland determined the King to dismiss the Whig Ministry. Fortune played into his hands. The death of Earl Spencer in the autumn of 1834 removed his son, Lord Althorp, to the House of Lords, and made it necessary to appoint a successor to Althorp as leader of the House of Commons. Lord John Russell was the obvious person for the position. But the King very much disliked him, and had said of him: 'If you will answer for his death, I will answer for his damnation.'

In November 1834, Lord Melbourne journeyed down to Brighton to discuss the position with the King. Melbourne seems quite to have expected that the King would dismiss the Ministry rather than consent to the appointment of Lord John. This the King decided to do, and Lord Melbourne returned to London, bearing with him the letter of summons to the Duke of Wellington. Melbourne, who knew of the divisions in the Cabinet and realised the blow to the Government's prestige caused by the loss of Althorp, wrote of the King's action: 'I cannot altogether blame him.'

But Lord Brougham, with less knowledge of the Government's difficulties but more of newspaper publicity, as soon as he heard the news, hurried round to *The Times*. From that paper many of the Ministers first learned of the fate of the Ministry, and read with astonishment Lord Brougham's comment on the position: 'The Queen has done it all.' It would have been equally sensational and more accurate if *The Times* had said: 'Lord Brougham has done it all.'

The King was furious when he read the announcement in *The Times* and immediately hustled all the Whig Ministers out of office and appointed the Duke of Wellington as a kind of Pooh-Bah Minister to hold all the Secretaryships of State in his own hands. The King summed up his feelings for Brougham by saying: 'I never want to see his ugly face again.'

The rest of the story is soon told. Wellington advised the King to entrust the formation of a Tory Government to Peel. Peel rushed back from Rome and formed his administration. In a letter to his constituents, now famous as the Tamworth Manifesto, Peel outlined the policy of his party and showed that they were not wholly unfavourable to social reforms. In the General Election that followed, the Tories did well, but they were still in a minority. They were defeated in the House of Commons in 1835, and Peel resigned. The Whigs returned to office with one notable exception. No place was found in the Cabinet of 1835 for Lord Brougham.

William IV's action in dismissing the Whigs in 1834 is the last occasion on which an English sovereign has exercised his prerogative of dismissing his Ministers. The General Election which followed shows that the dismissal was unjustified, as the Ministry still retained the confidence of the electors. The King's tactics have been much criticised. It is argued that the performances of Lord Brougham, the divisions in the Whig Cabinet and the elevation of Lord Althorp to the Peerage must have soon destroyed the Ministry; that the King had but to wait for the collapse; that by dismissing them he gave them time to recover and reorganise. All this is no doubt true. A wiser King or a more deceitful one would have acted differently, but he was neither a wise nor a deceitful man. He had lost confidence in his Ministers; he had a reasonable excuse for dismissing them; it was not in his character to stand by while they smashed themselves. His action is only an example of his straightforwardness.

The Reform Bill and the struggle with the Whigs spared the monarchy but not the King. It destroyed his popularity. Stones were flung at his carriage in the London streets, and there was a dramatic incident at Ascot races when he thought that he had been shot and fell back crying, 'Oh, God, I am hit.' It was nothing worse than a small stone. As he drove down to dissolve Parliament in the summer of 1832, people did not even trouble to lift their hats, still less to open their mouths. The

King spat out of the window of his coach. It was probably a survival of his sailor days and not disgust at his reception, but someone in the crowd cried out: 'George IV would not have done that.' In two years his popularity was gone and people could compare him unfavourably with George IV.

This loss of popularity, together with the turmoil of the Reform Bill, affected his character. The agitation of the Reform Bill was like some interminable scenic railway which whirled him down a series of ever more terrifying precipices and left him at the end shattered and exhausted. The memory of those thrilling, terrible months remained, and resulted in his showing a good deal of what his secretary called 'nervous excitement.'

There was never any escape for him from politics. Even the calm of domestic life at Windsor or at the Pavilion at Brighton, where he spent much time on account of the Queen's partiality for bathing, was disturbed by the cursed Bill. His illegitimate children, the FitzClarences, were violent reactionaries who were much at Windsor and Brighton, and alternately bullied and alarmed their poor old father. The Queen and his sisters, the Duchess of Gloucester, Princess Augusta and Princess Sophia, were all extreme Tories. It is true that Lord Grey always maintained that, apart from improving his manners, the Queen had no influence over him at all; and the Princess Augusta once said: 'The Queen, like my good mother, never interferes or gives an opinion. We *may* think, we *must* think, we *do* think, but we need not speak.' It may, however, be imagined that their nervous, gloomy faces were not without their effect on the King, and he once confided to the Duchess of Gloucester: 'I feel my crown tottering on my head.'

The good-natured, breezy King strolling through the streets of London or offering people 'lifts' in his carriage had given place to a tired, eccentric, rather bitter old gentleman. This was particularly unfortunate in a man like William IV, who was constitutionally incapable of hiding his feelings. He frequently insulted the Whig Ministers whom he disliked, and often had to apologise for these outbursts. An example of this was when he said to a Minister: 'Mind me, my lord, the

Cabinet is not my Cabinet; they had better take care or, by God, I will have them impeached.'

But these outbursts were far more serious when they were directed against his sister-in-law, the Duchess of Kent. To a highly developed capacity for irritating the King she added much of her husband's self-righteousness. In a series of tours she introduced the Princess Victoria to the people of England as 'your future Queen,' and hardly softened the King's irritation by adding, with her sweetest smile, 'I hope at a very distant date.' It was after one of these tours that the King burst out, speaking of the danger of a revolution, 'I shall defend London and raise the Royal Standard at Weedon: the Duchess of Kent and the Princess Victoria may come in if they can.'

The Duchess of Kent brought up the Princess Victoria to regard the Court of King William and Queen Adelaide in much the same light as the smoking-room of a club for retired admirals. The Duchess would never have dreamt of allowing the Princess to go there alone. The result was that the King and Queen saw very little of their niece. They were both devoted to children, and felt themselves ill-used by the Duchess.

But the climax was reached in 1836, when the Duchess appropriated seventeen rooms in Kensington Palace to her own use. She had previously asked the King's permission, which he had refused on the ground that she already had a perfectly adequate suite there. The Duchess quietly took the rooms. The King happened to go to Kensington Palace and was told what the Duchess had done. He returned to Windsor rightly feeling that he had been grossly insulted. The Duchess of Kent and Princess Victoria were paying one of their rare visits to Windsor to celebrate the King's birthday. A large dinner was given in honour of the event. Over a hundred guests were present. The Princess Victoria sat opposite the King; the Duchess of Kent sat on his right.

In replying to the toast of his health, he expressed the hope that his life might be spared nine months, so that the Duchess of Kent might not be Regent, and he referred to the Duchess as 'a person now near me, who is surrounded by evil advisers and who is herself incompetent to act with propriety in the station in which she would be placed. I have no hesitation in saying that I have been insulted — grossly and continually insulted — by that person . . .'

Mr Greville, who was by no means favourable to William IV, said that nothing could be more reprehensible than the Duchess of Kent's behaviour. But of course that did not excuse such an insulting outburst from a man to a woman in public, from a host to his guest in public. It would not have happened at the beginning of his reign, and it was only a further proof of the extent to which the excitement of his position unbalanced his judgment, which was never strong.

The King's wish was granted, and 24th May, 1837, when the Princess Victoria celebrated her eighteenth birthday and became old enough to rule without a Regency, saw him still alive. But all that year he had been failing, and King Leopold, who found Belgium too small a country to satisfy his ambition and capacity for intrigue, was scratching away to his niece Victoria to advise her how to act when the great day came and the King was no more.

At the beginning of June, the public knew that the King was seriously ill with heart trouble and was unable to rally. With a flash of his old spirit he said to the doctor: 'I know that I am going, but I should like to see another anniversary of Waterloo. Try if you cannot tinker me up to last over that date.' The doctors did their work, and he lived over 18th June to the morning of the 20th, when, after muttering, rather surprisingly, 'The Church, the Church,' he died.

The occasional blunders and many oddities of King William should not blind us to the difficulties of his position. Tossed on to the throne at sixty-four, he had few of the qualities and none of the training of a King. It is, of course, no defence of a King to say that he lived in difficult times. There could be no harsher criticism than to say of him that he would have made an excellent country gentleman or a wonderful father. But the remarkable thing about William IV was that, with no political experience or qualities, he kept his throne and avoided a revolution in the most perilous political crisis in

English history. He was by character frank, stupid and obstinate, characteristics which were accentuated by his early training, but he was redeemed by just that gleam of greatness which made him conscious of his defects and made him eager to rely on the advice of those whom he trusted. He described himself as trying 'to avoid obstinate adherence to prejudices which would be ill-suited to the times and the circumstances under which he had been called to the sovereignty of the country.'

THE FITZCLARENCE FAMILY

CHILDREN OF THE DUKE OF CLARENCE AND MRS JORDAN

George Augustus
Frederick   (1794-1842) Created Earl of Munster 1831, from whom the present Earl is descended. Lieutenant of the Tower and *aide-de-camp* to Queen Victoria. Committed suicide.

Henry   (1795-1817) Died as a captain in India.

Frederick   (1799-1854) Lieutenant-General in the Army.

Adolphus   (1802-1856) Rear Admiral: naval *aide-de-camp* to Queen Victoria.

Augustus   (1805-1854) Rector of Mapledurham in Oxfordshire.

Sophia   (?1792-1837) Married the first Lord De'Isle and Dudley.

Mary   (1798-1864) Married General Fox.

Elizabeth   (1801-1856) Married the sixteenth Earl of Errol, from whom is descended the Duke of Fife who married the late Princess Royal.

Augusta   (1803-1865) Married first the Honourable John Kennedy Erskine and secondly Lord John Frederick Gordon.

Amelia   (1807-1858) Married the tenth Viscount Falkland.

NOTE – The younger sons and daughters were given the rank and title of the younger children of a marquis in 1831, with the exception of those daughters who were already of a higher rank through their husbands.

CHAPTER IV

❦

EDWARD AUGUSTUS,
DUKE OF KENT

2ND NOVEMBER, 1767, was one of those November days on which, in the country, it is possible to feel the last glow of summer still hanging in the air and to indulge in the melancholy enjoyment of decay, but which, in a city, is unutterably depressing when every building seems to exude a dank and blanket-like depression. Indoors, even in the poorest quarters of eighteenth-century London, in the squalid alleys behind the Strand or in the dark horror of the hovels by the river, it was possible with a little light and a handful of coals to keep up the fiction that the gloom was all outside. But in Buckingham House it was almost gloomier inside than out. Behind heavily shuttered windows, the Queen lay waiting her fifth child, while Court officials in mourning tiptoed outside her door.

King George III's favourite brother, Edward Duke of York, was lying in St James's Palace awaiting burial on the following day. A young man, who at the age of twenty-five had exhausted the pleasures of England, he had set out at the beginning of 1767 in search of new experiences abroad. Reaching Monte Carlo in August, he was so stimulated by the ladies of Southern France and performed such prodigies of dancing that he fell into a violent perspiration. In this heated condition, he exposed himself to the night air and within a few hours was dead. It was, perhaps, not particularly sad, but on the day before his funeral everyone remotely connected with Royalty, and every Royal Palace, was draped in black magnificence in honour of what then was called 'the approaching solemnity.'

In this atmosphere King George's fourth son was born and was christened Edward after the stricken Duke of York. As he was ever one to improve on occasion, he used to say in later life that 'the circumstances of my birth were ominous of the life of gloom and struggle which awaited me.'

Many years later, when the Princess Victoria stood close to the throne, public curiosity was roused to know something of her father, Prince Edward. Old Bishop Fisher of Salisbury, known from his partiality for crowned heads as 'The King-fisher,' used to hold forth to a crowd of callers in his London home about the time when he was tutor to Prince Edward. He would speak of the harsh punishments given to the Prince by the King, and, with shaking head, would ask, 'When was it otherwise, in childhood or manhood? When and where?' Then he would tell his great story, how he could remember a clock at Kew Palace which had once belonged to the Duke of Gloucester, Queen Anne's son, and which the King prized very much but which to the Bishop's eye seemed only 'old-fashioned and clumsy.' Prince Edward deliberately smashed it. The King punished him. It must be admitted that the punishment was richly deserved. But the Bishop thought otherwise: he had seemingly no eye for naughtiness or for good clocks.

In fact, whatever the Bishop and the Prince himself may have said, there was nothing unhappy, gloomy or struggling about Prince Edward's childhood. When he was nine, he went to live in one of those delightful red-brick houses on Kew Green, with a large garden behind and the Green in front. Till 1779 he shared this house with Prince William, and when Prince William went to sea, Prince Edward found himself, at the age of twelve, the sole occupant of a very comfortable establishment. There was a governor with two tutors to culti-vate his mind, two pages to care for his appearance, a porter and night-watchman to admit his visitors, and three maids and a housekeeper to keep his house clean and to supply him with food. A grateful country spent £2,000 a year on his food and £200 a year on wine and beer for him. The only criticism that could fairly be made of this life was that, far from being gloomy and struggling, it was too gay and easy for someone who in later life was not to enjoy an enormous income. From the age of nine till he was seventeen the Prince can have had few desires ungratified.

Consequently the next period of his life came as a very disagreeable surprise. In 1785, when he was seventeen, he was sent to Luneburg in Hanover to start his training as a soldier. There was a Royal palace at Luneburg, and the Prince lived there till, in 1787, he was transferred to Geneva. Instead of his gentle tutors, and all the comforts of Kew, he was accompanied by a fierce military person – the Baron Wangenheim – who acted as his governor. The Baron was allowed £1,000 a year for the use of the Prince, which was increased when they went to Geneva to £6,000. The Baron spent the money in maintaining a comfortable establishment with plenty to eat and drink, and doled out 31s. 6d. a week as pocket money for the Prince.

All went fairly smoothly till they reached Geneva in 1787. The Prince was now twenty, his tastes and desires had naturally developed since the old days at Kew, and endless meals, however tasty, with the Baron and a carefully selected company had become hopelessly tedious. He made up his mind to live a Prince's life on 31s. 6d. a week. Though he was completely ignorant of money matters he wrote to his father, to ask that a part of the £6,000 might be transferred from the Baron to him. But the Baron, nervous that he would have to do without his little delicacies, prudently intercepted the Prince's letter to George III. It was hardly surprising that the Prince was heard to say: 'I have so seldom found a gracious answer to any of the little trifling requests that I have made him [the King] that I am now very shy of asking.' But there were always plenty of people in Geneva ready to come forward to lend him money, particularly as he spent it lavishly in their own town to maintain his position as leader of their social life.

In the winter of 1789, finding the Baron particularly intolerable and the society at Geneva particularly dull, the Prince decided to bolt for England. He arrived in London in the middle of the night in January 1790, not expected by a single member of his family, and found a bed at a hotel off St James's Street. The following day the Prince of Wales and the Duke of York, who were then on the worst possible terms with George III, came and led him off to Carlton House. No doubt they loved their brother Edward but, for the moment, his chief attraction lay in his disobedience, which they felt would infuriate the King, particularly when he heard how warm a welcome they had given him. So angry was George III that he ordered Prince Edward to go to Gibraltar in ten days' time, and absolutely refused to see him except for ten minutes on the morning he set out.

In 1790, Prince Edward was in his twenty-third year. He was more than six feet tall, and in appearance greatly resembled his father. He was intelligent, orderly, a stern soldier, very conscious of his dignity as Prince Edward of England, but capable of a certain deliberate graciousness. He was never drunk, because that would have entrenched on his dignity.

He had two obvious failings which had been exacerbated by his five years abroad. He was wildly extravagant. Every penny that he could lay hands on was spent in an effort to shine upon the world in the true glory of a King's son. He left Geneva heavily in debt, and, in a memorandum on his debts to the Prince Regent in 1815, he wrote of the three years in Geneva: 'Where he was incapacitated from enjoying those indulgences which not only princes, but private gentlemen expect at a certain age and borrowed money to procure them.' It was not so much these indulgences that led him into debt but the sight of dull, continental gentlemen leading the way where a Prince of England was too poor to follow.

His other obvious failing was that, as a soldier, he was completely inhuman and bestially severe with his troops. Military opinion in Europe just before the revolutionary wars had crystallised into an extraordinarily narrow view of warfare. Machines having just begun to impress themselves on the human mind, it was everywhere believed that if a squad of soldiers could be sufficiently trained so as to march and manœuvre in perfectly mechanical unison, they would be invincible. The Prince was too apt a pupil of this system. He

returned to England convinced that the rod of iron was really
a magician's wand which would transform the British soldier
into the finest fighter in the world. He had all that fussy attention to detail which invariably accompanies the officer who is
trained for war but never tastes it, whose only experience of a
battlefield is a rather tiring field day with his friends.

His admirers, who tended to increase when his daughter
became Queen of England, agree in attributing these weaknesses in his character to the five years he spent abroad. 'A
British Prince must be nurtured on British ground,' they have
cried, apparently forgetful that till Prince Edward was seventeen, at which age nurturing days are done for most people, he
lived exclusively in England, surrounded by English people.
They have blamed the King for sending his son abroad, for
putting him under that rather gross creature, the Wangenheim, and for keeping him too short of money. But George III
can hardly be blamed for sending his son to what was then regarded as the best military training in Europe. In England
there was no provision for the training of officers, still less of
Field-Marshals.

But it would be idle to argue that the Prince was not nursing
a grievance as the boat carried him away from England. He
had not been allowed to state his case but had been simply
pushed out of the country. How was he to pay his debts? Why
should the Duke of York be allowed to stay in London with a
large grant from Parliament, while he, with nothing from his
country, was sent to toil in an outpost of Empire?

II

When he reached Gibraltar, Prince Edward tried to forget
his troubles by flinging himself heart and soul into his work as
Colonel of the Royal Fusiliers. He rose from bed very early to
inspect, to drill and to order floggings. All day there were men
in motion, obedient to his orders, deploying over the scorched
acreage of the Rock. At night there was gossip with his
brother officers on the state of discipline.

A more unfortunate post for someone of the Prince's

martinet tendencies than Gibraltar cannot be imagined. Soldiers on parade always drove him slightly mad, in much the same way that donkeys on the green affected Miss Betsey Trotwood, and Gibraltar was nothing but a parade-ground. Such civilian life as there had been, which at best was composed of Jewish shopkeepers, had been killed by the prolonged siege. There was never any escape from the parade-ground, and his mind was frenzied with thinking about the state of the soldiers' discipline. Men and officers grumbled about his tyranny together.

News filtered back to London that the troops in Gibraltar were discontented, and in May 1791, with a rare spark of genius, the Government ordered the Prince to North America, where any parade-grounds there may have been were conveniently lost in the forests and plains. And in North America the towns, where French and English lived together in the fashions of half a century earlier, civilised a soldier's life with a faint echo of Louis XV and Madame de Pompadour.

The evening before he left Gibraltar an extravagant banquet was given in his honour. Fifty musicians played a grand march as he walked up the length of the banqueting-room to his seat, which was underneath a canopy of pink silk, on which the figure of Fame was precariously perched, while to the left of the canopy was a statue of Minerva pointing upwards to the figure of Fame. Immediately above the Prince's chair was an enormous rising sun. The feast went none the less merrily because each officer felt, as he cast a frugal eye at the expensive glittering canopy with its classical imagery and symbolical heavenly bodies, that in many ways Gibraltar's gain was Canada's loss. For the credit of Gibraltar had been exhausted in gratifying the tastes of this magnificent Prince. He had to sell his equipment to pay off the most pressing of his creditors, and he issued bonds for £20,000 repayable at the end of seven years, with interest at 5 per cent., for those who could be persuaded to trust him. It was a considerable sum to be squeezed from the Rock.

As his ship rolled over the Atlantic, the Prince cannot have thought that his prospects were any better than when he landed at Gibraltar a year before. His debts had grown, and after a year's exile from England he was only banished still farther away. Accustomed as we are to present-day populations and modern means of communication, it would be easy to make the mistake of regarding this move to North America as important preferment from a rather large fortress to a vast continent. But in the eighteenth century the world was Europe. People sometimes travelled to America or India, some even discovered Australia, but it was always thought rather odd if they returned. Canada was vast, remote, un-European and so unimportant. It is true that during the 1760's and 1770's when the English had just captured Canada from the French and still possessed the United States, they looked upon the continent of North America, which was completely British, as a kind of showpiece, like some glorious vegetable marrow remarkable for its size. But they very much lost interest in it when it was broken in half by the successful revolt of the United States. Canada was certainly not preferment. It was a little reminder that the rod of iron must not be flourished in the polite precincts of British Europe. Let the Prince try it in the ruder, more democratic atmosphere of the New World.

But Prince Edward could never learn from adversity. His first action on reaching Quebec in June 1791 was to order a large and expensive equipment, while his credit was still good. Discipline remained his god, to whom he was quite ready to sacrifice his popularity with his men and his personal comfort. And his god was no respecter of persons: prince-colonel and private soldier were each equal in the eyes of discipline. Perhaps, really, the god demanded that soldiers should parade as soon as it was light, but the prince-colonel rose while it was still dark, fortifying himself with a cup of coffee (made overnight) for the labours of the day. The men began to grumble and grouse; even some of the officers suggested a lightening of the *régime*; but the Prince refused to listen. Desertion became common. A deserter was caught: the Prince ordered him 999 lashes, the maximum allowed by the regulations. Driven to desperation, a group of the soldiers decided to seize the Prince and to kill him. Their secret was badly kept, and the ringleaders were court-martialled. One of them, Private Draper, was sentenced to death; the others were ordered lashes of varying hundreds. On the day fixed for Draper's execution the soldiers marched from Quebec to a place about two miles outside. Prince Edward was at their head: behind the soldiers marched Private Draper, in grave-clothes, his coffin carried in front of him and the regimental band playing funeral dirges beside him. When they reached the gallows the Prince walked towards the condemned man and said: 'Draper – you have now reached the awful moment when a few moments would carry you into the presence of the Supreme Being. As the son of your sovereign whose greatest prerogative is the dispensation of mercy, I feel myself fortunately able to do that which, as your colonel, the indispensable laws of military discipline rendered it impossible for me even to think of.' Draper was pardoned, but even this was an expensive lesson, as the coffin and grave-clothes were presumably a slightly gruesome addition to the Prince's debts.

But while the Prince was very unpopular with the soldiers, Canada offered relaxations from soldiering which were lacking in Gibraltar, and with the civilian population of Canada he was very popular. When he reached Quebec, in answer to the citizens' address of welcome he had spoken of 'the pleasure it would give me if I should be fortunate enough to find the opportunity of being personally serviceable to you.' During his stay in Quebec he did his best to carry this out. One evening each week his house was put at the service of an amateur society of musicians which he had organised. He was one of the leaders of Canadian Freemasonry. He founded Sunday free schools in Quebec. And his popularity reached tremendous heights when one night there was a serious outbreak of fire, and the citizens watched the massive figure of the Prince, black and sweaty, leading the improvised fire brigade. During the first elections held in Canada there was a certain amount of rioting among the French Canadians to compensate themselves for electoral disappointment: the Prince went down to the scene of the disorders and, mounting a chair in the street, called out to the rioters: 'Let me hear no more of these odious distinctions of French and English. You are all his Britannic Majesty's beloved Canadian subjects.' It was an obvious, but effective, remark.

Then his choice of a mistress tended to increase his popularity in Canadian society. Naturally in Quebec, with its French influences, there was no squeamishness about such things: it was politely recognised as inevitable in a healthy young Prince, cut off from his home and in no position to marry. An imported English mistress could not have been popular: a series of discarded Anglo-Canadians must have sooner or later caused a scandal. With judicious passion, Prince Edward allied himself to someone unmistakably French – Madame Alphonsine Thérèse Bernadine Julie de Montgenet de St Laurent, Baronne de Fortisson who, as Madame de St Laurent, remained to all intents and purposes his wife for nearly thirty years. As no scandal ever dragged her from the protecting shelter of the Prince, and as in later years, out of respect to Queen Victoria, it was always politely recognised that she had never existed, very little is known of her. She was presumably a Roman Catholic, as she retired to a convent when the Prince married. She was always rather slightingly referred to by the Prince's brothers as 'Edward's French lady,' but she was devoted to him, and added a touch of gaiety and lightness which was completely lacking in his own character.

It has been suggested that she was some relation of the famous French Canadian family de Salaberry, with whom the Prince was on the most affectionate terms. He was unceasing in his efforts to improve their position, and hardly a packetboat passed from Canada to England without a letter from the Prince to the English Government demanding some recognition or preferment for Monsieur de Salaberry or some position in the Army for one of his sons, with frequent complaints at the way they had been neglected. When one of their children was born, Madame de St Laurent wrote enthusiastically to the mother: 'Hurrah! Hurrah! Hurrah! a thousand rounds in honour of the charming *souris* and the new born . . . Oh no I was never so happy in my life. I have this moment sent the news to our dear Prince . . . in the meantime I embrace the whole household without distinction of age or sex.' This son was christened Edward, and both the Prince and *Madame* stood as godparents.

It seems a far cry from Madame de St Laurent and the de Salaberry family to Private Draper: from the beloved Prince fighting the fire in Quebec to the tyrant of the parade-ground. It is difficult to believe that a man who in private life was affectionate and considerate, and who was so beloved by the Canadians as to be regarded as their patron saint, became transformed by the sight of a dirty button on a soldier's uniform, or a shuffling, ill-timed boot on the parade-ground, into a violent, sadistic lunatic. The explanation of this dual character is that by nature the Prince was kindly and affectionate, and only a mistaken sense of duty made him cover these virtues up in a *façade* of formal severity. His life in Canada was of great benefit to his character because it gave him frequent escapes from the parade-ground and few opportunities to play the Prince. The Canadians were not impressed by magnificence and they encouraged him to be natural.

But in the winter of 1793 the musical evenings in Quebec, the shooting-parties at Haldimand House, where he lived in the country, his friendship with the French Canadians, were all interrupted by his being ordered to join the British troops in the West Indies. For a moment he paused, while an enormous outfit, such as became a major-general in the British Army, which he had recently been created, was collected in Quebec. Then nothing could hold him, not even the fact that he must pass through the unfriendly United States, as the sea passage was too dangerous in mid-winter. Like some legendary Viking this tall, princely warrior moved out from his northern fastnesses. He crossed Lake Champlain into the United States, and, looking back, saw his equipment, piled high on three sledges, skimming towards him over the frozen lake. But no ice that nature formed could bear such princely extravagance, and with a protesting crack it gave way, and the maps and the plans, the uniforms and the books, the saddles and the wines, were lost for ever in its icy depths.

Even this disaster had its compensations, for the good republicans of the United States were so impressed with the simplicity with which a son of the tyrant of England went to the wars that they treated him with great respect. At Boston a deputation of the citizens asked to call on him, provided it could be arranged after six o'clock when their work was over, and they explained that their call was 'dictated by the principles of common civility . . . and possibly urged by an unwarrantable anxiety to have an interview with your Royal Highness.'

From Boston the Prince went by ship to Guadelupe, where he joined the English force under Sir Charles Grey. The object of the English expedition was to capture the French islands among what are now known as the Leeward and Windward Islands, which plot out an exact semicircle between the larger islands of Cuba and Haiti and the mainland of South America. In island after island the *tricolor* ran down and the Union Jack ran up, and the Prince fought most recklessly in order that another unimportant island might be added to his father's possessions. Sir Charles Grey sent back glowing accounts of his bravery, and Parliament thanked him for his services, a tribute which was particularly gratifying, as his brother, the Duke of York, was never thanked by Parliament for his services in the field. But in spite of all this the Prince seemed no nearer a Parliamentary grant and recall to England, and he wrote gloomily to a friend: 'The West Indies! The wish entertained about me in certain quarters when serving there was that I might fall.' He could never help regarding himself as a child of sorrow, but the only people who wished him dead were the French Republicans, who had been trying to withstand his onslaughts on their islands.

The campaign came to a triumphant end in the early summer of 1794, and the Prince returned to North America as commander of the British troops in Nova Scotia, and landed at Halifax in June 1794. Halifax is one of the most eastern points in North America and, being therefore one of the nearest points to France, its citizens confidently expected that the French would land there. It was improbable that the French would have been able to spare soldiers to worry the extremities of the British Empire, but if they had decided on a spectacular raid they would no doubt have chosen Canada, in the certainty of receiving help from the French Canadians and in the hope of an upward thrust from the Americans. At any rate, hope of battle springs eternal in the martial breast, and Prince Edward and the army of Nova Scotia made themselves ready. It was decided in advance where the French would land, and the ground bristled with traps, bastions and fortifications. The Prince thought the discipline of the soldiers very bad and, while they hoped and worked, the rod of iron whirled above them.

But after years of waiting the only link with the enemy which ever came was three young brothers, the eldest of whom had fought for Revolutionary France in the Netherlands. They were the Duc d'Orléans, the Duc de Montpensier and the Comte de Beaujolais. They had been obliged to escape from their own country, and hoped to find a refuge in the New World, which their near relationship to Philippe Egalité made impossible in the unrelenting Courts of Europe. They were almost destitute, and the Prince entertained them generously and lent them £200. No doubt in the midst of their misfortunes the Duc d'Orléans and Prince Edward mourned the fate of Princes born in the second half of the eighteenth century.

But time brings its revolutions, and with an indulgent shrug of the shoulders we can read, half a century later, how the daughter of Prince Edward, as Queen of England, was received in France with the utmost magnificence by Louis Philippe King of the French, who fifty years before had been glad to borrow £200 from her father to eke out his salary as an American schoolmaster. Together Queen Victoria and the King drove through crowds yelling: '*Vive la reine: vive le roi,*' and the Queen noted in her diary: 'The King repeated again and again to me how happy he was at the visit, and how attached he was to my father.'

But the Prince had been looking forward to receiving Frenchmen with a totally different welcome. News had reached him that his younger brother, Prince Ernest, had lost his left eye in fighting the French, and that his youngest brother,

Prince Adolphus, had been badly wounded while serving with the Duke of York. Why should he, an equally mettlesome Hanoverian, have to wait for an enemy that never came? But he stuck to his post in the hope that he would be appointed commander-in-chief of the British Army in North America. However when, in 1795, the position fell vacant, a septuagenarian general was sent out from England to fill it. The officers, exhausted by the Prince and fretted by his discipline, began to whisper that at last he would be off. He wrote to his father asking to be allowed to come home. Permission was refused.

The Prince made up his mind that he would now have to stay in North America until the peace. He sent to England for another outfit, which was captured by the enemy, and he sent to Quebec for Madame de St Laurent, who arrived safely, with nothing worse than a cold. To celebrate her arrival he decided to build her a house. Halifax is built by the side of a basin of water which goes inland for a distance of six miles, and it was at the end of the basin, about six miles from the town, that the Prince decided to build. It was high, rather desolate country, covered in trees and undergrowth, but he railed off several hundred acres, and with an army of resident workmen attempted to subdue it. The house itself was small, being two stories high and built of wood. Standing slightly away from it was a rotunda, with a large gold ball on the top, and it was in this building that the Prince's band played so that the sound should be gently wafted across to the house. But the great charm of the place lay in its view of the Atlantic across Halifax Harbour, and the workmen who lived on the estate were employed in making narrow walks through the thickest part of the trees, out of which the stroller suddenly burst into a clearing with a magnificent view of the sea. In each of these spaces a Chinese temple, covered with bells, was placed for Madame de St Laurent, so that the ground was soon broken up with hundreds of these vistas and pagodas. In 1860 the Prince of Wales visited the place, and wrote to Queen Victoria that the rotunda alone remained. 'I send you a piece of sweet briar from it which I thought you would like to have.'

Here the Prince delighted to entertain the Nova Scotians.

Excellent food and drink were provided, but no excesses and no gambling were allowed; just a little music from *Madame* after dinner. And society at Halifax was quite transformed when it was known that the Prince disapproved of gentlemen getting drunk and joining the ladies, and far worse of the ladies merely laughing at their drunken frolics, and that he and *Madame* could never be persuaded to accept invitations to Sunday card-parties.

So, with soldiering relieved by little social functions, the years passed on. Then one day in October 1798 the Prince was returning from a field day on horseback, when a few planks, that had been put over a stream, gave way under him and he was heavily thrown. *Madame* was frightened, and sent for the doctor. The Prince did not mend, and the doctor tactfully said that only the waters of Bath could put him right. He reached England just before Christmas 1798 and, with *Madame*, was quite cordially received by the Royal Family.

In March 1799 he was given a Parliamentary grant of £12,000 a year, and in April he was raised to the Peerage as Duke of Kent and Strathearn and Earl of Dublin. Ever since 1790 the Duke had been expecting – and spending – his Parliamentary grant. He argued, from the fact that the Duke of York had been given his grant at twenty-one and the Duke of Clarence his at twenty-three, that he could have expected his long before he was thirty-one. Pitt told him that having been abroad he had been forgotten: but people do not forget their sons, even when they have seven, especially one like the Prince, who was constantly reminding his father of his existence by a number of querulous letters. It certainly seemed unjust that Prince Ernest, who was four years younger, should have received his grant on the same day as the Duke of Kent. There seems no good reason why the Duke of Kent was not given his Parliamentary grant when he was thanked by Parliament at the close of the West Indian campaign, except that George III was not fond of him and that bad reports of his harshness were finding their way to England. The financial position of the Duke was serious: there were debts still unpaid in Geneva; £20,000 of debts in Gibraltar; since 1790 he had been in receipt of £5,000 a year, which, for the eight years he had been in North America, totalled £40,000. This sum did no more than cover the expenses of his various equipments. His house at Halifax, his living expenses there and in Quebec for the past eight years, were all debts that would take many years of his grant to wipe off.

But his professional career seemed brightened by the news in May 1799 that he had been appointed commander-in-chief of the forces in British North America, in succession to the septuagenarian general. He set sail with *Madame* in July.

He arrived at Halifax and settled down to enjoy his new dignity. A shower of promotions fell on the de Salaberry family, an outfit which cost £11,000 and contained a library of 5,000 volumes was ordered from England, and when he went for a short visit to Annapolis, on the west coast of Nova Scotia, he was able to order unruly soldiers at Halifax to be flogged by means of a system of telegraphic signals placed on the hills between the two towns. With one secretary and five under-secretaries he slaved away at the details of his command for fourteen or fifteen hours on end. Rather proudly he wrote to a friend that he could not find a single moment of leisure time to count on from break of day to close of night. He had come out full of high hopes that he would be appointed Governor-General of Canada, but at the end of 1799, he was writing sadly to Major de Salaberry:'. . . As to the idea, my dear Major, that the time has arrived when it would be advantageous to place me at the head of the Civil as well as the Military Government believe me your wish cannot be realised, for under the rule which the present Ministers have established as to the Princes of the Blood, the thing is impossible.'

Early in 1800, hearing of the proposed Union with Ireland, he fancied that the position of commander-in-chief in Ireland was exactly what he wanted; so, on the plea of biliousness brought on by application to business, which had deprived him of exercise, he wrote to the Government asking to be re-called. He left Halifax on 3rd August, and the citizens turned out in great force to line the streets through which he and his party would walk down to the ship. The Duke, with his height accentuated by the plume of the Fusiliers, towered above the crowd, and smiled and bowed in answer to their cheers. He left them as they had ever found him: 'the affable prince and polished gentleman.' But in the barracks eleven soldiers were waiting to be executed, which fact caused one of the Duke's warmest admirers to say: 'His Royal Highness's discipline was strict almost to severity.'

III

When the Duke landed in England at the beginning of September 1800, he did not make the mistake, which he had made ten years earlier, of hob-nobbing with his elder brothers but hurried down to Weymouth to pay his respects to the King. He stayed there for three weeks, taking hot sea baths for his rheumatism, and then rejoined *Madame* in London. They were both rather crotchety, he with his rheumatism and a little chest trouble, she with a severe cold, all of which were attributed to the climate of Canada. They were very busy settling into their house, which the Duke had taken in Knightsbridge. Nominally a bachelor, he had apartments given him in Kensington Palace but it would not have been proper or possible for *Madame* to live there. He was very careful not to do anything to offend his father and, when the King was rather ill at the beginning of 1801, he wrote that '*Madame* and I consequently abstain from any amusement whatever.' He occupied himself writing sharp letters to the Prime Minister, because he found that his successor in Canada had dismissed Major de Salaberry from one of his lucrative posts. In June 1801 he wrote to the major :'. . . You will be, I am sure, pleased to know that I continue for the present to hold my appointment as Commander-in-chief in America, my leave having been extended for another year. I know not if I will ever again be obliged to cross the ocean, but in spite of the attachment which I bear you all, I shall be inclined to do what I can to prevent it.'

Early in 1802, a complete surprise to him, came the offer of the Governorship of Gibraltar. He made up his mind to accept it, but was rather chagrined when the King said to him, as they were saying good-bye, 'Now, sir, when you go to Gibraltar do not make such a trade of it as when you went to Halifax.' He reached Gibraltar on 10th May, 1802, exactly eleven years after the Government had removed him from there because of the mutterings of the soldiers at his severity. It was a curious appointment, in many ways reminiscent of Pitt's treatment of the Duke of York, recalling him from Flanders in 1794 on the grounds of incompetence and then, in 1799, reappointing him to the same command. The explanation probably is that, since 1791, the discipline of the Gibraltar garrison had been growing steadily worse, till the Government felt that the abuses which had developed in all ranks must be put down, even at the risk of a certain amount of discontent. At the same time the Duke of Kent, renowned as a disciplinarian, was in need of an appointment. And without very much consideration of the circumstances, the authorities must have offered him the post.

The Duke of York, perhaps knowing more about his brother, would seem to have had some qualms, for he wrote to him: '. . . I consider it my duty on your assuming the command of the garrison at Gibraltar, to make your Royal Highness aware that much exertion will be necessary to establish a due degree of discipline among the troops: and which I trust you will be able gradually to accomplish by a moderate exercise of the power vested in you.' But to ask the Duke to use his powers with moderation in the face of disorderly soldiers, was like asking Miss Trotwood to send her servant with the polite suggestion that the donkey boys should keep to the road. Lack of discipline roused him to a frenzy which kept its grip on him until discipline was restored. Almost his first remark on landing in Gibraltar was that the Guard of Honour lacked steadiness.

It was hardly surprising. There were in Gibraltar, which is only two and a half miles long and varies in width from a quarter to three-quarters of a mile, no less than ninety wine houses. Drunkenness was no offence in the soldiers, except for those actually on duty. A contemporary wrote of Gibraltar: 'It is indeed distressing to see whole bands of soldiers and sailors literally lying in the streets in the most degrading state of inebriety.' Distressing is the right word: it was not wicked, because there was nothing else for the soldiers to do. The 'town' of Gibraltar consisted of one main, but narrow, street where there was a kind of recreation room for the men, with ancient English periodicals; off this street were a few alleys of squalid hovels; no communication with Spain was allowed in time of war so that the food had to be brought by sea from the coast of Africa; plague frequently cut off communication there, when the garrison had to rely on salt meat; there was always a scarcity of water. Stronger incentives to drunkenness than salt food, lack of water and boredom cannot be imagined.

But the Duke had no sympathy. Remarking that 'Drunkenness is the bane of the soldiers,' he closed fifty wine shops. By Christmas 1802 an elaborate code of orders had been drawn up which, apart from purely military questions of life in barracks and discipline on parade, probed most searchingly into every moment of the soldier's life. They were to get up at 3.30 in the summer, 4.30 in the autumn and the spring, and 5.30 in winter. No officer or soldier was ever to be seen, on or off parade, with an umbrella. The officers' hair was to be cut once a month, always in the first week of the month, and the most minute instructions followed as to how it was to be cut, and the exact proportion of pomatum and powder to be used so as to avoid, on the one hand an excessively stiff appearance, and on the other the clothes being covered in powder. The same directions followed for the men, except that they were not to grow whiskers, but were to be shaved up level with the corner of the eye. Regulations for the price of washing to be charged by the wives of the N.C.O.'s and soldiers were laid down. Sergeants were never to drink or mix with corporals or private soldiers; corporals were never to drink or mix with private soldiers. Owing to the heavy rains soldiers were to be allowed to wear greatcoats when mounting guard at night, but to prevent this indulgence from injuring their good appearance, the officer, on the return of daylight, was to set every man to untie his hair, comb it well through and tie it afresh, and the officer was then to inspect them minutely to see that their clothes were properly brushed.

But perhaps more serious than anything was the rule that no soldier was ever to enter a wine shop. They were allowed to buy wine at the regimental canteen, or beer at three specified houses which were licensed to sell malt liquor. And they were to be cautioned by their commanding officers on the eves of Christmas, St George's, St Andrew's and St Patrick's days against entertaining the idea that any day was to be considered privileged for intemperance and indiscipline. So the code of orders continued for more than three hundred closely printed pages.

But on Christmas Eve 1802, after hearing the fatal news that the following day was not to be considered privileged for drunkenness and merriment, the second battalion of the Royals, which was the Duke's own corps, broke out from barracks. They tried to persuade the other regiments to join them but failed, and were even received by the 54th with a volley of rifle-fire, whereupon they returned to their barracks. On Christmas Day, the Duke came across and gave them a thorough dressing down, but they were not further punished, which can only be explained by the nervousness of the authorities at the effect of punishment on the loyal regiments. Two days later one third of the soldiers of the 25th Regiment broke from barracks and attacked the quarters of the Royals. It was a very serious disturbance, rightly called a mutiny, which was not finally quelled till one o'clock in the morning; a few lives were lost and several soldiers wounded.

Apparently the Royals and the 25th Regiment had agreed to mutiny together on the Christmas Eve, but the pay of the 25th Regiment was, for some reason, not distributed then, so that the men of the 25th were fairly sober on Christmas Eve, at any rate too sober to join the Royals when they came clamouring outside. Naturally the Royals taunted the 25th with cowardice. Two days later the 25th were paid their money, they beat up the quarters of the Royals instead of the Duke of Kent. Discipline was restored. The ringleaders were punished, three with death and the others with lashes, and the whole affair seemed soon forgotten.

The Duke and his code of orders were entirely responsible

for the mutiny, and nothing but good fortune saved a much more serious outbreak in which the Duke might have lost his life. The attitude of the private soldiers towards him was summed up by a survivor fifty years later: 'The Duke of Kent! I recollect him well. He was a very bad man. He would not let us drink.' If the officers did not actually organise the disturbance they were passive sympathisers, and Major-General Barnett, the second in command of the garrison, was heard to say: 'It is the best thing that could have happened: now we shall get rid of him.'

Exaggerated rumours of the disorders reached England but no official account came from the Duke till the end of January 1803. The Duke of Kent always maintained that the Cabinet was divided as to who was to be blamed for the mutiny, but that the Duke of York insisted on his being recalled. And when at the beginning of March the Duke of Kent's secretary, Captain Dodd, reached Gibraltar with letters of recall for his master, the Duke was not only furious but taken completely by surprise. He was ordered to return immediately and hand over the command to the next senior officer, Major-General Barnett. The Duke had of course no option in the matter of returning to England, but to hand over the command to Barnett was more than he could bear. He had always disliked the General and suspected him of disloyalty: and he therefore decided, in spite of his orders, to stay on in Gibraltar until the arrival of his successor, Sir Thomas Trigge. Sir Thomas was astounded on sailing into Gibraltar to see the Royal Standard still flying, and wrote to the Government that the Duke had presented him with a copy of his code of orders and had dwelt much on the quiet state of the garrison. Sir Thomas added that the standing orders were certain to produce disaffection in both officers and men, and that the quiet state of the garrison might be dated from the day when the Duke announced his departure.

But, as the Duke sailed back to England, he had no doubt that he was scandalously ill-used. He had been ordered by the Government to restore discipline in the Gibraltar garrison. He had done so, with what he regarded as a little incidental discontent. He could only attribute his recall to the jealousy of his brother, the Duke of York. It is of course true, as a warm partisan of the Duke of Kent has said, that 'if he had done nothing: but had winked at the drunkenness and the un-steadiness of the men, he would never have been recalled and there would have been no scandal.' He certainly experienced the penalties, without the rewards, of virtue. Unfortunately he could not see that what he understood by discipline was some-thing so ridiculous and so impossible as to justify the Govern-ment in thinking that the disorder of other generals was far preferable to the discipline of the Duke of Kent.

For three months the Duke had been breathing fire and slaughter in Gibraltar, and he was determined that not one breath should escape his brother. He wrote five abusive letters to the Duke of York in June, attempted to appeal to the Cab-inet over his head, and demanded to be court-martialled. The Prince of Wales wrote to the Prime Minister: 'Edward were neither officer nor man if he did not complain.' Early in 1804 he met the Duke of York at Windsor and upset his father by calling him, before them all, 'a rascal.'

But after this relief he nursed his grievance in private and only mentioned it to his friends. He wrote to an officer who had served with him in Gibraltar lamenting his inability to help him, adding: '. . . I fear there is but little chance under existing circumstances of so much good fortune falling to my lot as my being thought of for any command. You who know how matters stand between me and a certain quarter will under-stand this without my saying more.' And in his letters to Major de Salaberry there were frequent outpourings against the Duke of York.

After five years, in which he had been absolutely ignored except for the empty honour of being created a Field-Marshal, he made one last bid for professional notice. Early in 1808 rumours reached him that the Spanish Government, under Joseph Bonaparte, was threatening to attack Gibraltar. The Duke was still Governor of Gibraltar, drawing the emoluments but absolutely forbidden to visit his Government. He may perhaps have had visions of another famous siege with himself

in the rôle of defender and, after it was over, a portrait by
Lawrence of Field-Marshal His Royal Highness the Duke of
Kent holding, like Lord Heathfield, that massive key which
cannot really have been very serviceable in preventing the
capture of a rock. At any rate he wrote to his father asking to
be allowed to resume his duties. '. . . To your Majesty, who
yourself possess so nice a sense of honour, it is quite unnecessary for me to represent, that on the result of your decision upon
this request, which I beg leave in the most dutiful, yet in the
strongest manner to press upon your attention, everything
most dear to me in life, I mean my character as a man, my
professional credit as a soldier, is at stake.' The King curtly
refused and the Duke of York, to whom he had sent a copy of
the letter to his father, replied:

> Horse Guards,
> Feb. 6th, 1808.

Dear Edward,

   . . . It is at all times a matter of great regret to me to recall
to your recollection the unfortunate events which led to
your return from that fortress and which have already, and
must ever preclude the confidential servants of the King
from advising His Majesty to permit you to resume your
station there.

   I had hoped from the number of ineffectual applications
which you have at different times made upon this unlucky
subject that you would have been prevented from renewing
them . . .

> I am, etc., etc.,
> Frederick.

This letter from his brother roused all the Duke of Kent's
slumbering fury. For three months he bombarded the Government with letters demanding to know what were the grounds
on which they had decided that he was never to return to
Gibraltar. Lord Castlereagh, with whom the correspondence
was conducted, politely but firmly refused to give any information.

All that year the Radical papers were full of attacks on the

Duke of York, accusing him of jobbery and incompetence as commander-in-chief, and holding up the Duke of Kent as a pattern of what a soldier Prince should be — brave in the field, capable in command and uncomplaining at the monstrous behaviour of a jealous brother. Just before Christmas 1808 a daring pamphlet appeared, called, *Observations on His Royal Highness the Duke of Kent's shameful Persecution since his removal from Gibraltar*, which published a number of confidential letters which had passed between the Royal brothers. The pamphlet was so outrageous in its disclosures and attacks on the Duke of York that even the Prince of Wales was roused, and sent for the Duke of Kent to ask him to take steps to deny that he had had anything to do with it. After a long discussion between the brothers it was decided that any denial would only give additional publicity to the pamphlet. However, in January 1809, when the House of Commons was discussing the Duke of York's administration of the Army and the disclosures of Mrs Clarke, it was decided that, in view of the general belief that the Duke of Kent was behind the attack on his brother, a public statement was necessary. The Duke of Kent was recovering from influenza and he wrote to a friend that he had 'already gone through all the discipline of medicine, the lancet, etc., which has made me as weak as water': but as soon as he was well enough he went down to the House of Lords and made a dramatic statement that, whatever professional differences there might have been between him and his brother, he entertained the highest respect for him, and believed him wholly incapable of acting in the manner imputed to him. All the arguments against giving publicity to the differences between the Duke of York and the Duke of Kent, which had been used against his denying any knowledge of the pamphlet which had come out just before Christmas, applied with equal force to this public statement. And after the statement, the world believed, largely because it made the scandal even more delicious, that the Duke of Kent was really behind the attacks on his brother. This was so generally believed, even by his family, that in July 1809 the Duke of Kent put a number of written questions to his private secretary Major

Dodd which, with that gentleman's answers, were written down and sworn before a Peer of the Realm. The paper was then circulated among the Royal Family. Major Dodd swore that the Duke had never encouraged the attacks on his brother nor had any dealings with the parties concerned in bringing forward the inquiry in the House of Commons. The questions and answers were none the less readily distributed, because they occasionally showed the Christian resignation of the Duke of Kent.

Question: 'What were my expressions on the subject of the pamphlets which appeared passing censure on the Duke of York, and others of my family, and holding up my own conduct to praise . . .?'

Answer: 'I have invariably heard your Royal Highness regret that any person should attempt to do justice to your own character at the expense of that of the Duke of York or any other member of your family. — T. Dodd.'

Question: 'During the ten years you have been my private secretary, when in the most confidential moments I have given vent to my wounded feelings on professional subjects, did you ever hear me express myself inimical to the Duke of York, or that I entertained an expectation of raising myself by his fall?'

Answer: 'Never! I have very frequently heard your Royal Highness express yourself very differently. — T. Dodd.'

But there was only one question that really touched on dangerous ground.

Question: 'Have you ever to your recollection, expressed yourself, either by words or in writing, either to Colonel Wardle or Mrs Clarke . . . in any way that could give them reason to suppose that I approved of the measure or would countenance those concerned in bringing it forward?'

Answer: 'Never! But I have on the contrary expressed myself that your Royal Highness would have a very different feeling. — T. Dodd.'

As the year 1809 drew to a close Mrs Clarke surveyed her handiwork and was proudly conscious of having put down the mighty from his seat. While she felt satisfied with the disgrace of the Duke of York, she was not so satisfied with the triumph of the humble and meek in the person of the Duke of Kent. Having exposed the frailties of one Duke, she felt qualified to deal with the other, and early in 1810 appeared her celebrated pamphlet *The Rival Princes*, in which she showed that the Duke of York had fallen a victim to the jealousy of the Duke of Kent. The Duke of Kent came in for a full share of those sarcastic sallies which had so delighted the House of Commons in the previous year, but perhaps the most painful was the reference to *Madame*: '—the Duke's affection for his old French lady, whom, he lamented, he could not marry was a proof of his steady disposition and domestic good qualities, added to which he regularly went to church.'

The most serious point for the Duke was that the book alleged that Major Dodd was hand in glove with Wardle and Mrs Clarke before, and during, the Parliamentary inquiry, and that Major Dodd had promised Mrs Clarke in the Duke's name £10,000, and promotions and places for her various families, legitimate and illegitimate. According to Mrs Clarke, Colonel Wardle always called her 'the Duke of Kent's little mortgage.' As soon as the pamphlet was published the Duke of Kent issued a counterblast by publishing his *Questions and Answers* to Major Dodd.

Picking one's way through the labyrinth of lies with which every passage in *The Rival Princes* is embellished and obscured, it is tolerably clear that Mrs Clarke believed the Duke of Kent to be behind her and that, when and if he became commander-in-chief, he would see that she was not a loser for siding with virtue. That Mrs Clarke believed the Duke of Kent to be behind her, supplies a motive in her attempt to expose the Duke of York. She certainly did not proceed against the Duke of York out of jealousy. There was nothing of 'heaven's rage or hell's fury' about Mrs Clarke. Her heart had been given too often, and returned unbroken, for that. She was not jealous but mercenary. Both Wardle and Dodd were men of straw, and could not have afforded to pay her any considerable sum of money. It seems to have been one of her rare flashes of truth when she said that Dodd had told her that the Duke of Kent would pay all her debts and give her an annunity of £400. Of course, in the *Questions and Answers,* Dodd denied this on oath before a Peer and a Prince, but it was only Major Dodd's word against Mary Ann Clarke's. Truth was, I think, on the side of frailty. How, otherwise, is it possible to explain Dodd's prominence in the intrigue, and that drive with Wardle and Mrs Clarke to the Martello Towers? Wardle and Mrs Clarke would have never tolerated Dodd's interference as a mere independent busybody. It is only possible to explain his eminence in their councils on the footing that he held himself out as the agent for the Duke of Kent.

But whether the Duke of Kent knew anything of Dodd's activities is far more questionable. It is significant that all the preparations between Mrs Clarke, Dodd and Wardle, were made immediately after the Duke of Kent's passage of arms with his brother and the Cabinet, over his return to Gibraltar in 1808. It is significant that both the Prince of Wales and the Duke of York believed their brother to be behind the disclosures. And, above all, the Duke always remained on friendly terms with Dodd. In April 1810 he wrote to Louis Philippe on this subject:

'As for my former secretary, I will only say that in spite of everything you may have seen in the papers, he is more to be pitied than blamed in many things and the imprudent things which he has unfortunately done have come from too great enthusiasm for my service and too lively a sense of all the injustices we have suffered. It is eight months, since he voluntarily retired from my employment, believing it a necessary sacrifice to public opinion but he can certainly say, with a clear conscience, without having lost any of my esteem for him.'[1]

In this murky glow faded the glory of the Duke's military career. Just occasionally his Field-Marshal's baton was dragged out of its case to attend a review, and he would sit his horse, grimly watching defects in the troops which he was powerless to correct. Once he took his daughter with him, when she was

[1] Translated. The Duke used to write curious Anglo-French letters to Louis Philippe: e.g. 'Le paquet de lettres . . . à été remis à Guillaume, qui lès a fait au quartier Hartwell; where they will have been very welcome, I apprehend.'

three months old, to a review on Hounslow Heath, and the stern disciplinarian had the mortification of hearing the Prince Regent call out to him, in front of everyone, 'What business has that infant here?' It was perhaps natural, but hardly wise, for Queen Victoria to refer so proudly to the fact that she was a soldier's daughter.

IV

For fifteen years after his return from Gibraltar the Duke was in retirement, forced on him by an increasing load of misfortunes. It is true that in 1810 he was reconciled with the Duke of York, though without enthusiasm. He wrote to Louis Philippe thanking him for his congratulations on the reconciliation, admitting its convenience, but adding that he did not think it would be of any advantage to him. The Duke of York was mildly amused at his brother's pompous sensibilities, and at the family dinner-party after Princess Amelia's funeral, said with a sly wink, 'Though this is a sad occasion I must drink the health of poor Edward.' But, of whatever advantage this reconciliation may have been to him, it had long ago been set off by his quarrel with the Prince of Wales, which – as may be supposed – was only due in the Duke's eyes to his efforts to do good and avoid scandal.

The Duke of Kent was on friendly terms with Sir John Douglas, an officer in the Marines, whose wife was a close friend of the Princess of Wales. In 1804 Sir John had been flabbergasted to receive a letter, accompanied by an indecent drawing, explaining that his wife had admitted another gentleman to her bed. Both the Douglases were certain that the letter and the drawing came from the Princess of Wales. Sir John showed both to the Duke of Kent, who, after a careful examination, agreed that it was the Princess's writing and wisely begged Sir John to forget it, as a little unfortunate obscenity of the Princess's. But Sir John was a knight, and keenly felt the slur on his honour: he was barely persuaded not to prosecute the Princess, and poured out his wounded feelings to his friends. In 1805 the story came to the ears of the Duke of Sussex, who hurried off to Carlton House to tell the Prince, and added: 'The Duke of Kent has known it for a year.' The Prince angrily sent for the Duke of Kent and asked why he had kept to himself a matter which so closely concerned the honour of the Royal Family. The Duke explained that he had kept it to himself to avoid scandal, and added, quite gratuit- ously, to avoid further misunderstandings between the King and the Prince. The Duke made a careful memorandum of the interview, and wrote that the Prince had said: 'that if he had not placed the most entire reliance on my attachment to him and he was pleased to add, on the well-known uprightness of my character and principles, he should certainly have felt him- self in no small degree offended at learning this from others.' The sarcasm was lost on the Duke. He had made a powerful enemy in his elder brother, who ever afterwards, complained of his treachery and deep-laid plans and always referred to him as Joseph Surface or Simon Pure. How powerful an enemy, he was to find out in 1814, when his debts became quite un- manageable.

From 1799 to 1806 the Duke's Parliamentary grant was £12,000; in 1805 all the younger Royal Dukes, including the Duke of Kent, were given a lump sum of £20,000 each from the droits of the Admiralty, and in 1806 their grants were raised to £18,000 a year. As the Duke kept his post as Governor of Gibraltar, his military pay and the rangership of Hampton Court brought his total income up to £24,000. But by 1807 his debts were more than £200,000.

It was not in the Duke's character to admit that his debts were due to extravagance and to a taste for splendour. Instead, he pestered the Government with elaborate memoranda as to the more favourable financial treatment given to the Dukes of York and Clarence, and the large sums he had lost through the accidents to his various equipments. No doubt he had been un- fortunate. In addition, he had been less generously treated than his brothers, his Parliamentary grant being longer de- layed than in the case of any of the Royal Dukes, but neither of these facts explained a debt of £200,000. In any event, it would have been impossible for the Government to suggest that the country should be called on to pay £200,000 to the Duke of Kent. In 1807, the Duke handed over half his income to trustees to pay the interest on his debts and lived on £12,000. *Madame*'s allowance was cut down from £1,000 to £400.

But the income of £12,000 which, after this, the Duke enjoyed was sufficient for even a man like the Duke of Kent, to whom four houses were a necessity. All might have been well if, at the end of the war, his creditors had been satisfied with the regular payment of their interest and had not begun to press for the return of their capital. Not knowing which way to turn, the Duke sent a memorial to the Prince Regent detailing once again his losses in the colonies and the preferential treatment given to his elder brothers. It was accompanied by a private letter.

> Kensington Palace,
> June 13th, 1815.

My Dear Brother,

The recollection of those habits of unreserved confidence in which it was my good fortune to live with you in former days, and of the innumerable marks of friendship and affection which I almost daily received at your hands, added to that warm attachment which I must ever feel for you to the latest hour of my existence as ever having been my steadiest friend in many of the most trying moments of my life, renders it impossible for me to reconcile it to my feelings, to leave it to your Ministers to be the first to acquaint you with my having addressed through them an official appeal to your justice for relief, at a moment when, overwhelmed with embarrassments, I could no longer refrain from taking that step . . . It has been unavoidable for me to introduce a comparison between the Duke of Clarence and myself . . . and I rely only on your knowledge of my character to acquit me of the most distant thought of wishing to draw any inference therefrom invidious to a brother, to whom, from habits of our earliest infancy, I am bound by ties of the warmest affection. I therefore consider it needless to attempt the justification of a step which, I am sure, will be viewed by you exactly as it is intended by me ... and permit me to add one request, which is, that you will judge my claim from your own upright just mind and good heart, as then I can not doubt of the result being favourable to my interest.

    With every sentiment of the warmest devotion and attachment,

        I remain,

            My dearest Brother,

                Your faithful and affectionate,

                    EDWARD.

But the only reply to this faintly pathetic document from 'that upright just mind' was a formal message of regret sent through Lord Liverpool that nothing could be done. But the Duke was obliged to do something. He handed over three-quarters of his income to trustees, one of whom was the Radical, Joseph Hume, and the other the philanthropic Socialist and partner of Robert Owen, William Allen, who were to deal with his creditors as best they might, while he went to live abroad in Brussels on £7,000 a year.

The Duke did not fly the country like the traditional debtor, a little out at elbows and anxious to hide his face in a strange land. He took the largest house he could find in Brussels. For a year it was filled with carpenters, bricklayers, painters, glaziers, architects, embellishing it for a Prince of England. *Madame* was fond of fresh air, so that the large garden must be entirely laid out anew; stables and coach-houses were built in the latest English fashion, and it became quite one of the sights of Brussels to see the arrangements being made to house the English Prince's stud. After all, a Prince must live.

If we had to judge the character of the Duke of Kent simply by his professional career, by his relations with his family, and by his misfortunes, we could only think of him as combining the qualities of Mr Micawber and Mr Pecksniff. As a brother he reeked of principle and virtue, and in misfortune he was an almost nauseating victim of circumstances. He had nothing in his character — and this was partly due to his upbringing — to enable him to face misfortune. As a youth he had firmly believed that everything conspired to make a Prince's path through the world easy and glorious. He had set out full of high hopes and full of high principles and, when disaster overtook him, he could not imagine that it might be himself who was to blame. When he saw his elder brothers roystering through life, generally in a state of tipsy infatuation but far more successful than himself, with his sober ways and his devotion to 'his old French lady,' he was stricken by the injustice of it all and, instead of facing misfortunes, comforted himself in querulous tartuffery.

But, as he grew older the quarrels with his brothers and his professional career occupied him less and less, and his other activities show him to have possessed far more agreeable qualities. In politics he was an advanced Whig though, apart from supporting the claims of the Roman Catholics, he was never prominent in party struggles. He was uncomfortably conscious of the miserable state of the poor, and was a tireless worker for charity. Much of his creditors' money found its way into the coffers of such organisations as the Society for Propagating the Gospel in the Highlands and Islands of Scotland, the Westminster Infirmary, the British School of Industry, the Lying-in Charity for Delivering Poor Women at their own Habitations, the Bible Society, the Literary Fund for Distressed Authors, the Philanthropic Harmonists — to mention a few of the fifty-three charities he supported. In 1816 he presided at seventy-two charity meetings and, in that year, was given the Freedom of the City of London 'for the distinguished manner in which he had exerted himself to promote every object of benevolence throughout the United Kingdom.'

He was far in advance of contemporary opinion in believing that charity was not enough to solve the prevailing distress, and at a public meeting said that 'it was evident that no charitable provision or establishment could remedy the evil of a depressed working class.'

But perhaps his naturally generous and lavish character was

shown at its best in his home life. Of his four homes he was seldom at the Pavilion at Hampton Court; Kensington Palace was his official headquarters, from whence his correspondence was addressed and where he received callers. His apartments there were done up in a magnificent style in 1807 at a cost of £13,000. A special bedroom was fitted up for Louis Philippe. But when he was in London the greater part of his time was spent in the house at Knightsbridge with *Madame*. It was here that they made a home for the various children of Major de Salaberry who were sent over to England to serve in the Army. In 1807 their godson Edward came over, and spent all his vacations with them while he was at Woolwich. His first letter from England, when he must have been fifteen, gives a delightful picture of the Duke and *Madame*.

Kensington Palace,
30th Dec. 1807.

My Dear Papa,

    . . . I have not yet got a letter from my dear Mamma but I hope to have one quickly, which I shall look for impatiently. I am at present staying with H.R.H. the Duke of Kent at Kensington Palace, where I have fine apartments. H.R.H. and Madame de S. Laurent are at present at Knightsbridge which is some distance from here. It is a superb mansion beautifully furnished: I have dined there several times. I dined there on Christmas Day with the Duke of Orleans and his brothers. I have been at the Opera with H.R. Highness and Madame, when I saw the Duke of Cambridge to whom I was presented as the godson of H.R. Highness and Madame. I have also seen the Swedish Ambassador the same evening. I have been at the play with H.R.H. H.R. Highness has given orders that we shall always have music at dinner. The dinner is at seven o'clock which is supper for me. The Duke and Madame have been very kind to me, and their kindness if possible is greater every day.

    I hope my dear papa you will write me by every mail: the letters cost me nothing: they all come first to H.R.H.

and then to me: the postage is paid at the Palace where I now am . . .

Adieu my dear papa, I believe I shall see you before long, and I am with the most lively affection,

Your devoted and obedient son,

EDWARD ALPHONSE DE S.

Madame de St L. has given me six guineas since I came to England, a jolly sum for me.'

It was a terrible grief to the Duke when Edward was killed in the storming of Badajos, after his two elder brothers had died in India, and the Duke wrote to de Salaberry: 'There are not in the world two persons who have mourned the cruel death of your dear Edward so much as the two old friends [the Duke and *Madame*] who write to you to-day.'

But *Madame* was not overfond of London and, in one of her letters, she says: '. . . Adieu, dear and ever dear de Salaberry, I have only a minute left to dress and go out. It is go and come from morning till night. Ah! London, I will not call you a hole – the greatest and most beautiful city in the world – but every place has its drawbacks.' And the happiest time for both *Madame* and the Duke was when they were at the Duke's home in Ealing, Castle Hill Lodge, a pleasant, low house surrounded by forty acres of park land, in the middle of what was then a village. There was a winding drive up to the house, which the Duke always kept brilliantly lighted at night and from which by day there was a fine view of Harrow. There was a system of bells from the porter's lodge at the entrance gates, up to the house, so that there were always six footmen standing at the front door when anyone called and, if a person of any importance was expected, the house steward, who was an elderly Frenchman, would be there as well. The outside of the house was not particularly impressive: it was classical in design, though disfigured by Mr Wyatt in one of his whimsical Gothic moods. Inside, the house was not only impressive but quite unlike anything ever known in England. There were scores of menservants, always with new liveries, their hair perfectly dressed and powdered by a resident hairdresser who was kept for the purpose. Every morning each servant had to present himself before the Duke to show that he was perfectly well dressed and clean. Apart from meal-times, the servants might never be unoccupied and every visitor could not help noticing that the inside of the house was speckless. In the sitting-rooms the walls were hanging with bell-ropes, each of which called a particular servant. The Duke always got up at six, and a fire had to be lit for him at five. One servant, therefore, stayed up all night and slept by day so that there should be no danger of the fire not being lighted. The house was filled with musical devices, cages of artificial singing-birds, organs with dancing horses, and musical clocks. At night all the corridors and halls were lighted with hundreds of coloured lights. Naturally the Duke had a fine library. He owned the expected standard English books; he also possessed a military library with numerous maps and plans and also books on contemporary problems with a bias towards the Left. Perhaps less expected was a very fine copy of Eikon Basilike, and a small library of medical books.[1]

A young officer in the Duke's regiment who was asked out to breakfast at Ealing was astounded at the state and ceremony with which the servants prepared the meal. They finally handed a massive tea-caddy to the Duke, which he unlocked, saying to his guest: 'Take a lesson from me – you are just starting in life – never be above attending to particulars, ay, and minute particulars . . . What is a trifle? Nothing that has reference to our comfort, our independence or our peace.'

And a middle-class judge who spent a night there was nearly startled out of his wits. He was changing for dinner, and thought he must be in Elysian fields when he was shown a carefully concealed door which opened into the closet, where there was a running stream and a fountain playing. It was autumn, and when the judge looked out of the window the next morning he saw the lawn was covered in fallen leaves. Within a quarter of an hour, a gardener and six under-gardeners had cleared up every leaf and twig. At breakfast, he

---

[1] An interesting article on the Duke's library was published in *History Today* for October 1969, written by Mollie Gillen.

noticed the Duke get up and speak in German to someone
behind a glass door in the dining-room and, just as the judge
was lifting his cup of tea to his lips, there came a sudden burst
of music from thirty wind instruments which, with the players,
had been hidden behind the door. (This band played in Ealing
Parish Church when the Duke was at Castle Hill.) The tune
was the dirge written for the judge's son, who had been killed
in the war. The judge burst into tears at this delicate attention,
and the Duke took his hand, saying: 'These are tears which do
none of us any harm'; and the band then broke into less
harrowing melodies. Afterwards the judge, who as a youth
had seen Lord Chesterfield, wrote to a friend that the Duke of
Kent was distinguished by a grace of manner compared with
which Lord Chesterfield was a dancing-master. The Duke of
Wellington used to say that he never knew a man with more
natural eloquence than the Duke of Kent.

It is easy to see in the domestic economy of Castle Hill
Lodge the same thirst for perfection which had proved the
Prince's undoing as a soldier. The home of a Prince of England had to be slightly different from that of other men. But, if
visitors could once get over this oddity in the Prince's character,
they were all charmed by his kindness, his intelligence, and
what in the language of the day they spoke of as 'the manly
good sense of his character.' His kindness certainly could not
be better shown than by his faithfulness to *Madame*, who,
middle-aged and rather foreign, must have quite upset the
perfection of Castle Hill. He wrote to de Salaberry in 1814
'. . . I am sure you will be pleased to know, that what our life
was when we were beside you, that it has continued during
the twenty years that have passed since we left Canada, and I
love to think that twenty years hence it may be the same.'

v

On 6th November, 1817, the Princess Charlotte had died.
A few weeks afterwards the Duke and *Madame* were at breakfast, and the Duke tossed her over the paper to read, while he
opened his letters. Suddenly he was disturbed by hearing a gasp

THE HOUSE OF SAXE-COBURG

Francis Frederick, Duke of Saxe-Coburg.
(1750–1806)

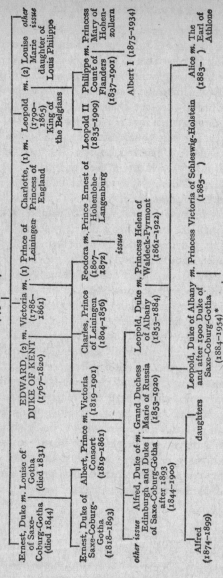

* Struck off the roll of the Order of the Garter in 1915 and deprived of all his English honours in 1919 because he fought for his country.

and a gurgle. For a few moments he thought that *Madame* was going to die: but, when she had sufficiently recovered, she pointed to the paper, where it said that it had become essential for the succession that the Duke of Kent should marry.

The Duke decided to confide in Mr Creevey, who had the ear of all the Whig leaders and happened to be then in Brussels. The Duke explained that the Regent and the Duke of York would almost certainly never have heirs, and that if the Duke of Clarence did not marry he would be next in succession. 'God only knows,' he said, 'the sacrifice it will be to make, whenever I shall think it my duty to become a married man. It is now seven and twenty years that Madame St Laurent and I have lived together: we are of the same age, and have been in all climates, and in all difficulties together, and you may well imagine, Mr Creevey, the pang it will occasion me to part with her ... She is of very good family and has never been an actress, and I am the first and only person who ever lived with her. If Madame St Laurent is to return to live amongst her friends, it must be in such a state of independence as to command their respect. I shall not require very much, but a certain number of servants and a carriage are essential.'

But servants and even a carriage without the Duke meant nothing to *Madame*, and she offered to remove to a convent. The offer was accepted, and while she was expiating in the rigours of convent life those twenty-seven happy — if canonically sinful — years, the Duke was preparing to make his sacrifice. After a short courtship, he married the Princess of Leiningen. She was Prince Leopold's sister, a widow with two children, and was thirty-two years old, 'short, stout, with brown eyes and hair, and rosy cheeks, cheerful and voluble, and gorgeously attired in rustling silks and bright velvets.' She was a typically capable Coburg.

They were married according to the Lutheran Church on 29th May, 1818, and were re-married in the drawing-room at Kew before Queen Charlotte on 11th July, 1818. A family party, with the Regent leading the cheers, wished them Godspeed for Amorbach. This was a small territory, between Hesse and Baden, which the Duchess ruled as Regent for her infant son, and which had been given to the Princes of Leiningen in exchange for their own lands on the Moselle, which had been overrun by Napoleon. The Duke borrowed £10,000, and ordered a small army of English artisans to be sent out to Amorbach to transform the castle into a place fit for a Prince of England. The workmen had just begun to pull down and build up, to enlarge and embellish, when the Duchess announced that she was pregnant.

The Duke had no money, but he was determined to return to England. At about the same time it was announced that the Duchesses of Clarence and Cambridge would await their lyings-in at Hanover, but although two Kings of England, George I and George II, had been born in Hanover, the Duke made up his mind that nothing but London would do for his child. Money was the difficulty. He was absolutely without the means of paying for the journey. At last his trustee, William Allen, sent a draft on Frankfurt. It was not large, and all ideas of grandeur had to be abandoned. The Duke himself sat on the box of the coach and took the reins, while the Duchess, with only two months to go, her daughter, Princess Feodore with a pair of Russian lap-dogs and her song-birds, a nurse and a lady's maid, rode inside. The news that the Duke would not trust his wife to anyone else, but was himself driving, was very tenderly received in England, though an Englishwoman who saw them jogging along through France reported that it was 'an unbelievably odd caravan.'

They reached Kensington Palace in the middle of April, and the Duke had had his own way. He settled down with satisfaction to wait events. At the end of April he wrote to a friend that 'I trust my countrymen will duly appreciate the great sacrifice and exertion made by her in travelling at a period drawing so near her confinement . . . [and then followed a reference to the Regent] . . . with regard to congratulations from a certain quarter, to which you allude, I could say a great deal, but as harmony and peace is my object, I had much rather the world should think that everything was most cordial between us than the reverse. It now only remains for me to assure you that all is going on as well as I could possibly wish, and I trust that your prayers and those of my other friends will be realised in witnessing a prosperous result to the Duchess's present interesting situation.'

On 24th May, 1819, a daughter was born. The Duke was not disappointed, and wrote to a friend: 'As to the circumstance of the child not proving to be a son instead of a daughter, I feel it due to myself to declare that such sentiments are not in unison with my own: for I am decidedly of opinion that the decrees of Providence are at all times wisest and best.'

The Duke had manfully done his duty in providing for the succession, and expected that a grateful country would now relieve him from his embarrassments and make it possible for him to live in England. George III, on one occasion, complained to the Duke that he made too much of a trade of his profession and, if the King had been in his right mind in 1819, he might well have complained that the Duke made too much of a parade of the functions of motherhood. He wrote off to his friends of 'our duties in giving it maternal nutriment on the soil of England,' and, when someone wrote to congratulate him on the news that the Duchess was herself nursing the baby, he replied how happy she was 'that an office, most interesting in its nature, had met with the wishes and feelings of society,' and later he wrote of the weaning of the child: 'we do not expect, at earliest, to be able to get over that arduous charge until the second week in November.'

But whether these performances might have touched the generosity of the public was never known, because the Regent would not hear of the public being approached. His only anxiety was that the Duke and all his family should go as soon as possible to the distant obscurity of Amorbach. Though he had never loved the Princess Charlotte, this ostentatious breeding reminded him too forcibly that he had failed to provide the country with an heir. Prince Leopold, drawing £50,000 a year from the country and ever anxious to please the Regent, frugally offered to defray the expenses of the journey to Amorbach. But the Duke of Kent decided that his daughter must be kept before the British public, especially as the Duke of Clarence's child had only lived a few hours, and she was therefore in direct succession to the throne, and he made one last effort to find sufficient money to make it possible for him to live in retirement in England.

As far back as 1815, his principal creditors had had the property at Ealing valued, when it was declared that, while a house of that size, furnished in that style, could not be built for less than £100,000, the intrinsic value as it stood was not more than £51,000. Perhaps naturally, plashing fountains and purling brooks in the water-closets were not the choice of ordinary mortals, and the creditors, recognising that it would have to be sold at a terrible loss, held their hand. After the birth of his daughter, a bright idea struck the Duke, and he decided to ask Parliament for leave to dispose of Castle Hill Lodge by lottery. The matter was brought before the House of Commons in July 1819, and the supporters of the Duke occupied the House with all the disasters which had dogged him since he was eighteen and of the preferential treatment given to the Duke of Clarence. Passing delicately over the Duke's dislike of lotteries, his friends dwelt at length on his charitable nature, and it was clear that they were making a clever appeal to free him from embarrassments so that he might be able to devote money to his charities. In short, the appeal was to be 'Buy a share in the Duke of Kent's lottery and help to spread the gospel among the heathen.' But the House of Commons was rather shocked and the motion had to be withdrawn.

In September the Duke was sadly writing to a friend: '... and I now candidly state that after viewing the subject in every possible way, I am satisfied that to continue to live in England, even in the quiet way we are going on without splendour and without show, nothing short of doubling the £7,000 will do, reduction being impossible in an establishment like ours where there is not a servant idle from morning to night.'

He found some respite from his financial worries by toiling away at his charities and made up for curtailed subscriptions by repeatedly acting as chairman. He was, too, much occupied with Mr Owen's schemes for transforming the human race. It was through William Allen, who was also Robert Owen's partner, that the Duke had been introduced to the man whom many people have regarded as mad, and most Socialists as the founder of their creed. At the beginning of the nineteenth century, England felt the air oppressive with new ideas, when every philosopher was evolving new theories and every inventor thought he was charming away the world's troubles with the same ease that the South Sea Bubble speculators a century earlier thought that they were charming away poverty. Thus encouraged, Owen devised a world from which poverty, greed and ignorance were to be banished. It was one day in 1815 that the Duke of Kent had first called on Owen in Bedford Square and had been shown the cubes with which Owen had represented the numbers of the various classes of society, a tiny cube at the top representing the Royal Family and the nobility, and the Duke had said: 'I know that there will be a much more just equality of our race and an equality that will give much more security and happiness to all.'

Owen had, for many years, put his principles into practice on the banks of the Clyde at the New Lanark Cotton Mills, where the operatives lived in clean surroundings, where drunkenness and theft were practically unknown, and where some effort was made to educate as well as to exploit child labour. Leading members of the Tory Government, rich men of all creeds and parties, and some Bishops, were enthusiastic supporters of Owen's work until, in 1817, at a public meeting, he said that it would be useless to continue his villages of union and co-operation 'unless the world is now prepared to dismiss all its erroneous religious notions – for it will be vain to look for inhabitants to occupy them ... who can love their neighbour as themselves ... whether he be Jew or Gentile, Mahommedan or Pagan, Infidel or Christian.' For this speech Owen lost almost all his influential support. His religious opinions were suspect. In this crisis the Duke of Kent and the Duke of Sussex did not withdraw their support from him, and undoubtedly their loyalty did much to steady public opinion. Owen's London partners – particularly Allen, who was a Quaker – were much perturbed by his religious views, and went up to New Lanark to inquire whether the Scriptures were taught in the school. They were satisfied but nervous. The Duke of Kent then sent up his doctor to inquire minutely into the life at New Lanark with a view to publishing a report on Owen's system, to try and dispel public prejudice. The report was enthusiastic, and the Duke wrote to Owen: '. . . I am therefore now for myself fully satisfied with the principles, spirit and practice of the system which you advocate for new-forming the human character, so far as human means are concerned, and for new-governing the human race, and I acknowledge myself to be a full and devoted convert to your philosophy in principle, spirit and practice. But we must act with prudence and foresight. The English are emphatically a practical people and practice has great influence over them.'

In the autumn of 1819 the Duke was making arrangements to visit New Lanark, with the Duchess and his daughter, early in 1820, when they were to stay with Owen. The trouble and fatigue of the journey he dismissed as nothing, and gracefully added that 'the plain and simple accommodation which you will have to offer us is what we should prefer to any other.'

From all this it seems a little idle to speculate whether the Duke of Kent was a Socialist. Owen, by taking a slightly unfair advantage, did his best to persuade the world that he was. For, many years after the Duke was dead, Owen published a statement that the Duke of Kent had spoken to him at a *séance* with the agreeable news that there were no titles in the spirit world. Jeremy Bentham and President Jefferson had strongly corroborated this important piece of news. But in spite of this it would not be possible or fair to say more than that the Duke was the first patron of Socialism.

In the autumn more practical matters claimed his attention. Lack of money made it impossible for him to continue to live in London and, in order to escape the reproaches of his creditors, he was on the look-out for a place of retirement. His old tutor – 'the Kingfisher,' now Bishop of Salisbury – suggested Sidmouth as being out of reach of creditors and healthy for his family. Accordingly they set out from Kensington Palace at the beginning of December, and broke the journey at Windsor, where the old Princesses were delighted with 'the beautiful fat baby and the excellent good little wife who made Edward so happy,' and at Salisbury, where they stayed with Bishop Fisher and all the Cathedral clergy came to pay their respects.

The Duke did his best to keep up the fiction that it was a health trip rather than a flight, and wrote rather grandly to a friend: 'We intend wintering in the West in order that the Duchess may have the benefit of tepid sea bathing and our infant that of sea air.' There was admittedly a ring of truth in this, because the medical profession had recently discovered the sea. Chest weakness, rheumatism, exhaustion after nursing a baby, apoplexy, *tic douloureux* and many other affections were all said to be charmed away by the tonic properties of a few whiffs of ozone. Ladies and gentlemen only visited the sea: they did not live by it. That riot of red and yellow brick, that medley of classical and Gothic, that blending of Eastern pinnacle and German *schloss*, had not yet fantastically skipped down to the water's edge as the memorial of England's professional classes. In 1820 the red and green coast of South Devonshire was only marred by a few white splodges which were the houses for the visitors and the homes of the fishermen. One of these little splodges was Sidmouth, with hills at the back and high cliffs on either side, open only to the sea. Woolbrook Glen, where they stayed, was a small two-storied white house less than a quarter of a mile from the sea. Like all buildings which house a succession of families, it was very musty. There was just room for the family, a few servants, and the Duke's gentlemen. It was so close to the road that once, when a boy was potting sparrows with a gun, a pellet passed through the nursery window, at which the Duke gravely observed that his daughter had stood fire as became a soldier's daughter.

Devonshire's mild and humid air suited the Duchess and the Princess, and the Duke was well in all climates. He was so healthy that he used to say in reference to his brothers: 'I shall outlive them all.' On one of those close, soft and muggy January days peculiar to Devonshire, the Duke climbed up Peak Hill to see the view across the sea to Torbay. Without realising it, he had got soaked in the reeking air. A cold resulted, which he neglected, and within a week his lungs were affected. The wonderful properties of sea air which the doctors had discovered had endangered his life. Medical men, messengers from the Regent, and Prince Leopold dashed to Sidmouth. At Windsor the Princess Augusta was a little relieved on hearing that the Duke's own doctor had reached Sidmouth: 'a very discreet and a very bold physician: both of which qualities were necessary with such sort of colds as poor Edward's always are.' Blisters, bleedings, cuppings and leeches were tried, and the invalid lost a hundred and twenty ounces of blood. But the Princess Augusta lost all hope when a messenger hurried to Windsor with the news that the invalid had continued hiccups. On 22nd January he said to his wife: 'Do not forget me' and, after lapsing into unconsciousness, died on the following morning.

The coffin, seven feet in length and over a ton in weight, lumbered up to Windsor with stops at Bridport, Blandford, Salisbury and Basingstoke. The means for leaving Sidmouth, and the funeral expenses, were provided by Prince Leopold. To many people, particularly his brothers, the coffin contained all that was left of an unsuccessful, self-righteous pauper. But within a century his descendants were to sit on the thrones of England, Germany, Russia, Norway, Roumania and Spain. It is not fanciful to suppose that Queen Victoria, who raised the English dynasty from provincial to cosmopolitan importance, owed as much to the capabilities of her father as to the natural acquisitiveness of her Coburg mother.

CHAPTER V

❧

ERNEST AUGUSTUS,
DUKE OF CUMBERLAND

PRINCE ERNEST, the fifth son of George III, was born on 6th June, 1771. He lived with a tutor and his two younger brothers in a house on Kew Green till he was fifteen, when he went to the University of Göttingen in Hanover. In 1790 he was made an officer in both the English and Hanoverian Armies, and he served throughout the campaigns in Flanders of 1793, 1794 and 1795. In the winter of 1794-5, he commanded the Hanoverian troops in the exceedingly difficult task of maintaining themselves in Holland against the victorious armies of France. When the Hanoverians were obliged to withdraw to Germany, he continued to serve with them and did not return to England till 1799. In that year, when he was twenty-eight, he was given a Parliamentary grant of £12,000 a year and was created Duke of Cumberland and Teviotdale. From 1799 until 1813, he lived in a suite of apartments in St James's Palace or at Cumberland Cottage on Kew Green, and occupied himself with extreme Tory politics and the affairs of the Fifteenth Dragoons, of which he was colonel-in-chief.

This account of the Duke of Cumberland's early life – with the sojourn in Germany, the little experience of war followed by high command in two armies, the Dukedom and the Parliamentary grant – might well have been descriptive of any of the younger sons of George III. To the casual observer the Duke of Cumberland was merely one of the King's younger sons, but in fact he was pre-eminent among them in intelligence and bravery and differed from them in almost every characteristic.

On 5th June, 1771, only a few hours before the Duke of Cumberland's birth, Queen Charlotte rather startled society by appearing at a Court function. This bold display of her condition was, in the light of after events, fortunate, because some learned historian, steeped in the obscurer doctrines of heredity, would otherwise undoubtedly have proved that the Duke of Cumberland could not have been a son of the King and Queen. He would have argued that, while it is obviously possible for parents to have children who are totally unlike themselves, it is impossible for them to have a child who is not only totally unlike themselves but totally unlike its brothers and sisters. Yet the Duke of Cumberland achieved this triumph of impossibility.

Perhaps the most patent difference between him and his brothers was that, while they were all inveterate chatterers, he alone could hold his tongue. Mr Creevey was amazed, on sitting next to him at dinner at the Pavilion, to find a member of the Royal Family who scarcely spoke. All the sons of George III had abilities far above the average, but the Duke of Cumberland was the only one who harnessed his gifts to a definite purpose and drove them brilliantly and unscrupulously in an effort to triumph over the principles of progress.

Even in appearance he was totally different from his family. His brothers were, with the exception of William IV, tall and handsome, but an increasing plumpness gave them a homely, middle-class geniality. The Duke of Cumberland, handsome, very tall and very thin, was alone denied this softening influence of flesh. While they looked like comfortable merchants, he throughout all the eighty years of his life looked like nothing but an elegant cavalry officer.

And even his bravery was of a different quality from that of his brothers. They had that stolid indifference to danger which enables men to stay on the field of battle till they are victorious or killed or led away by their more prudent comrades. The Duke of Cumberland had not only that kind of bravery but, coupled with it, an active fierceness which his brothers lacked. In the autumn of 1794, while fighting with a French

Dragoon, he broke his sabre, parried his adversary's blow with the stump, and, while the Frenchman was getting ready to strike again, calmly lifted him from the saddle and carried him off to the English lines. The Frenchman, who had been encouraged by his Government to believe that all Princes were decadent, was no doubt too surprised to offer any resistance.

Then in politics he took a different line. His brothers had all, at some time of their lives, Whig sympathies. He alone had no truck with Whig politicians and Whig principles, and from 1799 onwards put his intellectual gifts and courage at the disposal of the High Tories. His maiden speech in the House of Lords was actually made on a subject far removed from Toryism, but on one which seemed to act like a magnet on Royal oratory – the Adultery Bill. The Bill was designed to prevent the marriage of the guilty parties to a divorce. The Duke spoke up for the fair sex: 'So few men are inclined to marry the women they have seduced, that it would be cruel to deprive the females of this last hope.' It was the only occasion that I have been able to discover, on which the Duke allowed even a faintly liberal sentiment to pass his lips.

When the Duke started his political career, the question of granting relief to the Roman Catholics was agitating the country. But in order to preserve the King's sanity, it was tacitly agreed by the leading politicians that the subject should never be mentioned to him. Thanks, however, to the activity of the Radicals, to whom the sanity of one man, whom they had long regarded as mad, did not appear as important as the freedom of thousands, the question was frequently raised in debate in both Houses of Parliament. In the course of one of these debates in 1805 the Duke of Cumberland said that with the last effort of his nature he would defend the establishment in Church and State, and added: 'All that can be given consistently with reason and conscience I am prompt to give. But the Constitution I cannot, dare not, will not give.' This is an amusing picture which he draws of himself, ready to give almost anything to the Roman Catholics, but reluctant to dole out the British Constitution. It is only marred by the doubt whether the British Constitution was really his to give.

From then onwards the Duke of Cumberland stood high in
the councils of reaction. In the long gallery of his apartments
in St James's Palace, the extremists of the Tory Party would
meet, and plot how they could cast the shadow of the past
across the bright hopes of the reformers. Inevitably these
gentlemen, 'hob-nobbing' in a Royal Palace, respected their
royal host and, when he added to his hospitality a fearless
Toryism, expressed in terms that were neither vague nor
flocculent, they began to think of him as a Tory leader. And as
faint whispers of these meetings reached the people of England,
they grew increasingly nervous of the Duke of Cumberland.

Their nervousness of his politics was accentuated by the fact
that almost everything that was known about him was un-
prepossessing. As a soldier he was known to prefer German
officers to English ones, because they were more servile. In his
own regiment, the Fifteenth Dragoons, he had caused the
greatest scandal by raising his cane to one of the English
officers. In 1810 one of the officers of his own regiment presented a petition to Parliament complaining of the systematic
unfairness of the colonel, the Duke of Cumberland. The cause
of the officer was warmly taken up by the Opposition and it
was shown that the military discipline of the Duke of Cumberland was quite as savage as that of the Duke of Kent. The
Fifteenth Dragoons was the only regiment in which the
punishment of 'picqueting' was still practised, when an
offender against military discipline was made to balance for
hours at a time on the pointed end of a stake fixed in the
ground.

In one respect, perhaps, the Duke was unfortunate in drawing on himself the disgust of his fellow countrymen. He had
been shockingly scarred on the left side of his face as a result of
his wound at the Battle of Tournai. With the heartless patriotism of a soldier's sister, the Princess Augusta said to Queen
Charlotte when he came back with his wound: 'Mamma, how
lucky it is that Ernest is just come so seasonably with that
wound in his face. I should have been shocked else, not to have
had one little bit of glory among ourselves.' Although the
Duke used to say that he had only one eye but that that one

was a regular piercer, and although he was always careful only
to allow his right profile to be painted, which showed an extraordinarily distinguished face, people meeting him could not
fail to be repelled by his appearance. It is uncertain whether
there was actually an eyeless socket, as some people said, or
whether 'the eye turned completely out of its place,' as Stockmar said. It was no doubt to try and cover what his sister called
'this little bit of glory' that the Duke, in later life, allowed his
whiskers and moustaches to trail over his face, which greatly
added to his German appearance.

And if people's knowledge of the Duke made them dislike
him, the gaps in their knowledge made them loathe him. They
had little knowledge of his vices but they filled in the gaps with
the most lurid colours. For the forty years of the Duke's life
up to 1810, the only tangible evidence of his 'gallantry' is in a
letter from Mrs Harcourt, who was the wife of one of the
British generals serving in Flanders in 1793. She had taken
the Duke, a young man of twenty-two, over one of the French
convents, which, in spite of the decrees of the Republican
Government, still existed in remote corners of France. She
had been greatly shocked when he attempted to kiss the Abbess
and persisted in ogling the nuns, though anyone who went
over a convent with one of the sons of George III can scarcely
have hoped to escape without a blush. Mrs Harcourt wrote
sadly home that she was afraid he was too wild for England.
But Mrs Harcourt was entirely wrong.

A little rollicking love-making would have done the Duke
no harm on his return to England. What did do him im-
measurable harm in the public esteem was that he returned to
England and set about his vices in an atmosphere of darkness
and obscurity. The newspapers openly jested of the latest
attachments of the Prince of Wales, all the world knew of the
Duke of Kent's '*Madame*,' the Duke of Clarence was to be seen
any day driving down to Bushey with Mrs Jordan, and the
Duke of York was often recognised bowling down the King's
Road to pay a call on Mrs Cary, who lived next door to the
Bishop of London at Fulham Palace. All these were public
scandals, but at any rate people knew the worst. Of the Duke

of Cumberland's vices they knew nothing but guessed the worst. In the Duke's bedroom in St James's Palace, where hundreds of pounds had been spent in hanging the walls with mirrors, the public firmly believed that every kind of decadent vice was practised.

By 1810 the Duke of Cumberland was already so unpopular that he was almost a rival to Napoleon for the national ogreship. Nurses were said to threaten their naughty charges with the words: 'Boney will come for you!' And mothers may well have cautioned their roving-eyed, venturesome daughters with the gruesome threat that 'Cumberland will come for you!'

II

But on the last day of May 1810, whatever had been obscure and dim in the private life of the Duke was exposed by the glittering blaze of scandal. That morning, as fast as fire, the news travelled that the Duke of Cumberland had murdered his valet in St James's Palace. It was not difficult for rumour to find a motive. Some assured their friends that the valet had been blackmailing the Duke by threatening to expose the dark secrets of his private life. But it was more generally believed that the valet, whose name was Sellis, had discovered the Duke in bed with Mrs Sellis. The Duke, or so the story ran, had murdered his valet, not to silence him but to punish him for daring to interrupt his master's pleasures. To support the theory that Mrs Sellis was the mistress of the Duke, it was recalled that the Princess Augusta and the Duke of Cumberland had been godparents to Mrs Sellis's last child. Some, who were very well informed, remembered that Queen Charlotte had presented Mrs Sellis with two yards of Indian muslin.

Despite the general belief at the time, which only grew stronger as the Duke grew more unpopular, it is certain that, far from murdering a valet, the Duke was almost murdered by one.

On the evening of 30th May, the Duke had returned to his apartments in St James's Palace about nine o'clock to change for a concert. Sellis had helped him into his clothes and had then been dismissed for the night. The Duke had gone out to his concert before half past nine. There were four doors in the Duke's bedroom. Two were merely the doors of closets. The third, which was by the head of the Duke's bed, led into the bedroom of his other valet, Neale. There was another door in Neale's bedroom which led into a passage at the far end of which was one door of Sellis's bedroom. If, therefore, Sellis had occasion to go to the Duke's room, he would ordinarily pass through Neale's room. The fourth door in the Duke's room led to the sitting-room and certain state apartments. These all opened out of one another and eventually led to the second door of Sellis's bedroom. It was possible for Sellis to approach the Duke's bedroom through the state apartments though he was not supposed to use this way, as the state rooms were shut up.

At about half past ten, one of the maids had seen Sellis standing in the door of his bedroom, half undressed. A little later the same maid had heard someone creeping through the state apartments. The Duke returned from the concert at about half past twelve and was in bed and asleep by one. In a written statement he described what happened: 'Being in bed and asleep he received two blows on his head which awoke him, and upon starting up he received two other blows upon his head, which being accompanied with a hissing noise it occurred to him that some bat had flown against him, being between sleeping and waking, and immediately received two other blows, there was a lamp burning in his room but he did not see anybody . . . he then got up and made for the door [the one leading into Neale's room] which opens at the head of his bed: he then received a wound upon his right thigh with a sabre. He then called out, "Neale, Neale, I am murdered." '

Neale dashed in and thinking the assailant was still there, he capered round the room brandishing a poker. He very soon tripped over the Duke's regimental sword, which was lying, with considerable bloodstains, on the threshold of the door which led to the state apartments. Neale then realised that the assailant had left. He supported his master to a chair. The Duke told him to rouse the servants at once and to stop anyone leaving the Palace. When the other servants had got up, the Duke told them to wake Sellis. They went through Neale's room and finding Sellis's bedroom door at the end of the passage locked, rattled it and screamed through the keyhole, with that excited exaggeration which murders at three o'clock in the morning perhaps excuse, 'Wake up, wake up, the Duke is murdered!' This startling news did not rouse Mr Sellis.

The servants then hurried back through the Duke's bedroom. They were surprised to find the doors of the state apartments unlocked, although the maidservant distinctly remembered locking them on the previous evening. When they reached this door of Sellis's bedroom, they heard from inside a suspicious gurgling noise. The porter opened the door and quickly cried out: 'Good God! Mr Sellis has cut his throat!' The guard were called, and the sergeant described at the inquest what they found: 'there was a bloody razor lying by Sellis's hand and a wash-hand-basin standing on the table with a little water in it, appearing as if someone had been washing their bloody hands in it. Sellis was quite dead when he [the sergeant] came into the room, but was not cold. There was no appearance of Sellis having struggled, his hands were straight down and the blood, all in a froth, running from his neck.'

The chain of evidence was completed when the servants found a lantern, together with a pair of slippers marked 'J. Sellis,' in the water-closet leading off the Duke's bedroom. Sellis had clearly gone through the state rooms to the closet off the Duke's bedroom at half past ten, when the servant said she had heard someone moving through the state apartments. He had hidden in the closet and attacked the Duke and then returned to bed after washing the blood from his hands. When the servants were clamouring at his bedroom door, he was undoubtedly still alive, but cut his throat, probably in a sudden access of panic, while they were going round to the other door of his bedroom.

The Duke's brain could be seen, pulsing, through one of the wounds on his head. He was wounded on the neck and the thighs, and his right thumb was almost severed from his hand where he had caught hold of his assailant's blade. The jury at the inquest was composed of shopkeepers. It could hardly be accused of sympathy for Royalty, especially as its foreman was Francis Place, that curious tailor, who behind the bales of cloth in his shop at Charing Cross, conducted some of the most virile Radical propaganda of the day. In face of the evidence and the Duke's wound, the jury, without retiring, brought in a verdict of suicide against Sellis.

But the public, in possession of a few facts but many prejudices, had unanimously decided on a verdict of murder against the Duke of Cumberland. They mainly relied on the Duke's own evidence, and argued that no man, defencelessly asleep in bed, could have lived through that series of sabre slashes which the Duke described. Certainly nothing could be less realistic than the Duke's comparison of those slashes to the flutterings of a bat. The public then pointed out the absence of motive, and, repeating Sellis's last words to his wife before the crime, 'Be sure and roast that piece of veal to-morrow,' asked if those were the words of a person setting out to commit a desperate crime. But anyone, even with a strong bias against the Duke, weighing up the little discrepancies, incidental to every violent death, with the unanimous evidence of the twelve or fifteen servants as to the movements of Sellis on the previous evening, as to the finding of his slippers and as to the time of his death, must recognise that such unanimity could only spring from truth.

At this distance of time the motive which inspired Sellis to try to murder the Duke can never be known. It would perhaps be easiest to dismiss him as a maniac. It was suggested by a contemporary that the real explanation of the crime was fairly simple. Sellis was a Corsican and a Roman Catholic. The Duke was a violent Protestant. The Duke was often heard mocking Roman Catholics to Sellis and making laborious Hanoverian jokes about the Pope. It seems possible that Sellis was inspired neither by madness nor outraged virtue but by the secret brooding of a sensitive mind over the brutality of a boring joker.

The Duke was critically ill and the Prince of Wales decided that he must be moved from the scene of the tragedy to

Carlton House. The Prince sent his own travelling carriage, with a bed made up in it, which had been used to take the Princess Amelia to and from Weymouth. After two months' quiet the Duke completely recovered, and it was from this period of convalescence at Carlton House that his influence over his eldest brother may be dated. This influence over his brother, particularly when the Prince Regent became King, deeply affected British politics and is one of the most inexplicable facts in the history of George III's family.

That it was based on brotherly love may be safely dismissed at once. Many years later, when the Duke of Cumberland's influence was at its height, George IV said of him to the Duke of Wellington: '. . . there was never a father well with his son, or husband with his wife, or lover with his mistress or a friend with his friend, that he did not try to make mischief between them.' And, on his side, the Duke of Cumberland made no effort to hide his contempt for his brother. In 1811, when the Regent had a bad attack of gout in the feet, the Duke of Cumberland went about saying that the 'illness was higher than the foot and that a blister on the head would be more efficacious than a poultice on the foot.' The Regent was pardonably furious when the remark was repeated to him. He refused ever to see the Duke alone again, but to avoid the public appearance of a quarrel, he agreed to be civil to him in the presence of other people. The Duke, however, forced his way into the Regent's private room and, although their voices could be heard all over Carlton House shouting at one another, within a few minutes they emerged together on their old friendly terms. Incidents of this kind gave rise to the belief that the Duke knew of some terrible secret of his brother's private life, and, by threatening to expose it, exercised a blackmailer's hold over him. This explanation was generally accepted by the Whigs and by the majority of contemporary opinion. The Whigs and contemporary public opinion had no more opportunity for knowing the facts than we have to-day. If their explanation of the Duke's influence was correct, it was a fact that could be known for certain by only George IV and the

Duke of Cumberland, and possibly by some of the Royal servants, the most discreet race on earth.

I am inclined to think that while there was little love between the two brothers there was even less of blackmail. The explanation of the Duke's influence probably lies in the fact that George IV was fascinated by the mental qualities of his brother, particularly as these qualities were all focused on a reactionary policy, which even as Prince Regent he had begun to think faintly attractive. From 1810, when he became Prince Regent, to 1830, when he died, the tide was running ever stronger in favour of Toryism. George IV, always indolent, never enthusiastic, allowed himself to be swept along with the tide. Unlike the many, progressive politicians who, when they are caught in such dangerous waters, deny that they are being swept along at all, he preferred to glide along in majestic dumbness and to comfort himself with the assurances of the Duke of Cumberland that the tide was really carrying them to the greater happiness of mankind. The function of the Duke of Cumberland was to make the King forget his Whig youth and that he had once been the devoted follower of Mr Fox.

How well the Duke knew his elder brother, even as early as 1811, is shown by his advice to the Tory leaders over the Regency question in that year. When the Prince of Wales was made Regent, certain limitations were imposed on him through fear that if he had the full powers of sovereignty he would dismiss the Tory administration and send for the Whigs. The Duke of Cumberland assured his Tory friends that there was not the slightest danger of this. The Tory Party would not listen to him. When the limitations on the Regency expired in 1813 and the Regent did not send for a Whig Government, the Tories had to confess that the Duke of Cumberland had been right. From then onwards they began to look up to the Duke as one of their leaders.

In 1813, when Napoleon's waning power made it once more possible for English people to travel abroad, the Regent and his Ministers were obliged to recommend the charms of the Continent to the Duke, in consequence of a disagreeable exposure in Parliament. This had arisen out of an election petition for the borough of Weymouth, for which a Government supporter had been returned. A Committee of the House of Commons, which had been inquiring into complaints of corruption at the Weymouth election, made its report at the beginning of 1813. It was shown that the Duke of Cumberland and two other persons were owners of the borough of Weymouth, by reason of being trustees under a will. It is almost unnecessary to say that with such a splendid opportunity for borough-mongering added to his office of trustee, the Duke became very active in the trust. So active, that when the Speaker sent down the writ for the election, the Duke of Cumberland intercepted it and delayed the election until the Tory Party was ready for the fray. A letter was read in the House of Commons from the Duke to a certain Mr Stewart, begging him to support the Tory at Weymouth and promising that if he did so he (the Duke) would use his influence with Lord Liverpool to secure him a place under Government. At such almost contemptuous interference in an election by a Peer the Whig pack went off in full cry for the Duke's blood, but the Tory whips were put on and the Duke was saved.

It is hardly surprising that the English Government decided that Europe, with its nobles, Kings and Emperors rising up to restore the old order, was deserving of a visit from the Duke of Cumberland. He left London on 29th April, driving in an open barouche with his equerry. He wore a green morocco travelling cap made in the Russian style, lined with fur and ornamented with gold lace and buttons. With his moustaches, whiskers and scars the whole effect, as an observer complained, was 'very outlandish.' In the autumn of 1813, he was with the Hanoverian troops, though not actively engaged, at the battle of Leipzig. The battle lasted for three days. The French suffered 50,000 casualties and the Allies an equal number. It is easy to picture the Duke of Cumberland, through the smoky confusion of the battle, aloof, weird and thin, glorying, not that Napoleon was beaten at last, but that the ancient ruling houses of Europe were at last victorious.

Conquest was in the air, and in the following year, 1814, the

Duke triumphed over the scruples of his first cousin, the widowed Princess of Solms-Braunfels, and announced his engagement to her. The lady was thirty-seven. She had first married a Prince of Prussia, and on his death she had been engaged to George III's youngest son, the Duke of Cambridge. She had jilted the Duke of Cambridge and married instead the Prince of Solms. She had sons by both her former husbands. She belonged to that quartet of sisters, of whom Queen Louise of Prussia was the most renowned, who at the beginning of the nineteenth century were famous throughout Europe for their beauty, and, with the possible exception of the Queen of Prussia, notorious for their frailty. But perhaps the most difficult thing to believe about them was that they were nieces of Queen Charlotte of England.

Nothing could better illustrate the Duke's utter contempt for public opinion or for the feelings of his family than his decision to marry the Princess of Solms. He must have known full well how grossly the Princess had insulted the English Royal Family, because George III's consent to her marriage with the Duke of Cambridge had actually been made public when she light-heartedly announced that she was going to marry this obscure Prince of Solms instead. Considering that the Duke of Cambridge had been always very popular, the jilting amounted to a national insult.

In August 1814, news reached the English Royal Family of the Duke's intended marriage. Queen Charlotte wrote most charmingly to her son. She explained that she could not 'think as a lover,' and strongly advised him not to come to England until the year of mourning for the Prince of Solms (who had only died the previous May), was past; she also thought it would be better for neither of them to come till Parliament had voted them the extra allowance which at marriage a Royal Duke was entitled to expect. She added that when they came '. . . all I can do will be to make a Dull House as little so as I can.' That the Queen was nervous of her future daughter-in-law's morals is obvious from the letter she wrote to the Duke of Mecklenburg-Strelitz, the Princess's father.

MY DEAR BROTHER,

... As I have reason to believe that paternal advice will have a salutary influence on your daughter I think I may confide to you what will be essential for the princess on her arrival here. The usages of this country being so different from what they are on the continent, in every respect, I fear that my son may not be sufficiently attentive to them. As this is for you alone, I confide to you, that it is not the fashion here to receive morning visits from gentlemen, to which she will be exposed, by the circumstances of the Duke being Colonel of a regiment, unless he himself introduces them to her: she should also be very circumspect in the choice of ladies with whom she shall associate, which will be so much the more necessary as the Duke has acquaintance among our sex, who, although not actually of bad conduct, might, however, become injurious to her in point of policy. I have found that the advice of the dear King 'of being uniformly polite to everyone, of doing nothing in the spirit of party, and of adhering closely to his family,' has been my surest guidance during my long residence here: and I think I cannot do better than to transmit those sentiments to you, dear brother and friend, as father to my niece and future daughter-in-law, which you will make use of in such a manner as you shall judge proper.

I have sent by the messenger six pounds of tea and two cheeses; eat the latter to my health: and in drinking the tea, remember a sister whose attachment for you will not cease but with death.

Sir, my dearest brother,

Your very affectionate sister and faithful friend,

CHARLOTTE.

While the Duke had only himself to thank for everything that happened, he certainly cannot have expected from his mother's letter the treatment that followed. He and the Princess were married in May 1815. The Queen met the Prince Regent at Ascot Races in the following June and told him that, owing to the unsatisfactory rumours about the Duchess of

Cumberland's virtue, it would be impossible for her to receive the Duchess at Court. The Regent wrote off to the Duke, advising him to come over at once to England alone. On 17th June, the Duke arrived in England. The Queen was obdurate and wrote to him as soon as he arrived that she absolutely refused to receive the Duchess.

The Duke met one of his sisters, the Princess Elizabeth, at a party at Carlton House and told her that in spite of everything the Duchess was coming to England with her brother, Prince George of Mecklenburg-Strelitz, whom the Duke described to his sister as 'a gentleman who will soon put my mother to rights.' The Princess repeated the conversation to her mother. The gentleman who was to put the Queen of England to rights, a fierce, empty-headed Prince, arrived and sent off a wildly abusive letter to the Queen. She described the letter as 'Revolting and Indecent,' and threatened to publish the whole correspondence.

It was an unnecessary threat, because in those warm, anxious days of June 1815 the whole affair was discussed with an excitement and interest only second to the possibilities of a British victory over Napoleon. When the news of the victory of Waterloo was broken to the Prince Regent at the Pavilion, he had an attack of hysterics and was obliged to drink a beaker of brandy to quiet his emotions. No doubt he had been anxious for a British victory, but his mind was far more upset and unbalanced by the complexities of the Duke of Cumberland's marriage. The King of Prussia was writing him furious letters complaining that Queen Charlotte's attitude was an insult to the memory of a Prince of Prussia who had been the Duchess of Cumberland's first husband. Prince George of Mecklenburg-Strelitz was now directing his 'revolting and indecent' pen at the Prince Regent. The Queen was pathetically writing, 'many has been the day, many the sleepless night through which this disturbing subject has engaged my thoughts.' The Prince Regent was himself in a position of difficulty, as, while he was trying to persuade the Queen to receive the Duchess of Cumberland, he was trying to persuade her not to receive

another frail daughter-in-law in the person of his own wife, the
Princess of Wales.

The public curiosity in the matter was crystallised in a
famous poem by Peter Pindar (junior), called 'Salms for a
Royal Duke':

> *And slighting British fair at home*
> *In foreign climes resolved to roam*
> *To seek a wife — He did succeed*
> *A lovely fair of German breed.*
> *Of Mecklenburg's illustrious house*
> *Soon blessed his arms a willing spouse.*
> *A tender dame of thirty-four —¹*
> *Two husbands she had wed before.*
>
>   . . . .
>
> *He married her, to England came —*
> *But did not bring the wedded dame: —*
> *This seemeth odd so very soon,*
> *When scarcely passed the honey-moon.*

In this atmosphere of rumour and scandal the Government
asked Parliament to vote an extra £6,000 a year 'to the Duke
of Cumberland on the occasion of his marriage.' But the Whigs
had not forgotten the Weymouth election. One after another
they got up to attack the Duke. One member said that 'whatever respect he might feel for the rest of the Royal Family, that
respect did not extend to the Duke of Cumberland and that no
person could go into society of any kind without having that
opinion supported (Hear! Hear!).' He added that 'the marriage was an improper one, however much the parties might be
suited to each other from their habits and morals.' Lord
Castlereagh was pressed again and again to state whether,
according to custom, he would move an address of congratula-
tion to the Queen on the marriage. The indignation of the
Whigs did not, on this occasion, rouse the enthusiasm of the
Tories, many of whom actually voted with the Opposition.
On the final vote there was a majority of one against the
additional grant. Such violently personal language can hardly

¹ Truth was sacrificed for the rhyme: her real age was thirty-seven.

have been heard before or since in the House of Commons, and it is certainly the only instance in comparatively modern times of a vote of money to a member of the Royal Family being refused.

It was not till ten years later, in 1825, that Parliament could be persuaded to vote this £6,000. The Tories were then only deceived into voting for it by its being ostensibly demanded for the education of the Duke's son. The Whigs fought hard against it, Mr Brougham remarking that the boy could be educated for £100 a year at the new university in London.

The unpopularity of the Duke during these years was almost incredible. It is impossible to explain it by the fact that he was an extreme Tory, or by the belief, still widely held, that he murdered his valet, or by the fact that he had married an immoral woman who, the Whigs believed, had murdered her two previous husbands, or even by the fact that in appearance and opinions he was completely foreign. The whole Royal Family was, during this period, extremely unpopular, but all the rest of the family together did not inspire the same feelings of loathing as the Duke of Cumberland. Peter Pindar, in 'Salms for a Royal Duke,' touched this when he made the Duke of Cumberland say:

> But say I've faults — to own the truth,
> Some faults of inexperienced youth.
> Are George and Frederick without blemish?
> They never found you half so squeamish.

The point, of course, was that many people disliked George IV and the Duke of York, but it was a dislike that was blunted by contempt, whereas in the case of the Duke of Cumberland this dislike was sharpened by fear. The people of England feared him for his talents, his unscrupulousness and his utter contempt for the decencies of political warfare. They really felt that he would stoop to any crime, not excluding the murder of the Princess Victoria, in order to block the path of progressive opinions in England.

It seems very difficult during these years to catch a clear picture of the figure who was the centre of all this abuse and

DESCENDANTS OF THE DUKE OF CUMBERLAND

ERNEST AUGUSTUS, DUKE OF CUMBERLAND AND KING OF HANOVER (1771–1851) *m.* Fréderica of Solms-Braunfels (1777–1841)

George V, King of Hanover deposed by Prussia 1866 (1819–1878) *m.* Mary of Saxe-Altenburg (1823–1907)

Ernest Augustus, Duke of Cumberland* (1845–1923) *m.* Thyra of Denmark, sister of Queen Alexandra (1853–1933)

Frederica (1848–1926) *m.* Alphonse, Baron of Pawel-Rammingen — *issue*

Mary (1849–1904)

Ernest Augustus, Duke of Brunswick (1913– 1918)† (1887–1953) *m.* Victoria, daughter of the Ex-Kaiser (1892–) — *issue*

Marie Louise (1879–1948) *m.* Prince Max of Baden who was Chancellor of the German Empire — *issue*

Alexandra (1882–1963) *m.* Grand-Duke of Mecklenburg-Schwerin — *issue*

Olga (1884–1958)

* Struck off the roll of the Order of the Garter in 1915 and deprived of all his English honours in 1919 because his son fought for his country.

† Made ruler of the Duchy of Brunswick on marrying the Kaiser's only daughter in 1913. Deposed in 1918. Struck off the roll of the Order of the Garter in 1915 and deprived of all his English honours in 1919 because he fought for his country.

scandal and unpopularity, chiefly because for sixteen years after 1813 he was largely abroad. Queen Charlotte never relented and never received the Duchess of Cumberland and, after her death, her daughters respected her wishes by refusing to acknowledge the Duchess. In such circumstances the Duke wisely decided to live abroad, a decision which was strengthened by the refusal of Parliament to grant him the £6,000, as living was considerably cheaper abroad than in England. For the greater part of the time they were abroad the Duke and Duchess lived in Berlin, as they were closely related to the Prussian Royal Family through Queen Louise. In 1817 the Duchess had a daughter who died at birth: and in 1819, three days after the birth of the Princess Victoria, she presented her husband with a fine healthy boy known as Prince George of Cumberland, afterwards the blind King of Hanover.

The Duke came over to England occasionally to stay with George IV at Windsor, and on these occasions renewed his friendship with the Tory leaders, with whom he was corresponding all the time he was abroad. But these visits were very rare, for the Duke no doubt felt that as long as George IV was King, England was safe for Toryism.

III

During the summer of 1828 the Duke stayed for several months at Windsor. George IV was now sixty-six, rather blind and tottery, sleeping badly by night but heavily by day, and inclined to cry on the least provocation but, to the few people who were allowed to see him, still capable of some of his old flashes of brilliance. The Duke of Cumberland may well have questioned whether his brother was any longer capable of withstanding progressive opinions and maintaining the sacred principles on which the House of Brunswick held the throne. But, with a large Tory majority in the House of Commons, with the Duke of Wellington, hard and crusted, at the head of the Government, and George IV snoozing away in Windsor, it seemed unlikely that any very radical changes could burst through such defences.

In June 1828, Ireland was listlessly smouldering, just as she had for the previous thirty years. But at the end of June, while the Duke of Cumberland was still at Windsor, she burst into flames. A popular Irish landlord, called Vesey Fitzgerald, who had consistently supported the claims of the Roman Catholics, was appointed President of the Board of Trade, and had, therefore, to be re-elected to the House of Commons by the county of Clare, which seat he held. No one can have ever thought that Daniel O'Connell, the leader of the movement for Roman Catholic relief, but himself a Roman Catholic and for that reason unable to sit in the House of Commons, would stand against a popular candidate like Fitzgerald. The election which followed must always remain the dream of every political candidate. For O'Connell, the election simply meant the marshalling of frenzied hordes into the polling-booths. Inside the booths the priests stood taking down the names of any who dared to vote against God, and openly stated that they would never administer the last rites of the Church to any who voted against O'Connell. Against this celestial corruption the landlords replied with terrestrial bribes and threats, but Fitzgerald, realising that the contest was unequal, wisely retired before polling-day. The Roman Catholics then announced that they would contest every seat in Ireland.

At the beginning of August the Duke of Cumberland left England for Berlin, feeling quite confident, from his conversation with Wellington, that the Government would deal faithfully with the ugly situation that had arisen. He had hardly left England when Mr George Dawson, M.P., Sir Robert Peel's brother-in-law, announced to a gathering of Orangemen that 'the Catholic Association can no longer be resisted.' The Duke of Cumberland wrote furiously from Germany to Wellington: 'The conduct of Mr Dawson is certainly, in my humble opinion, the most outrageous and wicked I have ever known . . . My dear friend, when I say this [referring to the fact that people would think that the speech had been caused by a change of opinion in the Government] do not believe for

The Duke of Clarence
as William IV,
by Andrew Morton

'An Illustrious Character'–
the Duke of Clarence,
by James Gillray, 1802

'A Rejected Trifle from Cumberland to Hanover'–
the Duke of Cumberland, *by J. Cruickshank*, 1814

The Duke of Cumberland,
by George Dawe

The Duke of Kent,
by William Beechey

The Duke of Sussex, drawn by the
Reverend Walter Sneyd and given to the
author by Mr and Mrs Robin Bagot

'Droits Droits Droits!!!'–a popular view of Parliament's grants to
the Dukes, by J. Cruickshank, 1808

one moment that I harbour a single moment's suspicion: for after all that has passed between us, I know most fully your sentiments and firm opinion upon this weighty and great subject.'

Meanwhile everyone in England was asking: Was Mr Dawson speaking for Sir Robert Peel and the Government? Then, at the beginning of December, a letter from the Viceroy of Ireland to the Roman Catholic Archbishop of Dublin was published, in which the Viceroy expressed his disappointment that 'Emancipation was delayed,' and advised the Archbishop and the leading Roman Catholics to propitiate Wellington. Once again the Duke of Cumberland scratched away, in his thick, illegible writing, fierce invective against everyone concerned, but affected to believe that Wellington would never desert 'the sacred principles.'

It is now generally conceded that Wellington and his Cabinet had made up their minds to yield to the Roman Catholic claims as early as August 1828, and that Dawson was in fact speaking the Government's mind, though of course without their authority. But Wellington was faced with two serious difficulties, which made it impossible for him to announce his intention in August.

Ireland was in a state of uproar, clamouring for Emancipation, but the very granting of Emancipation, which would soothe Ireland, might well have thrown England into an uproar. Roman Catholic Emancipation had long engaged the sympathy of the Whigs and of the great majority of Tories, but it was never a popular 'hustings question.' Canning and Lord John Russell might advocate it in the House of Commons, Sidney Smith might fulminate from the pulpit on its behalf, but it would scarcely have raised a cheer from a mob of Westminster electors listening to Sir Francis Burdett speaking on the hustings. Only fifty years before, London streets had run with blood and wine in a riot of violence and looting inspired by the cry of 'No Popery.' There was the danger that opponents of Emancipation would rouse the country with that recurring nightmare, in which the Englishman seems to smell the whiffs of incense and hear the patter of priestly feet.

The other difficulty was not so considerable but was more certain. It was George IV. Wellington rightly estimated that he had sufficient personal influence over the King to persuade him to agree to Emancipation. But Parliament was not to meet till February 1829. Wellington saw that if he obtained the King's consent in August there would be six months before the measure could be introduced, in which the King would be a prey to all the threats and whisperings of the Duke of Cumberland. He knew that the Duke of Cumberland would threaten the King with the terrible consequences of breaking the Coronation oath, in which he had sworn to preserve the Protestant religion.

For these reasons Wellington kept his own counsel and allowed the Duke of Cumberland to believe that 'the sacred principles' were safe in his keeping. But in January 1829 it was no longer possible or profitable for Wellington to conceal his intentions, and he wrote to the Duke of Cumberland that 'the King had given his consent to the consideration of the question by the Cabinet and that they were now proceeding at once to introduce a Bill for the Relief of the Roman Catholics.'

Wellington followed this up with a letter to the Duke on 2nd February, in which he strongly advised him not to come to England, as he would only find himself put forward as a leader of the Protestant Party. From the frank and almost tactless references to the possibility of the Duke's becoming King which followed, it is obvious what importance Wellington attached to his being kept out of England. 'I confess,' he wrote, 'that I cannot avoid looking forward to events which are in the hands of Providence: to misfortunes in the course of nature which may befall this country, which must bring your Royal Highness into a most exalted situation in the conduct of its affairs. I cannot think that if such events should unfortunately occur, it can be otherwise than a great disadvantage to your Royal Highness to be considered the leader of a party in the State, rather than the impartial arbiter of its destinies.' But as Wellington's messenger careered across Europe he must have almost passed one from the Duke of Cumberland carrying a brief note to Wellington, which said: 'So far as my *feeble efforts* can aid you in defence of our Church and State *you may depend on them* . . . I mean without loss of time to set off from here.'

Wellington at the moment had no intention of defending either Church or State, and the last thing he wished to depend on were those efforts which, as he knew only too well, far from being feeble, were of an abandoned violence. Wellington hurried down to Windsor and persuaded the King to write to the Duke of Cumberland telling him not to come to England. The King sent Sir William Knighton, who had been originally his physician and was now his private secretary, to take the letter and intercept the Duke at all costs. But that much-vaunted Protestant wind, which has blown so many undesirable characters to these shores, did its work with such unexpected speed that the Duke eluded Sir William. Ever a gallant man, it was perhaps fitting that he should arrive in London on Valentine's Day.

It would be an exaggeration to say that but for the arrival of the Duke of Cumberland the Roman Catholic Relief Bill would have been passed without any serious opposition. The Earl of Eldon, who for years had opposed any change in law or politics, would have fought the Bill to the end, but the Duke of Cumberland put backbone into the opponents of the measure. He had a genuine admiration for Lord Eldon, although, because of his comparatively humble birth, he always treated him as a respectable family retainer; and together they organised meetings of the opponents of the Bill in the Duke's apartments in St James's Palace.

It is very easy to ridicule the ferocity with which the Duke of Cumberland espoused the Protestant cause. But it must be remembered that he felt that that cause had been betrayed by Wellington, and what made him even more bitter was the knowledge that Wellington only favoured Emancipation as a sop to Ireland and not through conviction as to its justice. The Duke of Cumberland and the extreme Tories always argued that it would not have the effect of pacifying Ireland. Time proved that they were right.

But the Duke of Cumberland's main task was with the King.

If he could persuade him to withdraw his consent, the Bill was doomed. The King now spent most of his life in bed, only dressing for a few hours in the evening, dozing most of the day, and ringing his bell throughout the night to inquire the time or to demand a drink of water. He had already, with many tears, threatened the Cabinet that he would retire to Hanover and leave the government of England to the Duke of Clarence. But although he was half converted against Emancipation before ever the Duke of Cumberland saw him, the Duke played him with all the skill of the most experienced angler.

He was constantly with the King. They would joke together, the Duke referring with a savage smile to Wellington as 'King Arthur.' After convulsive laughter from the bed, the King would reply: 'Wellington is King of England, O'Connell is King of Ireland and I am only Canon of Windsor.' Then the Duke would solemnly speak of the opinions of 'our sainted father' on the Roman Catholic question. But the Duke finally hauled the King over to his side by his brilliant powers of distortion. He would hear that a certain Bishop was disturbed at some of the provisions of the Bill, and would dash off to Windsor with the news that the whole Church was in an uproar against the Bill. Having bribed a hundred men to hiss Wellington on his way to the House of Lords, the Duke of Cumberland hurried down to Windsor with the news that a vast mob, cat-calling 'No Popery,' had surrounded the Prime Minister. The King, who was completely out of touch with affairs, could not fail to be impressed.

Within a few days of the Duke of Cumberland's arrival in England the King was telling the officers of his household to vote against the Bill. On 28th February, Wellington saw the King and told him that the Government would resign unless he could assure them of his complete support, and Wellington pressed him strongly to order the Duke of Cumberland out of the country. The King kissed Wellington, but would not commit himself further. However, on 2nd March the King sent for the Lord Chancellor and asked him to take a letter to the Duke of Cumberland ordering him to leave England, but the letter went on to say 'that his mind was not made up and that later he might be glad of his assistance.' The Chancellor refused to take the letter, presumably on account of the last sentence.

Two days later Wellington, Peel and the Chancellor went down to Windsor. They pressed the King once more to send the Duke of Cumberland away. The King, fortifying himself with repeated sips of brandy, talked to them continuously for five hours, at the end of which they offered their resignations, which he accepted. It was a signal triumph for the Duke of Cumberland, who had always assured the King that he and Lord Eldon would be easily able to form an exclusively Protestant Government. For twenty-four hours they tried. But, while they would have had formidable debaters and a considerable following in the House of Lords, they would have been ridiculously weak in the House of Commons. The Duke of Cumberland had to tell his brother that it was, after all, impossible, and a messenger posted up from Windsor to Wellington to say that the resignation of the Government was not accepted.

However unpalatable the opinions of the Duke of Cumberland appear to modern tastes, they were firmly and uncompromisingly held. His opponents never had any difficulty in knowing where he stood; he was always slightly farther on the right than any other Tory. This was a merit which was acknowledged by Brougham: 'I also held him to be a fair open enemy, and not one who pretended to more liberality than he possessed, but was content to appear what he really was – a rank, violent, ultra Tory of the strongest Orange breed, and whose principles and propensities were purely arbitrary.'

In any case, it is difficult not to admire the speed with which Wellington's strong Government toppled down before his machinations. But the Duke of Cumberland's political weakness – and it is a weakness inevitable to all who are several centuries behind their times – was that, when he had the opportunity, he dare not put his principles to the test of office. A compact handful of reactionaries can always effectively storm and thunder on the extreme right, but scatter them among the

Government offices and the Government benches of both
Houses of Parliament and their own fire and fury will expose
the thinness of their support.

A wiser or less bigoted and a less sincere man than the Duke
of Cumberland would have bowed to the inevitable. But even
after his failure to provide an alternative Government he continued to worry the King till the King was heard, through an
open door, saying to him: 'My dear Ernest, do not talk to me
any more about it. I am committed and I must go through with
it.' The Duke spoke violently against it in the House of Lords,
describing it as 'one of the most outrageous measures ever proposed to Parliament' And when the Bill finally passed, he
was observed to leave the House of Lords looking 'like a disappointed fiend.'

Thenceforward his one object in politics was to drive
Wellington from office: as he used to say, 'Let who will be
Minister.' In this again he was completely successful, because
there can be no doubt that one of the chief causes of the fall of
Wellington's Ministry in 1830 was the consistent apathy and
occasional hostility of the extreme Tories, led by the Duke of
Cumberland. Wellington clearly saw this, as he wrote to a
friend in 1830 after the fall of his Government: 'The administration was beaten by two events. First the Roman Catholic
question . . . I don't think that the Roman Catholic question
ought to have estranged from us so many of our friends: or
that it would if the Duke of Cumberland had not exercised
over the late King the most extraordinary influence.'

It may well be imagined that the Duke of Cumberland, in
the irresponsible position of Cabinet-breaker, did not com-
mend himself to the people of England. But it is almost impossible to imagine the unanimous contempt with which all
sections of society, the two political parties and most of the
newspapers joined in what the Duke called 'the general hoot
against me.'

The Ministry never relaxed their efforts to force him out of
the country. It was even suggested that he should be sent to
supersede his youngest brother as Viceroy of Hanover, but, as
the Duke of Cambridge was efficient and popular, Wellington

refused to agree unless the Duke of Cambridge offered to re-sign. No doubt the Duke of Cambridge felt that there was no good reason why Hanover should become the dumping-ground for undesirable elements in the English Royal Family. It was certainly because of the anxiety to move him abroad that, in the summer of 1829, the Duke decided to settle perman-ently in England, and sent for the Duchess and his son to join him. *The Times* observed: 'It is generally believed that the Duke of Cumberland will become a permanent inmate of the Castle. It is said that his Royal Highness and his august family will occupy that portion of the building called the Devil's Tower.'

So much mud was thrown at the Duke that he stands out from the pages of history as a shapeless lump of filth, from which it is now almost impossible to scrape off the mud and see what manner of man it really concealed.

His contemporaries believed that he was a monster, capable of any wickedness. He wrote of himself: 'I am neither a Methodist, Saint or psalm-singer' – a summary of his charac-ter with which no one would quarrel. And when he goes on to say: 'but I trust I have a sound foundation of true religion, which my father possessed in the highest degree and which I imbibed from him,' it is only possible to add that, while the foundations may have been there, his life was not built on them.

The very day – 14th February, 1829 – that he reached London to defend the Protestant religion his name was con-nected with the most atrocious scandal that has ever been spread about the reigning family of a civilised country. Al-though it was not true it was widely and implicitly believed.

A certain Captain Garth swore an affidavit in the Chancery Division in an action he was bringing to enforce an agreement he had made with Sir Herbert Taylor. Sir Herbert, who had been private secretary to George III, Queen Charlotte and the Duke of York and was the intimate friend of all the Royal Family, had agreed to pay Captain Garth's debts and to allow him £3,000 a year on condition that Captain Garth deposited with Sir John Dean Paul, the banker, a box containing certain

papers of the greatest importance, 'referring to his rank and
situation in life.' Sir Herbert Taylor was then to affix his seal
to the box, which was not to be opened without his permission.
The explanation why Sir Herbert Taylor had not carried out
his part of the agreement was that Captain Garth had made
copies of the papers, which he had shown to the editors of
certain newspapers, probably for a consideration.

It was common gossip that Captain Garth was the son of the
Princess Sophia, George III's fifth daughter, who as a girl had
been extraordinarily beautiful. While the papers in Captain
Garth's hands were thought to indicate royal parentage, there
were references in them to the Duke of Cumberland which
were never made public, but which encouraged the belief that
Captain Garth was really the son of the Duke of Cumberland
and his sister, the Princess Sophia. It was widely believed at
the time; it has been darkly hinted at in various books on
the period; it is still whispered over the port – but it was not
true.

Greville was told the whole story by Lady Bath, who had had
it from Lady Caroline Thynne, who was about the Court when
Captain Garth was born. There was a certain General Garth,
who was one of George III's equerries and with whom the
Princess Sophia was so entirely in love that everybody saw it,
as 'she could not contain herself in his presence.' The only
reason why people doubted that General Garth was the father
was because, as Greville says, 'he was a hideous old Devil, old
enough to be her father and with a great claret mark on his
face.' But Greville goes on: 'This is no argument at all: for
women fall in love with anything – and opportunity and the
accidents of the passions are of more importance than of any
positive merits of mind or of body. Then they [the Princesses]
were secluded from the world, mixing with few people – their
passions boiling over and ready to fall into the hands of the
first man whom circumstances enabled to get at them.'

The Princess and her sisters lived at the Lower Lodge at
Windsor: the King and Queen, with their attendants, of
whom, of course, General Garth was one, lived at the Upper
Lodge. (The Royal Family lived in these lodges while Windsor

Castle was being restored.) On one occasion the Princess Sophia was unwell, and was moved up to the Upper Lodge to a bedroom immediately over General Garth's. The King and Queen went up to London and General Garth remained at Windsor. Nine months later the Princess was brought to bed. The scandal was thought to have been kept from George III by telling him that the Princess had been dropsical but had suddenly recovered, thanks to 'the roast-beef cure,' which he used to tell to people as 'a very extraordinary thing.'

Greville also heard, but indirectly, that Sir Herbert Taylor had said that the letters affecting the Duke of Cumberland were letters from the Princess Sophia to General Garth complaining that the Duke had attempted to assault her. Greville, in support of this, adds that it was notorious that 'the old Queen [Charlotte] forbade the Dukes access to the apartments of the Princesses.' But this hardly supported Greville's theory. It was a provision which applied to all the Royal Dukes, and not specifically to the Duke of Cumberland alone, and was dictated, not by prudence, but by common decency. The authority for this statement of Greville's about the letters affecting the Duke of Cumberland is very questionable. He wrote it down in his diary several days before his conversation with Lady Bath, and at a time when he knew very little about the affair except what he had seen in the newspapers.

However, while it is obvious that the Duke was not Captain Garth's father, it is more difficult to dismiss him from the affair altogether. What struck Greville as an observer was that 'there must be some cause for the universal and deep execration in which he [the Duke of Cumberland] is held – especially by his own family . . . Lord Bathurst told me that the only time he ever nearly quarrelled with the Duke of York was about Lady Bathurst's visiting the Duchess of Cumberland – they had a violent dispute [the Duke being against visiting her] in which he [the Duke of York] said, speaking of the Duke of Cumberland, "if you knew——" and then stopped.' But the Duke of Cumberland's disgraceful marriage is quite sufficient explanation for 'the execration of the Royal Family': at any rate, it dated from then.

There is a very curious letter from the Princess Sophia to Lady Harcourt written in 1794 which may well explain the whole of the scandal: 'Dear Ernest is as kind to me as it is possible, rather a little imprudent at times, but when told of it never takes it ill.' It seems possible that there was a certain amount of irresponsible foolishness between the Duke and his sister when they were both in their early twenties, in much the same way as the Dukes of Clarence and Cambridge professed an almost fantastic admiration for the Princess Mary. It was not entirely unnatural in a large, healthy family living under conditions of monastic severity. The Princess, in writing to General Garth, may well have referred to it in the same half-joking way that she did to Lady Harcourt. But in 1829 the Duke of Cumberland was too unpopular for the public to draw fine distinctions on his behalf; as Greville writes: 'Everybody believes that there is some mystery of an atrocious character, in which he is deeply and criminally implicated — it is all horrid — the Royal Family is dragged through the mire.'

But the noise and dust of this scandal had scarcely subsided when the public were once again unpleasantly reminded of the Duke of Cumberland. The story, which was spread in the newspapers, was that the Duke of Cumberland had called on the Lord Chancellor's wife, Lady Lyndhurst, and, finding her alone, had made a desperate attempt upon her person. After a scramble, she had managed to ring the bell. He was obliged to desist, but he was supposed to have said: 'By God, Madam, I will be the ruin of you and your husband, and will not rest till I have destroyed you both.'

It was, one feels, almost inevitable that the confidential figure of Mr Greville should have been strolling across Wimbledon Common on the day after this attack, when Lady Lyndhurst came driving along in her pony-chaise. Mr Greville climbed into the chaise and asked her to tell him all about it as they went spanking along across the Common. Lady Lyndhurst told him that the Duke had made a violent attack upon her, which she had resisted; that his manner and his language had been equally brutal and indecent; that he was furious at her resistance, and said that he would never forgive her for putting him to so much pain. It shows what an extraordinary character the Duke of Cumberland must have been that after a rebuff of this kind he stayed, according to Lady Lyndhurst, for two or three hours slanging the Government and in particular Lord Lyndhurst.

The Duke of Cumberland excused himself by saying that Lady Lyndhurst had previously made every kind of overture and advance to him. With a view, no doubt, to making mischief, he wrote to Lord Lyndhurst:

MY LORD, –

I think it necessary to enclose to your Lordship, a newspaper containing a paragraph which I have marked, and which relates to a pretended transaction in your Lordship's house. I think it necessary and proper to contradict this statement, which I need not say is a gross falsehood, and I wish, therefore, to have the authority of Lady Lyndhurst for contradicting it.

I am, my Lord, Yours sincerely,

ERNEST.

Lord Lyndhurst, acting on the Duke of Wellington's advice, refused to deny it, and the Duke of Cumberland eventually wrote a letter in the third person and in a very sneering tone alluding to 'the loose reports current on the subject,' and adding: 'The Chancellor may have his own reasons for not choosing to speak to Lady Lyndhurst on the subject.' The Duke had declared war on the Ministry after they had passed the Roman Catholic Relief Bill; it was characteristic of him to carry the war into the enemies' homes.

In February 1830, only six months after his attack on the Lord Chancellor's wife, the newspapers could again remind their readers of the villainy of the Duke of Cumberland. For some months the newspapers had been hinting at an *amour* between the Duke and the wife of Lord Graves. Lady Graves had been a celebrated beauty and the first lady to waltz in a London ballroom, but she was now more than fifty, with fifteen children, and she was obliged to wear spectacles. It seems unlikely that these fading charms can have made any great appeal to an experienced man of the world like the Duke. Lord Graves was a Lord of the Bedchamber to the King. He was living apart from his wife, but he was terribly distressed by the scandalous statements which were daily appearing in the papers.

One Sunday in February, Lord Graves wrote a note to his wife saying that he did not, for one minute, believe the unpleasant reports that were being circulated. He then made the fatal decision of cutting his throat, and was found dead a few hours after writing the note. His pen announced his belief in his wife's innocence: his razor told the world that a bitterly wronged husband preferred death to his wife's dishonour. With that furtive desire of all public servants to hush up anything that is of absorbing public interest, the coroner held his inquest at 7.45 on the following morning and attributed the suicide to a fit of depression, to which the nobleman was proved to have been subject.

This finding of the coroner's was in accordance with the evidence, but it could not be expected to satisfy public opinion. On the morning following the inquest *The Times*, forestalling the vulgarity of a later age, had a trenchant article under the heading of 'Melancholy Suicide in High Life,' in which it said: 'It is impossible not to connect this fearful act with a rumour which has been for some time in circulation and to recall the public attention, however painfully, to another suicide – an inexplicable and mysterious suicide – with which a name that has been so often mentioned of late was also connected.' This was, of course, a reference to Sellis's suicide in 1810, and inevitably had the effect of making the public believe that the Duke had murdered Lord Graves as well as Sellis.

Even in 1830 the position and influence of *The Times* was very different from the scurrilous prints which had been filled with attacks on the Duke: and the King himself was distressed at this article. The coroner wrote a letter to *The Times* explaining the facts, and the editor was shown Lord Graves's last letter to his wife, in which he had referred to the rumours as 'scandalous falsehoods.' *The Times* then withdrew their implications.

The owner of *The Times*, the editor of *The Times*, a few of the aristocracy, a handful of fair-minded people, believed in the innocence of the Duke, but no amount of denials affected public opinion, which had been prejudiced against him by what the paper itself described as 'that article we thundered out . . . which created so great a sensation.' The public felt that they had every ground for believing the Duke an adulterer and a double-dyed murderer.

IV

It is easy to see now, a century afterwards, that in 1830 the sun of Royal favour in which the Tories had shone for half a century was dimming as George IV slowly sank into death. It is easy to see that the gentle breezes of majorities in the House of Commons, which had lazily filled the sails of successive Tory administrations, were giving way to the rude blasts of popular opinion which were to smash them in the autumn of 1830. No group of men was less fitted to withstand a storm of public opposition than the Tories of 1830. They stood up against it, bleak and irreconcilable. Even the Duke of Wellington, muffled to the eyes in the glory of Waterloo, was to lose every shred of popularity in the storm. The Duke of Cumberland, far too courageous to leave the country and far too tenacious of his opinions to yield one inch, had, long before the storm broke, lost every stitch of reputation and every thread of popularity. It is, on the whole, surprising that he was not killed. He was always hissed when he was recognised in the streets, and he was once dragged from his horse by an infuriated mob outside the House of Lords.

With the accession of William IV, the Duke lost all his influence at Windsor. Shortly after he became King, William IV gave a banquet, at which the Duke of Cumberland was present, and gave a toast, the significance of which was observed by all: 'The land we live in, and let those who don't like it leave it.' But the Duke was too good a Tory to quarrel with his sovereign, and as the years went on he became increasingly friendly with his brother, a friendship which was assisted by

Queen Adelaide's great affection for Prince George of Cumberland and the fact that the Duchess was at long last received at the English Court.

In common with the other extreme Tories, the Duke did as little as possible to help the Tory Government at the General Election following George IV's death, an abstention which contributed to the success of the Whigs. But when the Tories were confronted with the full horror of the Reform Bill in 1831, steps were taken to unite the two sections of the party. Wellington evidently felt very sore at the way he had been treated by the Duke of Cumberland and his followers, and he wrote to the Duke of Buckingham that His Royal Highness had discontinued to do him the honour of noticing him. He went on: 'When His Royal Highness, or any member of the Royal Family, notices me, I consider that an honour is done me: but I have done nothing to deserve to be deprived of it ... I must wait with patience till the moment will arrive when His Royal Highness will think it proper to notice me.'

The Duke of Buckingham seems to have eased relations between the Dukes of Cumberland and Wellington. He sent the former some extracts from Wellington's letter, evidently including the passage about being noticed, a courtesy which Wellington said had ceased on 12th August 1829. In his reply the Duke of Cumberland disputed the date, saying that he had had a very unpleasant conversation with Wellington at Windsor in February 1829, and that they had not spoken since except at a Review in the Park. He said that on getting the Duke of Buckingham's letter he had gone to call at Apsley House, adding 'It appears to me that in times such as these, it is necessary for every well-wisher to his country, who is attached to the Monarchy and the Constitution to meet and resist the revolutionary Bill now pending in Parliament, which, if carried, must, according to my humble opinion, annihilate all our contributions both in Church and State, and sooner or later, lead to the repeal of the union.' From then onwards the Duke of Cumberland was always consulted on questions of policy by the leaders of the party. On the Reform Bill, how-

ever, the Duke followed his own judgment and was one of the
'Diehard' Peers who voted against the Bill when the majority
of the party abstained from voting in order to save the King
from having to create hundreds of new Peers.

And all this time the attacks on the Duke never ceased.
In 1832 he brought an action for libel against the publisher of
a book called *The Authentic Records of the Court of England for
the last Seventy Years*. The writer had accused him of murdering Sellis for a most revolting motive. The Duke himself gave
evidence showing the back of his head (where he had received
the worst wound) and his right thumb to the jury. He said: 'I
think in all I had seventeen wounds. I was in a state of agony,
I suppose, from six weeks to two months.' The jury, without
retiring, found for the Duke.

Then, in the September after the passing of the Reform
Bill, there was a very curious incident which occupied *The
Times* for several days. Two charming young ladies, the Misses
Ann and Lucy Perfect, were strolling along a path by the
Thames near their home at Hammersmith. It was about
five o'clock, and the light was beginning to fail, when they
heard a horse galloping towards them. As the rider came near,
he turned his horse off the road on to the path and the young
ladies had to lean back against some railings to avoid being run
down. The black silk apron which Miss Ann was wearing was
caught up by the rush of air and blown round one of the
horse's legs. The rider, as he dashed by, turned round and
laughed. The ladies who were positive that the rider was the
Duke of Cumberland, said that 'if only he had lifted his hat
they would have considered it a compliment.'

The following morning the Duke was hooted by a large
mob at Hammersmith when he drove to London from Kew.
The Times made it a question of national importance, and
published a poem of Tom Moore's on the subject:

> *The Duke is the lad to frighten a lass,*
>   *Galloping dreary Duke.*
> *The Duke is the lad to frighten a lass,*
> *He's an ogre to meet and the Devil to pass:*

With his charger prancing,
Grim eye glancing,
Chin like a mufti,
Grizzled and tufty,
Galloping dreary Duke.

Ye Misses, beware of the neighbourhood
Of this galloping, dreary Duke.
Avoid him all, who see no good
In being run o'er by a Prince of the Blood.
And as no nymph is
Fond of a grim phiz,
Fly, ye new married,
For crowds have miscarried
At sight of this dreary Duke.

The Duke of Cumberland was genuinely distressed. The doctors who were attending Prince George of Cumberland at Kew, and the Duke's servants, swore that he was at Kew the whole afternoon and evening in question. Even more important, a gentleman who had been to see a friend at Kew village had distinctly seen the Duke shooting wild duck in the grounds of Kew Palace at the time of the supposed outrage. The Duke sent one of his friends to apologise to the Misses Perfect and to explain that it was not he at all but one of his equerries, who had not been able to see properly owing to the fading light. It was only another example of the price the Duke had to pay for his political opinions.

It is perhaps almost impossible to avoid a certain feeling of sympathy for the Duke. In the eighteen-twenties, with the Tories entrenched in power, the Whigs had been nothing but an acid minority, and it was only natural for them to attack so powerful an opponent as the Duke of Cumberland with the utmost ferocity in their power. In the eighteen-thirties, when the Whigs were themselves in power, such attacks were less dignified and less justified. The Whigs owed a great debt of gratitude to the Duke of Cumberland. The very fact that he associated with their opponents must have driven hundreds of quiet, respectable voters into the arms of the Whig election-eering agents. Wellington once described the sons of George III as 'the damnedest millstones that were ever hanged round the neck of any Government.' In the eighteen-thirties the Duke of Cumberland was the damnedest millstone that was ever hanged round the neck of the Tory Party, and consequently he had a peculiarly buoyant effect on the Whigs. As long as the Tories were associated with a man who could only speak of the Whig Government as 'these rascally Ministers,' or could write: 'My opinion is, blow them up *at once*; when and how I care not, provided it be but done,' and who could actually vote against the opening of the Great Western Railway on the grounds that it would be very disturbing to the Eton boys, it was difficult to see the Tories ever gaining popular support.

But it was, of course, preposterous to expect that the Whigs should recognise the Duke of Cumberland as an ally and cease their personal attacks on him. Equity is a stranger on the political battlefield. At the time the Whigs could not see how valuable the Duke of Cumberland was to them. They only feared him as their sovereign if the Princess Victoria should die. In the House of Lords in the debate on the slavery Abolition Bill the Whig Lord Chancellor insulted the Duke in these words : 'It would give the man of colour as clear a right to sit in this House (if His Majesty should so please) as either of the illustrious Dukes now present (Wellington and Cumberland) whether the illustrious Duke who is illustrious by his deeds, or the illustrious Duke who is illustrious by the courtesy of the House.' In 1836, in the debate on the Orange Lodges, which were the organisation of the extreme Tories, the Radical, Hume, openly suggested that these lodges, with a membership of hundreds of thousands in England and Ireland, of which the Duke of Cumberland was Grand Master, were prepared at King William's death to rise and declare for the Duke of Cumberland as King instead of the Princess Victoria. In all the more scurrilous papers it was freely hinted that the Princess might meet with the same violent end as Sellis and Lord Graves.

The Duke met all these attacks with great dignity, and declared in the House of Lords that he was prepared to sacrifice the last drop of his blood in defence of 'that innocent person' (the Princess). And on another occasion in the House of Lords he boldly declared that 'he was scandalously attacked in a way that any man of feeling, of honour and of character in the country would resent. No man would like to be bandied about in such a way. He had been used cruelly: and for no reason but that he had stood forward boldly to declare his honest opinion.'

All through these fresh attacks the Duke was in great private distress. He had only one child, Prince George, who was a slim, handsome youth with none of the Hanoverian animal spirits. It is interesting to remember that Cardinal Newman, as a young man, was suggested for the tutorship to Prince George but, being under twenty-five, was thought too young for the post. In 1832 the Prince met with an accident at Kew which seriously affected his sight.[1] The boy grew rapidly worse. The doctors cheerfully assured the Duke that it was nothing but a little indigestion; but by 1833 the Prince was to all intents and purposes blind. The Duke and Duchess travelled with him to Prussia, where they had heard of a very good eye doctor, but nothing could be done. At the end of 1833 the Duke of Cumberland's sister, the Princess Elizabeth, who was Landgravine of Hesse-Homburg, was sadly writing of Prince George:'. . . to see that lovely creature led about . . . his good humour, his sweet way of expressing himself, his gratitude for every kindness is not to be expressed – but he certainly sees nothing, such a *real dear* as he is, it is enough to break one's heart.'

On William IV's death, as no woman might inherit the crown of Hanover, the Duke of Cumberland knew that he must be King of Hanover. If the Princess Victoria died, he would be King of England as well. Consequently, if Prince George lived, he was bound to be a King. Apart from his natural grief, the Duke had to bear the knowledge that his

[1] I have been unable to discover exactly what the accident was.

son, as a blind King, would be disastrously handicapped in ruling his country in the sound reactionary faith in which he had been brought up.

v

On 20th June, 1837, William IV died, and the Duke of Cumberland, at the age of 66, became King of Hanover. He consulted the Duke of Wellington as to how long he could stay in England. Wellington advised an immediate departure, adding: 'Go before you are pelted out.'

The Hanoverians were a faithful, simple people but the new King was not called to an easy throne. Ever since the German States had united in the War of Liberation to overthrow Napoleon, there had been throughout them all an upward thrust of Liberal opinion, which was like some jack-in-the-box temporarily kept in place by the petty sovereigns and archaic Constitution which had been fastened on the States after the war. As a result of the events of 1814 Hanover was promoted from an electorate to a kingdom. George III's youngest son, the Duke of Cambridge, a genial soldier, had been Viceroy of Hanover since 1814. In 1833, the Liberals of Hanover, inspired by the successes of the French Revolution of 1830, sprang up and demanded a more Liberal Constitution. King William the Fourth, acting on the advice of the Duke of Cambridge, granted his Hanoverian subjects a new Constitution.

As the new King of Hanover always referred to the mildest Liberals as 'canaille' or 'rank republicans' or 'the vilest radicals,' it was expected that his stay in Hanover would be short. To anyone regarding the age of the King of Hanover, the violence of his views and the rather opinionated Liberalism of the Hanoverians it seemed certain that his reign would set in a lurid, angry glow which would be prematurely obscured by the storm-clouds of revolution. In fact he lived to be eighty and reigned for fourteen years, passing from the rulers of Europe in a blaze of undimmed glory. He reigned during one of the most revolutionary periods in European history, when every sovereign was treating with revolution or losing his throne. The King of Hanover did neither.

He triumphed by no compromise with the enemy. He said himself, in one of his rather rare moments of accuracy, 'I command the respect of even the rankest Radicals . . . they know I play no dirty tricks.' Part of his strength in Hanover rested on the fact that the Hanoverians had to take King Ernest or leave themselves to be swallowed up by Prussia. This fact emphasises the extraordinary lack of male heirs in the English Royal Family. The family of Queen Victoria, as tracing their descent through a woman, were in this connection of no account. The Duke of Sussex had no legitimate heirs. The Duke of Cambridge loyally refused to listen to the whispers that he should supersede King Ernest and put himself forward as the Liberal candidate for the throne of Hanover. Prince George of Cambridge, the Duke's only son, had no intention of leaving England. In 1837, King Ernest was the only male descendant of George I who was willing and able to continue the connection with Hanover.

King Ernest arrived in Hanover at the end of June, and at once suspended the Constitution of 1833, and in November declared it null and void. He did this on the grounds that his consent to that Constitution had never been asked. Seven professors of the University of Göttingen protested against this arbitrary behaviour and three of them published their protest. The King immediately removed all seven from their chairs in the university, and banished the three who had published their protest from Hanover. This caused a far greater stir in Europe than the actual suspension of the Constitution, and it was proposed in the English House of Commons that by his action King Ernest had forfeited any rights to the crown of England.

In 1840, having governed for three years without any Constitution, he granted the Hanoverians his idea of what a Constitution should be. The Assembly, which corresponded to the English Houses of Parliament, was allowed to meet and express its opinions. Its debates were never to be reported. The Ministry was to be quite independent of the Assembly. It merely meant that the King doled out to his subjects the kind of rights which are to-day enjoyed by some of the more obscure debating societies. Yet in 1848 Prussia, with her far more Liberal Constitution and far more Liberal sovereign, and France, with her Parliaments and her flamboyantly *bourgeois* King of the French, were afflicted with revolution while Hanover was unscathed. The King dealt faithfully with any murmurings of discontent. In April 1848 he wrote to his friend Lord Strangford: 'They had the impudence to send a deputation to me . . . demanding me not to adjourn the Chamber during the holidays. I naturally refused to receive the deputation, burnt their petition and instantly adjourned the Chamber till the 8th of May.' At the end of May the good people of Hanover were stirred up by the arrival of a number of Communists from Berlin. There was a certain amount of trouble, and the revolution seemed on the point of breaking out. The King sent out his Prime Minister who, standing on a chair outside the Palace, said: 'The King is quite willing to listen to any reasonable complaints . . . but if you make demands upon him which he does not think consistent with his honour to grant he will immediately pack up his things, take the Crown Prince with him, be off to England and leave you to your own devices.' The 'Hanoverian Revolution' immediately subsided and, as a slight reward to the people for good behaviour, the King changed his Ministers and introduced a more Liberal Constitution.

His rule in Hanover was a remarkable personal triumph. He proved himself an efficient and laborious sovereign, who owed his success less to the rod of iron than to the fact that he was loved by many of his subjects and respected by all. But while he was absorbed by Hanover and delighted with the success of his Government, he never ceased to cast a regretful and anxious eye across to England. He said of himself: 'My heart, soul and thoughts are British and all that can raise its glory, fame and honour most sacredly dear to me.' He only went back to England once. As may be well imagined 'the glory, fame and honour' of England were hopelessly tarnished in his eyes by the Whiggery of Queen Victoria and the Free

Trade policy of Peel's Conservative Government. He spent the summer of 1843 in England.

That ancient question, whether his wife should be received at the English Court, which Queen Charlotte had so definitely decided many years before but which had agitated the old Queen's daughters, did not arise to embarrass Queen Victoria, for the Queen of Hanover had died in 1841. In 1815 the King had sacrificed an increased Parliamentary grant and the affection of his family to marry her, and, although she only occasionally visited England, being in habit and interests wholly German, the marriage was successful. When she died the King wrote of her: 'She possessed such a sweet and amiable character, that she knew how to tranquillise my mind when irritated and disgusted at all the ingratitude and hostility I met.' After her death her rooms were left exactly as they were when she died, at night candles were lighted, the pages and dressers were in attendance, and the King went regularly to pray at her bedside.

While he was in England in those long summer days of 1843, everything seemed forgiven and forgotten. It was one long round of fêting. All the ambassadors, the Tory leaders, the Whig leaders, society ladies and Bishops jostled one another to write their names in the King of Hanover's book at St James's Palace. The great houses of London, Stafford House, Cambridge House, Apsley House, threw back their doors that all the world might meet him. Lord Brougham, the great Whig ex-Chancellor, entertained him to dinner. The King drove up to Lincoln's Inn to dine in Stone Buildings with his old friend Sir Charles Wetherell. For the week-end he generally went down to his cottage on Kew Green with its small library where in the old days he and Sir Charles Wetherell and Billy Holmes, the chief Tory whip, had sat up to all hours of the morning discussing the rascality of the Whigs. Sometimes he went down to the country to stay with friends for the week-end. He actually returned on the railway from a visit to the Duke of Buckingham at Stowe, which was a great concession for one who always spoke of railways as 'those damnable railways' on account of the facilities they offered for transferring Radicals from one part of the country to another.

But there was one large house whose youthful mistress and master strongly disapproved of the cordiality with which the King was everywhere received, and which only once opened its doors to him. Queen Victoria and Prince Albert had no love for the King of Hanover and had hoped against hope that illness and old age would prevent his making the journey to England. Queen Victoria, with all her affections focused on her mother's family, the Coburgs, treated her father's family with cold disdain, and certainly did not satisfy the requirements of common politeness. The King of Hanover was deeply hurt by this treatment and he wrote rather sadly to an English friend: 'I have never partaken of the pleasures of your Court or know anything of its interior, having only once been asked to dinner by Her Majesty during my three months stay in England in 1843.'

Disagreement between Queen Victoria and the King of Hanover was probably inevitable. He could not help feeling her very existence a reminder of how nearly he had missed the throne of England. She was entirely influenced by her uncle King Leopold of the Belgians and her Whig Ministers, all of whom detested the King. The King for his part was no lover of the Coburgs and said of them: 'the spirit of intrigue exists in the whole breed, but, fortunately the main point fails with them – self conduct and good sense'; and of Prince Albert himself he once wrote: 'from all those who know him he is a terrible Liberal, almost a Radical ... I hear that he is still more dangerous than a Roman Catholic, being a sort of Freethinker and very light in his religious opinions.' But the disagreement was aggravated by the family obstinacy which both the King of Hanover and Queen Victoria inherited. In 1837 Queen Victoria showed good sense in wishing to be free from her mother who, however successful as a mother, was a tactless and impossible person. The Queen suggested to the King of Hanover that he should give up his apartments in St James's Palace and allow the Duchess of Kent to live there. The King, who was precluded from appreciating the Duchess of Kent's maternal capabilities and merely knew her as a very tiresome woman, sent word from Hanover that he would not dream of giving up his rooms.

An even more serious matter than the Duchess of Kent came between uncle and niece. There were certain jewels, including some particularly fine diamonds, which the King of Hanover claimed, as head of the family, under Queen Charlotte's will. Queen Victoria was in possession of them and refused to give them up. There was a very acrimonious correspondence on what Sir Robert Peel called 'this most embarrassing question,' and it was eventually decided to submit the question to arbitration. (It was eventually settled in 1857, substantially in favour of the King of Hanover.) The Queen caused great offence to her uncle by wearing the jewels. Busybodies kept him informed of all these things and he wrote very angrily to his friend Lord Strangford: 'I hear the little Queen was loaded with my diamonds . . . which made a very fine show.'

While the King was writing angrily to his friends in England, the Queen and her uncle Leopold, King of the Belgians, carried on a spiteful little correspondence about him. King Leopold referred to him as 'your immediate successor, with the moustaches' and Queen Victoria replied by calling him 'King Ernestius the Pious,' and wrote of his visit to England in 1843: '[He] arrived just in time to be too late [for Princess Alice's christening]. He is grown very old and excessively thin and bends a good deal. He is very gracious for *him*. Pussie [the Princess Royal] and Bertie [the Prince of Wales] were not at all afraid of him *fortunately*.'

But their most serious and their most public difference of opinion was on the question of Prince Albert's precedence. The Queen, after considerable difficulty, had persuaded her uncles the Dukes of Sussex and Cambridge to agree to Prince Albert taking precedence before them. Naturally the King of Hanover utterly refused to have anything to do with such an arrangement. He came to England in 1843 for the ostensible reason of attending the marriage of his niece the Princess Augusta of Cambridge to the Grand Duke of Mecklenburg-Strelitz. The marriage took place in the Chapel Royal on 28th June. There was a terrible tussle when the Royal Family retired to sign the Register. The Queen naturally signed first. Prince Albert stood on her left, waiting to sign after her. The King of Hanover stepped up on her right, and when she had signed took the pen out of her hand. It was only by a judicious use of his elbows in the King's ribs that Prince Albert was able to knock him out of the way and sign after the Queen. Perhaps honours were fairly easy, because afterwards, when the King and Prince Albert were strolling in the gardens of Buckingham Palace, the King suggested that they should go out in the street. The Prince objected on the grounds of their being troubled by the crowd, to which the King replied: 'O never mind, I was once quite as unpopular as you are and they never bothered me.'

In those fourteen years from 1837 to 1851 the King of Hanover stands out very clearly, narrow, rigid and stubborn in his opinions, but with something of the splendour, colour and eccentricity of the eighteenth century in the midst of the solemn, tall-hatted, black-coated nineteenth century. He never allowed old age to weaken his opinions or the force with which he expressed them, and even his ultra-Tory correspondent, Lord Strangford, may have been amused at reading the old King's views on the Great Exhibition of 1851: 'Even were I in England I would not put a foot in Hyde Park, as I disapproved of the whole thing and I feared it would bring all the ruffians and *canaille* from all parts of the world into the country which might lead to very serious mischief, but instead I would remain quietly and enjoy the fine weather and the sweet scents of my little cottage at Kew.' Or on the landed interest: 'England can stand many a blow and storms, but if the aristocracy and landowners are ruined, all is over . . . the whole of the riches of the country would by degrees come into the hands of Jews, manufacturers, calico-makers who would lord it over you all.' Or on Sir Robert Peel: 'When you have not been born or bred a gentleman you can not expect noble ideas or feelings: and great as Peel's talents are, and no one is readier to admit them than myself, you will always see the Jenny: the manufacturer's blood will show.'

It would, of course, be absurd not to recognise that there

were many disagreeable qualities in the King of Hanover,
which William IV summed up by saying, 'If anyone has a corn
Ernest is sure to tread on it.' He delighted in hurting the
feelings of his Hanoverian courtiers, and always fêted any
English visitors to Hanover and made it perfectly clear to the
Hanoverians that he was English in affections and sympathy
and that nothing but a disagreeable sense of duty made him
devote his time to Hanoverians. At dinner one night, he said
before all his Hanoverian courtiers, to an English woman,
who had lost her way in Hanover, 'Pish! Nonsense! why the
whole town is not larger than a fourpenny bit.' On another
occasion a middle-aged lady appeared at his Court in virgin
white. The King deliberately pretended, with his bad sight, to
mistake her for the fireplace which was painted white, and
strolled up and started warming his back against her. And
everyone was nauseated by the sight of the King of Hanover
playing with his grandchild: the old King used to put out his
great tongue, and the child then bathed its face and hands in
the Royal saliva.

Of course he was not without his eccentricities. To the end of
his life he used to tie yards of cravat round his neck to prevent
his head from falling forward and to preserve the erect appearance of youth. In ordinary conversation, at the end of every
sentence, he always clicked his heels together. He never
smoked, except when he was out shooting and then not for enjoyment but to dry the air round him. But with it all there was
a great and unmistakable dignity about him. An Englishman
who saw him in the last year of his life described him 'as
enormously tall and finely made . . . as magnificent a specimen
of an English gentleman as I ever saw.'

He died on 18th November, 1851. He ordered that his
body might be shown to his subjects, so that they might take
a last look at one whose only object had been to contribute to
their welfare and happiness. When news of his death was
announced in England, *The Times* ostentatiously appeared
without a black edge and wrote of the deceased monarch
'the good to be said of the Royal Dead is little or none.' But
the Hanoverians, who had seen their sovereign slaving away

for them, unobscured by the mists of scandal and the acidities of party politics, put up a large equestrian statue to his memory and wrote on it:

> *Dem Landes Vater*
> *Sein treues Volk,*

which in English means, 'to the father of his country from his faithful people.'

CHAPTER VI

✿

AUGUSTUS FREDERICK, DUKE OF SUSSEX

In the eighteenth century, for the second time in her history, Rome was the capital of the world. It was inevitable in a century whose thought, literature and architecture looked for inspiration to the classical age.

The young Englishmen of the eighteenth century streamed out to Rome. A few came back laden with her treasures, all enjoyed her beauty, gladly lost their money to her princely families and bowed their stiff Protestant necks as the Princes of her Church swept by. In the last decade of the century, while His Most Christian Majesty of France struggled with his revolutionary subjects, Rome had never been so gay.

The Pope, Pius VI, in an effort to recall the mediæval splendour of the Papacy, was pouring out money upon the restoration of ancient buildings, the encouragement of art and literature, and the enrichment of his less deserving nephews. At their villas just outside the city the princely families of Rome were accustomed to give gorgeous garden parties, with rich wines and licentious songs accompanied by a guitar, after which the guests were often expected to change into peasant costume and rush and romp together in the full abandon of rustic men and maids. Then hosts and guests would dash back to the city to attend a formal dinner party or reception in one of the palaces. Life in Rome was one unending carnival of pleasure.

In the winter of 1792, a sad sufferer from asthma and therefore unable to winter in England, George III's sixth son, Prince Augustus, arrived in Rome. He was only nineteen, having been born on 16th February, 1773. In face he much resembled his eldest brother, the Prince of Wales, but he was very much taller, being more than six foot three inches high and proportionately burly. At the age of fourteen he had been sent to the University of Göttingen where his father thought his good sense would prove conspicuous. There was no doubt of his good sense, though it was at times obscured by an extraordinary vanity. A lady who congratulated him on his voice was amazed to hear the young Prince reply: 'I have the most wonderful voice that was ever heard – three octaves – and I do understand music.'

On arriving in Rome, he exchanged compliments with Pius VI and then set out to pay a call on a cardinal of the Roman Church, which set every tongue in the city wagging. The object of his call was a third cousin, twice removed, of George III's. But this gentleman was more than a mere collateral relation of the King of England; he was himself the King of England – Henry IX – the last legitimate descendant of James II, known as the Cardinal Duke of York or the Cardinal of York. He was wealthy, important and rather proud, but was always glad to receive Englishmen and to show them that he was not completely ignorant of their customs. Prince Augustus gave the Cardinal great pleasure by studiously addressing him as 'Your Royal Highness,' and the call was quickly returned.

In all this Prince Augustus showed that good sense to which George III had proudly referred; it was only unfortunate that with the spring, and his twentieth birthday, this excellent quality completely deserted him. He fell in love with Lady Augusta Murray, who, with her mother, Lady Dunmore, and her sister, Lady Virginia Murray, was visiting Rome. It is uncertain, from the conflicting accounts, whether this lady was only six years older than the Prince or eleven years older. At this time Lady Knight and her daughter, Cornelia, who was to win a small niche in history as lady-governess to Princess Charlotte, were in Rome. Lady Knight wrote: 'What is a youth of 20 in the hands of a woman of 30. Both my Cornelia and I would have thought it high treason to forward the match.'

The affair began with one of those minor civilities between the sexes which are fraught with so much danger for a bashful young man. Lady Dunmore, with her daughters, had been seeing the church of St Giacomo. Prince Augustus arrived with the same intention just as they were leaving. He noticed that the string of Lady Augusta's shoe was untied and knelt down to tie it up.

Henceforth the Prince became a regular visitor at the hotel where Lady Dunmore was staying. One day he came, armed with a copy of *The Tempest*, which he begged Lady Augusta to read. She found that the Prince had heavily marked the lines:

> *O if a virgin, and your affections not gone forth,*
> *I'll make you the Queen of Naples.*

This bold declaration was followed by a number of violent love-letters from the Prince to Lady Augusta. It was 'my amiable Goosy' and 'Ye Gods, my Gussy, how well you looked last night' and 'Where Goosy is not, is no pleasure for Augustus.' Whatever qualms Lady Augusta may have had as to the Prince's intentions must have been set at rest by reading: 'My heart's at ease . . . I feel its palpitations and say to myself: "It beats for Augusta, indeed it does"; and then I add "Goosy my Goosy has felt it." ' And she added, 'It is an honest heart.'

But the owner of this honest heart was precluded from marrying without his father's consent under the provisions of the Royal Marriage Act. As Lady Augusta was not of Royal birth, the Prince knew that it was useless to expect his father's consent to the marriage. However, by the middle of March he had committed himself as far as he could and Lady Augusta was in possession of the following vital document: 'On my knees before God our Creator, I Augustus Frederick promise thee Augusta Murray and swear upon the Bible, as I hope for salvation in the world to come, that I will take thee Augusta Murray for my wife: for better for worse: for richer for poorer: in sickness and in health: to love and to cherish till death do us part: to love but thee only and none other: and may God forget me if I forget thee. The Lord's name be praised! So bless me! O God! And with my hand-writing do I, Augustus Frederick this sign 21st March 1793 at Rome and put my seal to it and my name.'

But, at her time of life, Lady Augusta was not one to put her trust in princes. She wrote in her diary on 21st March: 'O Lord, Creator of all things, I am not worthy of the mercies you lavish upon me, but yet I dare not trust to them.'

Five days later, the Prince was almost pathetically writing to her: 'The rings have been exchanged mutually to-day and sanctioned by being put upon the Bible: for before I sent thee mine, I took a Bible in my hand: I knelt down: kissed it three times, and then laying it upon the Bible, repeated the oath I wrote thee last night [to marry her] and then kissed it and the Bible at the same time. More solemn it could not be.'

But the solemnity of the proceeding did not impress Lady Augusta, who was only to be satisfied by a religious ceremony, and she wrote in her diary: 'What are oaths unsanctioned there [in church]? They bind the honourable but they do not satisfy the world.' As the Roman Catholic Church would not marry Protestants, Lady Augusta occupied herself in searching for an American pastor and an Armenian Patriarch who, she had been told, were visiting Rome.

But the Prince was more orthodox and, hearing of an English clergyman, the Reverend William Gunn, who was acting as chaplain in Rome, he wrote frantically to Lady Augusta on 4th April, begging her to allow him to come that evening bringing Mr Gunn. 'O let me come . . . more than forty-eight hours have I passed without the smallest nourishment. O let me not live so! . . . If Gunn will not marry us, I will die . . . O Augusta, my soul let me try: let me come: I am capable of everything: I fear nothing . . . I am half dead. Good God, what will become of me? I shall go mad, most undoubtedly.'

That evening, shortly before eight, Lady Dunmore's carriage rolled out of the courtyard of the hotel, to attend a party at the Venetian Ambassador's. In her absence the Prince and Mr Gunn slipped into the hotel. With no other witnesses, a ceremony of marriage was performed. For many succeeding nights the Prince climbed into the hotel.[1]

In the summer of 1793 Lady Dunmore and her daughters moved to Florence. The Prince followed them. While they were here, Lady Dunmore noticed that Lady Augusta did not look particularly well. She prescribed all sorts of violent purges, but at last the Prince had to tell her that time alone would cure Lady Augusta, as in a few months she was expecting a baby of which he was the father. In August the Prince was recalled to England, as his governor had no doubt hinted to the Royal Family that the Prince was forming a dangerous attachment. Lady Dunmore and her daughters followed him to England and lived together at 16 Lower Berkeley Street, where the Prince continually visited them.

During the first three Sundays in December the congregation at St George's, Hanover Square was not particularly interested to hear the publication of the banns of marriage between a Mr Augustus Frederick and a Miss Augusta Murray. The marriage was very quietly performed at the end of December, the bride explaining her condition by saying that 'she had married Mr Frederick in Italy when he was under age and so she decided to be re-married.'

On 13th January, 1794, a son, Augustus Frederick, was born. On 15th January, the owner of the 'honest heart' called to see his son, and on the following day left the country, leaving his wife to face the wrath to come. The King and Queen had known of the affair almost from its inception, and Queen Charlotte said to the Princess Elizabeth, when Lady Dunmore and her daughters arrived in England in the autumn of 1793: 'I see it is not all over by the agitation Augustus is in.'

[1] The Reverend William Gunn was rector of Sloyle in Norfolk. In 1793 he was travelling in Italy for his health. He became friendly with Prince Augustus. He went to the Prince's lodgings on 4th April when he found the Prince, Lady Augusta and a Prayer Book. He read the necessary office, made out a certificate: the three of them swore to keep the marriage secret, and Gunn's part in it likewise secret. The Duke's gratitude was real and lasting; he made Gunn his senior Chaplain, and gave a chaplaincy to Gunn's son. When he was 80 poor Gunn was much flustered by a summons from Sir Augustus d'Este to give evidence about the 1793 'ceremony.' I thank Mr Michael Rivière for letting me have a copy of his article on Gunn which was published in *Norfolk Archaeology*.

The King no doubt ordered the Prince out of the country in January 1794, partly to get him away from Lady Augusta and partly on account of his asthma; for, as the Prince himself wrote, 'he was only sleeping one night out of six.'

As soon as the Prince was out of the country, an application was made to the ecclesiastical courts, which were then the appropriate courts for dealing with divorces and nullities of marriages, that the marriage should be set aside on the ground that the King's consent had never been obtained in accordance with the terms of the Royal Marriage Act. The decree, annulling the marriage in St George's, Hanover Square, was pronounced by the Dean of Arches in the summer of 1794 and this functionary simply dismissed Mr Gunn's performance in Rome as 'a show and effigy of marriage.'

But that 'honest heart' was undaunted by the fulminations of King, Privy Council, and Dean of Arches. He was in Italy till September 1794, when he was ordered to Berlin. From here he arranged for Lady Augusta to join him with feigned passports, by which means they were able to outwit the King, who had given strict orders that Lady Augusta should not leave the country. For some years they lived quietly and happily in Berlin.

At the beginning of 1800 the Prince sent Lady Augusta back to England in the hope that the King would think the affair was at an end, and that, as he was now twenty-seven, steps would be taken to give him his Parliamentary grant, which would make him independent of his father. Later in 1800, when there were no signs of the Parliamentary grant, the Prince joined Lady Augusta and they lived together in Hertford Street and at 40 Lower Grosvenor Street. It was now that Lady Holland said in her amiable way that she thought he had thickened in mind and body since she had known him in Rome. Once more the Prince's asthma obliged him to winter abroad and early in 1801 he set out for Lisbon.

He wrote enthusiastically from on board ship how he had heard of a small island off Poole — Brownsea Island — which was to be rented for £250 a year and which he thought would suit them very well, and he felt confident that the Dorsetshire air would cure his asthma. He wrote to his son for his seventh birthday, addressing the letter to 'the Prince Augustus Frederick.' A little later he wrote to Lady Augusta: '. . . to leave you I must not only be the most infamous wretch in the universe, but also the greatest fool existing.' He attributed all the difficulties they were experiencing to the interference of 'H.R.H. the P. of W.' In August 1801 a daughter, Augusta Emma, was born.

But that year it was all over, and the Prince was not only the 'most infamous wretch' but 'the greatest fool existing.' At the end of 1801, he was given his Parliamentary grant of £12,000, which was raised to £18,000 in 1806, and created Duke of Sussex, Earl of Inverness and Baron of Arklow. Whether it was made clear to him that he would never be given his Parliamentary grant as long as he clung to Lady Augusta and that he preferred the solid worth of a Dukedom and £12,000 a year to the charms of a forty-year-old wife, or whether Lady Augusta was unfaithful to him, will never be known for certain, though at the time both explanations of his conduct were suggested. He allowed her £4,000 a year and the custody of the two children.

In 1806 he brought an action to restrain her from using the Royal Arms and calling herself the Duchess of Sussex. In 1809 he brought a second action to take the children away from her, as he understood she was bringing them up to believe that they were a Prince and Princess. Henceforward Lady Augusta was known as the Countess d'Ameland and the children as Augustus d'Este and Mademoiselle d'Este, after a common ancestor of the Duke and Lady Augusta. The children lived with the Duke, and he was a kind and affectionate father to them.

II

There is nothing in the account of the early years of the Duke of Sussex – with his beautiful voice and passionate love-letters – to suggest that he was to be famous, neither as a great singer nor as a great lover, but as a great Whig. He was, in fact, the most consistently Liberal-minded person of the first half of the nineteenth century.

All his brothers, with the exception of the Duke of Cumberland, claimed to be Whigs, and as young men the claim was justifiable. But as they grew older, and when their father went out of his mind, their Whiggery, which had chiefly existed to annoy him, became indistinguishable from violent Toryism. The Duke of Sussex started life with the Liberal views of his brothers and died with them. This was chiefly due to two causes.

Till 1806 the Duke of Sussex was hardly in England at all, on account of his asthma. When the first violence of his passion for Lady Augusta had passed, and when he had ceased to devote eight hours a day to the cultivation of his 'three-octave voice,' he spent his time in study. The excitements that life offered in Germany or Lisbon, where most of these years were passed, were not sufficient to draw him from his books. But if, during these years, he had been in London with his brothers, the calls on his time for pleasure and duty, inevitable to one in his position, would have made study impossible. As it was, he returned from the Continent in 1806, at the age of thirty-three, with a fine collection of books, a unique collection of the manuscripts of Italian opera, several hundreds of Bibles and a well-stored mind. It is not perhaps too flattering to the Whigs to say that such equipment made him naturally more favourable to their party, which always claimed to follow where Reason led the way.

And, in addition to the opportunity of educating himself, there was another cause for the permanence of the Duke's political views. He was no soldier. Being patriotic, he was colonel of a rather obscure force of Volunteers, known as 'The Loyal North Britons,' and when there were any threats of disorder in London he was at his post. It is recorded that he sat up with his men till five o'clock in the morning when the London mob rioted because of Sir Francis Burdett's imprisonment. To his Whig mind, the Loyal North Britons, being Volunteers, were the only constitutional force in England. But the colonelcy of this force, if not of equal eminence with the rank of Field-Marshal enjoyed by his soldier brothers, and if it did not entail work of so precise and laborious a nature as that of the regular soldier, at least left him free to continue his studies. Nothing can have been more crippling to Whig principles than service with the regular Army. The Duke of Sussex was spared this. Whig principles were more likely to flourish in his library at Kensington Palace than in the barrack-rooms of his brothers' regiments. Socially he was perhaps the easiest of the Royal Dukes. When he came back to England he formed the Neapolitan Club, which met for dinner in Willis's Rooms. Membership was confined to men whom the Duke had known in Naples. At a dinner in 1806, at midnight, a little dwarf, about three foot high, wearing a court suit ran on the table through decanters and dessert to make obeisance to the Duke. His Royal Highness stayed till five o'clock in the morning, laughing and singing to the last.

Having formed his opinions, the Duke of Sussex was not the man to flinch from expressing them, in spite of his position. In 1810 he treated the House of Lords to a burst of eloquence on the British Constitution, opening with the impressive words: 'May God forget me, if I forget the Constitution of my country,' and ending with a description of the Constitution as 'the great beacon of civil, constitutional and religious liberty, in the midst of a subjugated and desolated world: that Constitution for which my family have pledged themselves to live and die.'

On most of the important debates on the Roman Catholic question between 1810 and 1829, the Duke was a frequent and erudite speaker in favour of Emancipation. With doubtful relevance, he would trace the history of the doctrinal disputes which had shaken the Church of Rome in the Middle Ages. The Members of the House of Lords were surprised and bored at the flood of Royal learning, and on one occasion a Tory Peer mournfully whispered to his neighbour: 'His Royal Highness is deep in the Councils of Trent,' to which his fellow-sufferer replied: 'I could wish it was the river.'

If on occasions the opponents of Emancipation found his speeches rather tedious, they had no reason to complain of boredom when he attacked the methods which the Protestants were employing to keep up the spirits of the No-Popery party. In 1812 he said in the House of Lords: '. . . Every horrible story of murder, perjuries and a long *et cetera* of crimes is conjured up, collected and adorned with the phrenetic tales of heated and rank imaginations, such as the ghosts of murdered Protestants heard at Bambridge to cry out for vengeance against bloody Papists: and calculated for no other purpose than to frighten thoughtless children, like a Guy Faux, or to disturb the midnight slumbers of antiquated maidens.'

And his final speech on the Roman Catholic question when Emancipation was, at last, in sight, was sane and dignified: 'My Lords, I am no persecutor . . . I am in all sincerity of heart *pacis amicus, persecutionis osor*. I love my country, I cherish her institutions, and I look for pardon and salvation in the pale of her Established Church: but this Church, if I have read what she teaches right, tells me not to look for impossibilities: for such I maintain are identities of faith among so many millions.'

It is, no doubt, not very difficult for a member of the Royal Family, or for a member of the nobility, to propound progressive opinions in the House of Lords. The most he need fear is a stern rebuke from the succeeding speaker and the probability that his friends will think him a little mad. But it was a very difficult and far more courageous thing when, in 1814, the Duke of Sussex made what amounted to an attack on the Prince Regent in the House of Lords. He was risking far more than the polite disagreement of his fellow Peers: he was rousing all their capacity for toadying to the Regent. The topic itself, the Regent's treatment of the Princess Charlotte, was certain to cause a storm at Carlton House.

Princess Charlotte was a lumpy, affectionate creature, who had lived in great retirement but who presented to the people of England a fresh and youthful appearance and had become a popular idol. Her position was in unique contrast to that of any other member of the Royal Family. In 1814, she was eighteen and, for the purposes of sovereignty, being of age, there was great activity among the Princes of Germany, both young and old. The finest plum on the matrimonial tree was hanging in luscious perfection, waiting to be plucked. The Prince Regent as a father-in-law, the Princess of Wales, a little wicked and very crazy, as a mother-in-law, were objections that faded into insignificance before the project of winning the future Queen of England's hand. One of those extraordinarily unattractive Princes of Orange who have periodically cast a calculating, matrimonial eye on the English throne was first in the field. The Regent accepted him as a son-in-law. After a short experience of him, the Princess Charlotte broke off the engagement. The Prince Regent was furious, and on 14th July went round to Warwick House, where his daughter lived, soundly rated her and dismissed her immediate attendants. As soon as her father had left, the Princess hurried out, called a hackney coach off the stand at Charing Cross, and drove to her mother's house in Connaught Square. Her mother and father were then on the worst possible terms, and she was only occasionally allowed to see her mother. There was nobody but the servants at Connaught Square, because her mother was away at her house at Blackheath.

Princess Charlotte then sent a note to Mr Brougham, her mother's legal adviser, and also to the Duke of Sussex, asking them to come round and help her. The Duke was dining with a friend when the note was brought to him. He said: 'Charlotte wrote a most illegible scrawl so I did not attempt to read it, but put it in my pocket.' However, when a second note followed, he thought it must be important and, excusing himself, hurried round to Connaught Square. Here he met Mr Brougham and also the Duke of York, who had been sent round by the Prince Regent to try and persuade the Princess to return. It was then late at night, and the danger was that, if the Princess stayed there till the morning, news of the escapade would spread and the mob would surround Connaught Square to prevent their darling from being dragged away to the clutches of a tyrannical father. The Duke of Sussex asked Mr Brougham whether they would be legally entitled to resist if the Prince Regent sent to carry her off by force. Mr Brougham replied: 'Certainly not.' The Duke then turned to his niece and said: 'Then, my dear, you hear what the law is, and I can only advise you to return with as much speed and as little noise as possible.' At two o'clock the Princess obediently set out for Carlton House. So far the behaviour of the Duke of Sussex had been unexceptionable.

A few days later, the Princess managed to smuggle a note from Carlton House to the Duke of Sussex. She complained that she was practically a prisoner and was allowed no opportunity for seeing her friends or writing to them. On 17th July the Duke wrote a strong letter to the Prime Minister (Lord Liverpool) alluding to the rumours that the Princess was treated with 'violence and rigour' at Carlton House, reminding him that sea-bathing was vitally important to her health and demanding to be allowed to see her. He threatened to raise the whole matter in the House of Lords unless he received a satisfactory answer.

Two days later, on 19th July, the Duke of Sussex rose in his place in the House of Lords. He confessed to a 'considerable degree of embarrassment,' but that 'a sense of rectitude' induced him to put certain questions to Lord Liverpool. He put five questions: the first as to whether the Princess had been allowed to see her friends; the second as to what he called 'the free exercise of her pen'; the third as to her personal liberty; the fourth as to the prospects of her being given sea-bathing; the fifth as to when she would be given an establishment of her own. Lord Liverpool seems to have hesitated to make any reply at all, and briefly stated that such 'questions would bear by implication a disagreeable appearance, as uninvited as it was unnecessary.' The Lord Chancellor (Eldon) thought it incumbent on him to administer a rebuke to the Duke, and he consequently indulged in a panegyric on the conduct of the Regent, whom he called 'that Great Person.' The Duke was dissatisfied, and said that he would raise the subject again a few days later.

Meanwhile, and probably as a result of this publicity, the Princess had been moved to Cranbourne Lodge, at Windsor, and had been seen out riding in Windsor Park. Consequently the Duke withdrew his motion in the House of Lords. In announcing this on 25th July the Duke could not resist giving

Lord Eldon a rebuke, which Hansard reports as follows:
'Before he sat down, he begged to address a few words to the
noble and learned lord on the Woolsack, who was forward in
stating responsibility in his Majesty's servants, for the advice
they may have given on this occasion. He would quote the
words, he believed of Lord Bacon, that "reading made a
learned man, writing a correct man and conversation a ready
man." He would further remark that retirement, coercion and
seclusion were not the means calculated to instruct and give
Princess Charlotte of Wales the most favourable idea of the
beauty and advantages of the glorious constitution of this
country.' Even Whigs like Lord Grey, while questioning the
Duke's tact, were amazed at the courage he had shown in
raising the topic.

The Prince Regent sent for the Duke after this episode and
gave him a sound rating in that virile English which was
always heard to perfection when one Hanoverian quarrelled
with another. They were never afterwards on terms of even
common politeness. When Queen Charlotte's will was read,
the Regent, after keeping the Duke of Sussex waiting for four
hours, sent a message that he had better come again the next
day but that the will had just been read. When the disagreeable
quarrel between George IV and his wife was at its height in
1820, the Duke of Sussex ostentatiously drove to call at Bran-
denburg House at Hammersmith, where Queen Caroline lived.
A few days later he went to stay at Battle Abbey, and the crowd,
who knew of his visit, took out the horses and dragged his
carriage up to the Abbey, calling out 'The Queen and Sussex
for ever.'

On another occasion, when George IV was King and the
Duke was presiding at a dinner of the Society of Arts, he
turned to the toast-master to give the toast of the King, but
added, 'No cheering.' Inevitably an outraged patriot called out
from one of the lower tables: 'I love my King, I venerate the
name of his sire – what, no cheering?' 'No – no cheering,' the
Duke called out. The patriot resigned from the society.

These things were duly reported to George IV, and it is
hardly surprising that when he was dying, and the Archbishop

of Canterbury had come to prepare him for death, the Archbishop should have said: 'Rumour has it, that your majesty is not on the best of terms with your brother, the Duke of Sussex,' and urged him to a reconciliation. But an olive-branch – in the shape of an enormous invalid chair which had been made for the Duke of Sussex when he could not lie down at night because of his asthma – was already lumbering down from Kensington Palace to Windsor Castle. No doubt they were reconciled. But his quarrel with his eldest brother was not entirely disadvantageous. The fact that he could look for no little sinecures like Rangerships of Royal Parks, or for any increase in his Parliamentary grant, made it easy for him to prosecute the Whig cause with a gay, abandoned recklessness. He had nothing to lose.

So far as London was concerned, he was active in all progressive and philanthropic causes in much the same way as the Duke of Kent had been. He was a freeman of the City and Grand Master of the Freemasons. He was associated with many charities. He laid the foundation-stone of the University of London – one of the great Whig enterprises of the early part of the nineteenth century. He was friendly with Robert Owen, and when he went, with the Duke of Kent, to see Owen's famous cubes, representing the population in the various classes of society, and saw Owen pick up the tiny cube representing the Royal Family and the Lords Spiritual and Temporal, the Duke of Sussex 'impulsively pushed the elbow of his Royal brother saying, "Edward, do you see that?" '

But the Duke of Sussex was the only member of his family, at that time, to carry these activities into the provinces. He attended meetings in many parts of the country in support of Queen Caroline, and called down on his head the vituperation of the whole Tory Press for attending the Fox dinner at Norwich in January 1820. At that time Norfolk, inspired by the politics of Mr Coke at Holkham, was predominantly Whig. The Duke, who was a close friend of Mr Coke's and was godfather to his eldest son, stayed at Holkham, and drove over to Norwich with Mr Coke. The dinner was to serve the double purpose of commemorating the birthday of Fox and protesting against the arbitrary behaviour of the existing Tory Government.

Lord Albemarle was in the chair, and gave the toasts of the King and the Prince Regent, which were drunk in solemn silence, but the toast of the Constitution according to the Revolution of 1688 was greeted with loud and long applause. On the immortal memory of Charles James Fox being proposed, a local worthy stepped forward and sang a dirge:

> *Come to his tomb, but not to weep;*
> *There Freedom's holiday we keep,*
> *The sacred altar let it be*
> *Round which we vow to liberty.*

and after this the Duke of Sussex's health was given amid loud cheers, and was drunk with 'nine times nine.'

At the end of the Duke's speech, the local worthy again stepped forward and sang (more brightly):

> *The trumpet of liberty sounds through the world,*
> *And the universe starts at the sound.*
> *Her standard, Philosophy's hand has unfurled,*
> *And the nations are thronging around.*

The chorus was taken up by the rich port-wine voices of these enthusiastic Whigs:

> *Fall, tyrants, fall, fall, fall.*
> *These are the days of liberty.*
> *Fall tyrants, fall!*

Loud above them all was heard the famous three-octave voice of the Duke of Sussex. It was especially unfortunate that, while these festivities were at their height, the Duke of Kent was breathing his last at Sidmouth. The Tory Press poured out their wrath on the Duke of Sussex, who had preferred his bacchanalian Whig orgies to the decencies which were due to his brother. The Duke had only heard of his brother's illness when he reached Norwich, and he said in his speech that he knew his brother, Edward, would have said: 'However ill I may be, do you go and meet them.'

Two years later he paid a visit to another Whig stronghold – the north-east coast. He stayed first at Raby Castle in
Durham, where Lord Darlington lived; Mr Brougham and
Mr Lambton (afterwards the famous Whig leader, Lord
Durham) being invited to meet him. From Raby Castle he
moved on to Howick, where Lord Grey lived. At every place
of importance the crowd insisted on taking the horses out of
his carriage, whereupon he would stand up in it so that everyone might see him, while the people, flaunting their Whig
favours, cried out: 'Sussex for ever, Sussex the friend of the
people.' He drove in to Newcastle from Howick to lay the
stone of the Library and Philosophical Building, where he was
greeted with the utmost enthusiasm.

These activities were regarded with extreme disfavour by
George IV and the leading Tories. At that time there was
practically no political activity of any kind in the constituencies
except at election-time: politicians never dreamt of conducting
a 'raging, tearing campaign' in the country. To attend an
occasional dinner, with the oratory and high places mono-
polised by the nobility, was the maximum exertion of a
Member of Parliament out of election-time at the beginning
of the nineteenth century.

The massive figure of the Duke of Sussex, standing up in
his carriage, beaming and bowing, as he drove through a blaze
of blue and orange, scandalised and frightened the Tories who
were sourly peeping at him out of their windows. The Duke
himself, with pardonable exaggeration, regarded these ex-
cursions as the only link between the Royal Family and the
people. They could be more accurately described as the most
important link between the Whig politicians and their supporters in the country. To the Tories they were only another
proof of what they had always believed, namely, that when the
Revolution came there would be no Republic, but a new
sovereign in the shape of King Augustus. Remembering the
activities of the Duke of Orleans in the years before 1789, and
how the Palais Royal, where he lived, had been the rallying-
ground for all discontents against the Government and the

Royal Family, people began to think of the Duke of Sussex as a second Philippe Egalité.

III

But in 1830 everything changed. George IV died, and Windsor Castle and the British Government were now no longer dominated by the Duke of Cumberland. The latter left Windsor, and the doors of the Castle were flung hospitably open to welcome the Duke of Sussex. William IV succeeded George IV; the Duke of Sussex succeeded the Duke of Cumberland.

The Duke was made Ranger of a Royal Park, the first honour that he had received from the Crown since he had been made a Peer, and the only emolument he ever enjoyed apart from his Parliamentary grant of £18,000. He attended King William's first levée in July 1830, and, as the Tory leaders noticed the triumphant air with which he welcomed his Whig friends, one of them noted in his diary: 'His smile seemed to say "We shall do them yet." '

He was, of course, a convinced and enthusiastic supporter of the Reform Bill. He used such influence as he had with the King to persuade him to support the Whig Ministry through their difficulties in carrying the Bill. He presented a monster petition to the House of Lords, signed by hundreds of thousands of people, asking that the Lords should not delay the passing of the Bill. When the Bill finally passed its third reading in the House of Commons in the autumn of 1831, it was sent up to the House of Lords. It was a foregone conclusion that the House of Lords, swamped with Tory Peers, would reject the Bill. But the Whig Peers made a valiant effort to make up in oratory and argument what they lacked in numbers.

The Duke of Sussex rose to speak on the sixth night of the debate on the Bill. The occasion must have been unique, as witnessing the House of Lords attempting to shout down the brother of the sovereign. He stood up amid a perfect roar of 'Question! Question! Question!' and it was some moments before he could begin his speech. Even when he had begun there were what *Hansard* discreetly described as 'signs of impatience.' The Duke did not allow these interruptions to overawe him and remarked: 'I certainly have party feelings, but these feelings do not prevent me from respecting those who differ from me.' And he can have hardly softened the feelings of indignant Tory noblemen by saying: 'I know the people better than many of your lordships do. My situation, my habits of life, my connection with many charitable institutions and other circumstances on which I do not now wish to enter minutely, give me the means of knowing them . . . .I have gone to the mechanics' "societies," I have visited their institutions and seen their libraries. At Nottingham they have a Library that would do credit to the house of any nobleman . . . Now have not these men as good judgment as your lordships?'

And dealing with some trumpery argument about the French Revolution which had been used by a Tory speaker, the Duke said: 'If I were to use an expression which, perhaps, is not very courteous in this House but which nevertheless is strong and comprehensive, I should say that this is a mere humbug.' But in spite of all these efforts, the House of Lords persisted in rejecting the Bill.

In the critical days of May 1832, when William IV had dismissed Lord Grey and the Whig Ministers and had shown every sign that he would rather see the Bill wrecked than consent to a wholesale creation of Peers, the Duke of Sussex went down to Windsor and presented the King with a petition from Bristol, demanding that he should create the necessary Peers. The King was so angry that he wrote to the Duke forbidding him to come to see him again.

William IV refused to go down to the House of Lords and give his consent to the Reform Bill in person, despite the entreaties of the Ministry. The King's anger against the Duke was not lessened when it was reported that while the commissioners were giving the Royal Assent to the Bill in the House of Lords, the massive figure of the Duke, wearing the Star of the Garter, was observed standing by the throne. Mr Rush, the American Ambassador, who once called on the Duke of Sussex, described his ardour for constitutional liberty as rising to an 'eloquent boldness.' It was hardly an exaggeration, when he was not afraid to show in public that the King had done wrong in not going down to give the Royal Assent to the Bill in person. All the old complaints that he was plotting for the throne and that he would be the 'Louis Philippe' of England were revived. But in point of fact the Duke was only a fearless, convinced Whig, to whom the crown of England was not such a desirable object as to those who invented these stories about his ambition. It was not till August that his quarrel with William IV was patched up.

In 1833, as chairman at a complimentary dinner in Norwich on the retirement of Mr Coke from the House of Commons, the Duke was able to celebrate the twin triumphs of Catholic Emancipation and Parliamentary Reform for which the Whigs had laboured for half a century. In proposing Mr Coke's health, he outlined the varying fortunes of the Whigs during the previous fifty years. He said that he himself had opposed the war with Revolutionary France in 1793 although he and they were called Jacobins at the time, which he called 'a foul name that affrights ladies at the tea-table.' He went on: 'I scorned the imputation because my own conscience (the Duke here emphatically laid his hand on his breast) told me of the honesty of my proceeding.' It may be doubted whether this statement was strictly accurate because during 1793 he was not concerned with the honesty of his proceedings but in proving to Lady Augusta Murray the honesty of his heart. He ended with a warm eulogy of Mr Coke, who, in reply, said of the Duke 'the more I have known him the more I have loved him. A more liberal-minded person in everything that pertains to the rights and liberties of mankind does not exist.'

The Duke, in replying to his health, perhaps warmed by the excellence of the wine, described the Tories as the dirty, factious, pusillanimous party and said he had never had anything to do with them and trusted that he never would. He then wound up the proceedings with dozens of toasts which included every Norfolk Whig Peer, the officials of the county and the Bishop and, finally, 'our best canvassers – the witches of Norfolk – the Ladies.'

Of course, in the light of present-day knowledge, it is easy to smile at the simple faith and simpler enthusiasms of Whigs like the Duke of Sussex. They personally enjoyed not only as elegant a civilisation but as high a standard of intellectual companionship as was ever experienced in even Greece or Rome. They appreciated it. And the reason why they set such store by the Reform Bill was that it was to be the foundation of a vast structure of Reforms within which 'the people' were to enjoy the privileges of the few. The Duke himself, speaking in the House of Lords in answer to Queen Victoria's first speech from the throne in November 1837, thus summed up the Whig faith and Whig hopes: '. . . I cannot resist to express my hope and belief that when the chronicles of this century shall have to record the annals of this reign, which has begun so auspiciously (and I pray God to continue for many, many years) they will not have to write in characters of blood, but have to commemorate the triumph and glorious consequences of peace – the strict observance of the laws of the country – the security of person and property – the diffusion of knowledge – the advancement of arts, manufactures and science – the general occupation and employment of all classes of society, and the extension of commerce over the whole surface of the world.'

From this account of the Duke's Whiggish zeal it would be easy to think of him as that repository of all boredom – a human being whose sole interest is party politics. But his whole idea of life was on too magnificent a scale for him to fit himself into the cramping rôle of the political hack. He was a politician simply because politics was the only channel through which he could hope to conduct the amenities and sympathetic influences of the age to the poorer citizens. He was fortunate in living to see a substantial part of his ideal translated into fact. It was good fortune that was deserved, because the Duke had made considerable sacrifices for the progressive cause, and the thirteen years from 1830 to 1843, in which he lived to enjoy its triumph, made some amends for a life which would otherwise have been at best curious and in all probability futile.

His unfortunate marriage to Lady Augusta Murray, and

the fact that after they separated he was too loyal to think of marrying anyone else, made him the least important member of his family. His brothers were admittedly of no greater importance than he until the death of the Princess Charlotte, when wives, grants from Parliament and the hopes of a nation lifted them in a blaze of publicity from obscurity. But no bride was ever discussed for the Duke of Sussex. The existence of Lady Augusta made it impossible for him to draw his sword in what Peter Pindar calls 'Hymen's war terrific.' He was left in an obscurity which was increased by his disagreement with George IV.

And, having sacrificed much of the importance of a Prince to marry Lady Augusta, there were none of the compensations of family life. After their separation, Lady Augusta, who lived to a considerable age, did not make it possible by dying for the Duke to marry again until 1830. The Duke was fond of his children, and possibly his daughter was some reward for the sacrifices he had made. She was a large, bouncing miss, whose English appearance suggested that her name 'Mademoiselle d'Este' hid an interesting scandal. Her mother always called her 'the Princess Emma' and made valiant efforts to marry her to Prince Leopold after Princess Charlotte's death.

But the Duke's son, Augustus d'Este, added to his father's embarrassments. After a rather unusual education which involved going to both Harrow and Winchester, he went into the Army. He became in time an equerry to his father and accompanied him on his various visits in the country. The Duke was evidently fond of him and wrote to Mr Coke: 'without vanity I can say that he is a very fine fellow.' But in 1830 Captain d'Este began to give his father considerable anxiety. That year marked the accession of William IV and the acknowledgment of his bastards. Captain d'Este argued, with some logic, that if bastards like the FitzClarences were to be raised to the dignity of an Earl's family, a legitimate son like himself should be made at least a Duke, if not a Royal Duke. William IV's answer to this reasoning was to make Captain d'Este a Knight. Sir Augustus was not satisfied with this honour and threw himself on the mercy of the legal profession. We should add that d'Este at this time was beginning to show symptoms of disseminated sclerosis.[1] He had, shortly before this, attempted to become engaged to Queen Victoria's half-sister, Princess Feodora of Leiningen, and had been particularly annoyed by an insulting letter from his father, no doubt reminding him of the difference between a Royal Princess and a Royal Bastard.

The lawyers were able to comfort him. They explained that, as the marriage of the Duke and Lady Augusta at St George's Hanover Square had been declared invalid, his only chance was to base his claim on the first 'ceremony' in Rome which, it will be remembered, had not been declared invalid by the Dean of Arches, because there was not sufficient evidence that it had ever taken place. The lawyers ingeniously argued that the Royal Marriage Act could not apply to a marriage that had taken place outside England and that therefore the ceremony in Rome was lawful. They argued that in any event the Royal Marriage Act could not have any application to Hanover and that as his parents had gone through a ceremony of marriage, which was never disputed, he was a Prince of Brunswick-Luneberg who could certainly claim the crown of Hanover if the Duke of Cumberland and his son were to die. Fortified by this opinion, Sir Augustus d'Este travelled to Germany in 1832 and started to prosecute his claim to be a legitimate member of the Brunswick-Luneberg family before the diets and potentates of the Empire.

The scandal of these proceedings filled the English newspapers just at the time that the Duke of Sussex had been forbidden the Court, and the King was still further annoyed with his brother, although the activities of Sir Augustus d'Este were conducted without the Duke's inspiration or approval. In fact it ruined the friendly relations between the Duke of Sussex and his son. After the Duke's death in 1843, Sir Augustus d'Este claimed his father's Peerage, basing his claim on the marriage in Rome. The House of Lords decided that the claim had not been made out. An interesting repercussion of the case was

[1] Sir Augustus's illness was the subject of a small book, which included his own diary of his symptoms, by Mr Douglas Firth, which was published in 1948.

that Sir Augustus's counsel, Mr Wilde, afterwards Lord Truro, married the Duke's daughter, 'the Princess Emma.'

But in addition to his disastrous marriage, there were two other factors which continued to reduce the Duke's importance as a Prince of England. Till 1817 his sufferings from asthma had been so great that for months at a time it was impossible for him to lie down in bed. In 1817 the complaint completely and mysteriously left him, but it left him convinced that he was a most delicate man. He used to say that if the doctors could open his head they would discover some peculiar deformity.

He was consequently always very careful of his health and adopted some unprincely and slightly eccentric precautions. Perhaps the most pronounced of these was the black skull cap he always wore. (At the urgent request of the artist Hayter he left off his cap to sit for his portrait in the painting of Queen Victoria's Coronation, but it gave him a severe cold, which developed into a sharp attack of asthma.) He was constantly worrying over his health and once, when he was staying at Bognor, he drank by mistake a very strong embrocation which was intended to rub on his chest. He at once realised his mistake and swallowed a quantity of warm water which, in the words of The Times, 'had the effect of bringing the perilous dose off his stomach.'

Then, to add to these misfortunes, he found himself in 1832 becoming rapidly blind as a result of cataract. With his confidence in science, he decided to submit to the operation for its removal, which was then both novel and dangerous. He had to wait till the cataract was sufficiently hard to be removed and almost his last public appearance was at the dinner to Mr Coke at Norwich in 1833. He was just able to see to read out at the dinner an abusive, anonymous letter he had been sent, though he characteristically added that his blindness made him read it so badly, which he thought he had better make clear as, otherwise, the Tories would certainly say that he was drunk. The period of waiting till the operation could be performed and the precautions which were necessary to complete his recovery occupied two years. When it was all over, and he took the chair as President of the Royal Society, he said that he felt the novelty of his situation as though he was entering on a new tenure of existence.

And the other fact which reduced his importance as a Prince was the family complaint of shortness of money. He had none of the wildly extravagant ways of his elder brothers, but his money was exhausted in maintaining considerable grandeur for himself and purchasing curios and rare books. In 1838 he took the step of resigning from the Presidency of the Royal Society and gave as his reason the fact that his Parliamentary grant of £20,000 was not sufficient to cover the expenses of entertaining the members of the Society at an evening party, which it was customary for the President to do. After this the Radicals, who were well disposed to the Duke, proposed in the House of Commons that an increase should be made in his Parliamentary grant. About forty members voted in favour of this but the official Whig Party and all the Tories voted against it. *The Times* was very satirical on the subject:

> *A friend to the Whigs I have been and shall be,*
> *O Liberals, wherefore so stingy to me?*
> *Ye envy not Daniel O'Connell his rent:*
> *Ye paid off the debts of the Duchess of Kent!*
> *And then let me go, with a dog and a string*
> *To beg through the land — like the son of a King.*

> *Pity the sorrows of a poor old Duke*
> *Whose trembling limbs have brought him to your door*
> *With twenty thousand on his banker's book,*
> *He asks, for science sake, a little more.*

But the life of the Duke of Sussex had the fairy-tale quality of righting itself in the end. For many years he had been very devoted to Lady Cecilia Buggin, the widow of Sir George Buggin, a Knight and a person of some eminence in the City of London. In 1830 Lady Augusta Murray died, and marriage was once more a possibility for the Duke. He married Lady Cecilia on 2nd May, 1831. The marriages of the Duke of Sussex may have satisfied the consciences of the contracting

parties but they almost monotonously failed to satisfy the
provisions of the Royal Marriage Act. His marriage to Lady
Cecilia was, so far as the laws of England were concerned,
invalid. It was announced to the world by the Duke and Lady
Cecilia arriving in the same carriage for a party of Lady Grey's.
At the same time Lady Cecilia dropped the name of Buggin,
for which it is possible that she had little affection and to
which, having married again, she had now no right, and
assumed her mother's maiden name of Underwood. The
Duke's official home was Kensington Palace, but for some
years after they married Lady Cecilia lived at 5 Cumberland
Place just north of Oxford Street.

In 1840, Lady Cecilia was recognised by Queen Victoria
as her uncle's wife. The Duke of Sussex, as the elder surviving
son of George III in England, took precedence next to the
Queen. The Queen was always fond of him, but her affection
was doubled when he agreed to give pride of place to Prince
Albert by allowing the Prince to take precedence next to the
Queen. As a small reward the Queen created Lady Cecilia,
Duchess of Inverness. (It will be remembered that the Duke's
second title was Earl of Inverness.) Mr Greville was very angry
and wrote in his diary: 'It is called a recognition of the marriage which is just what it is not – it is a recognition of the co-
habitation, and if it is to be considered an approval of it, it is a
very indecent proceeding.' The kind of difficulties to which it
gave rise were well illustrated by the Duchess's first public
appearance after the honour had been made public. She and
the Duke went together to a ball at Lansdowne House. As they
entered the room the footman called out: 'His Royal Highness
the Duke of Sussex and Her Grace the Duchess of Inverness.'
Of course everyone knew, but on the face of it there was not
the slightest explanation of why the two names were coupled
together. She was noticed tucked under the Duke's arm and all
smiles and shaking hands in acknowledgment of the congratulations. But a more critical moment was reached when the
Queen arrived and went in to supper. She sat at a table at one
end of the room with the Duchess of Cambridge on one side

and an empty chair for Prince Albert on the other. The Duke of Sussex deposited his wife half-way up the room and went alone to pay his respects to the Queen, taking a seat at the supper table. The Queen then allowed the Duchess of Inverness to sit at her table, but only on condition that she came up after all the other Duchesses as the junior creation.

But in spite of these refinements of the official mind the marriage was completely successful. Of course physically the Duke was no longer attractive. The charming youth of more than six feet whom Lady Augusta had loved, was very different by the time he fell into the arms of Lady Cecilia Buggin. It is recorded that Lady Cecilia said to Mr Solomon Hart, who had painted the Duke's portrait for the Board Room of the Jewish Hospital in the Mile End Road: 'You have a difficult subject to treat in a corpulent man, but you have avoided coarseness and have made him look like a gentleman.'

Still, whatever his grossness and whatever his physical defects, there can be no doubt that the Duke of Sussex was a charming and lovable companion. His Whig associates loved him and always spoke of him as 'the good man.' Even Queen Victoria, whose youthful naughtiness had been checked by the threat that 'Uncle Sussex will come for you,' was devoted to him, and when he was dying she drove down in tears to Kensington Palace in an open carriage to inquire for him, although she was hourly expecting the birth of her third child.

The Duke of Sussex, in common with eighteenth-century nobles of progressive opinions like Philippe Egalité and Horace Walpole, combined the championship of progressive causes and a certain political austerity with an affection for splendour and comfort in private life. He was an enthusiastic gardener and his flower-garden at Kensington Palace was much admired. He showed his good taste in an age when the English sovereign had an embarrassing choice of untidy little palaces to live in – the Gothic handiwork of George III at Windsor and at Kew, the classical touch of George IV at Buckingham Palace or his fantastic production at the Pavilion at Brighton, by saying of Hampton Court: 'If I was King I would certainly live there and soon rout out the present inhabitants in the only Palace in England.'

His library was that of a collector and a prince. It consisted of some 50,000 volumes, and of these 12,000 were theological: these included bibles in all known languages including Esquimaux; there were many examples of the Greater and Lesser Polyglott Bibles and there were 273 English bibles beginning with the Myles Coverdale of 1535. Possibly this interest in theological matters explains why he put below the Royal Arms on his book-plate *Si Deus Pro Nobis: Quis Contra Nos*. In addition to serving his master in the library, T. J. Pettigrew, his librarian, was also his surgeon, and he acted as surgeon to the Duchess of Kent and Princess Victoria. In dedicating a printed catalogue of some of the contents of the library to his Royal Highness the Librarian wrote that the Duke's generous hospitality had made his house the resort of whatever is wise, and great and good. In his preface he expressed particular thanks to the Reverend Dr Samuel Parr — 'that most extraordinary individual' (Parr was a scholar of great attainments and a politician of opinions which were ardently left-wing). Pettigrew continues 'I shall never forget the delight and rapture of this venerable man, when I had the honour to conduct him through the extensive library — his astonishment at the vast treasures it contained, and his admiration of the spirit and taste of the illustrious individual who had formed the collection.'

His intellectual tastes were accompanied, as was inevitable in eighteenth-century persons, by a curious affection for the odd. He liked to be surrounded with unusual forms of life, and his rooms were filled with piping bullfinches and singing birds of every kind, while he had a small Negro page, whom he called Mr Blackman, to wait on him. He had the Hanoverian affection for clocks, and, as Kensington Palace clock struck the hour, there was a medley of martial airs and national anthems from the various clocks in the Duke's apartments. He kept eighteen watches in a glass case, the ticking of which his guests found very irritating. He had a gold watch with a miniature of Princess Charlotte's eye painted on the back. He had fifteen pairs of spectacles, a collection of coach whips, a mouth harmonium, and cases of less personal but equally curious possessions.

The Duke sat in the middle of this fantasy, and in the morning received his guests in his black velvet cap, elegant slippers, a violet satin dressing-gown and a white embroidered waistcoat. Much of his time was spent in his Library and, as he read, he would sketch in ink an elaborate hand pointing to any passage he thought memorable or with which he disagreed. In the British Museum is his own copy of Gladstone's *Church and State*, decorated with these pointing hands and covered with such comments as 'A most mischievous argument,' or, 'This is merely declamatory – no argument.' But far worse for the Duke's reputation, a gentleman bought one of his prayer-books at the sale after his death, and found the fatal pointing hand against the Athanasian Creed with the comment: 'I don't believe a word of it.'

In April 1843 the Duke was taken seriously ill with erysipelas. After living precariously on turtle soup and orange ices, he grew rapidly worse and on the morning of 21st April, realising that he had not long to live, he sent for his servants to come up and take their leave of him. As they came into the room, he made an effort to speak to them but fell back dead.

It was found that in his Will he had given directions that his body should be opened and examined, for he felt confident that there was a 'peculiarity in my conformation,' the knowledge of which might serve the interests of science. Many years before, in presenting a petition to the House of Lords that it might be made possible for surgeons to open the body of anyone after death unless such person had expressed a wish to the contrary, he had announced his intention of having his own body opened and had added: 'in quitting this state of existence, it may be some consolation to feel that, even after death, my bodily frame may advance that which I always desired during my life – the good of my fellow men.'

He also expressed a wish that he might not be buried at Windsor but might lie in the public cemetery in Kensal Green. It is curious to-day to walk through that cemetery and to see, among the vast contrivances of brick and stone which mark the resting-places of merchants and other men of wealth who had no family vaults to lay their bones in, a solid, grey mausoleum with the simple inscription 'In memory of His Royal Highness Augustus Frederick, Duke of Sussex, K.G.,' and inscribed on the other side of the mausoleum, away from the path, 'In memory of Cecilia Letitia, Duchess of Inverness, widow of the Duke of Sussex.' No one could doubt that underneath that stone was laid the finest product of the Whig tradition.

CHAPTER VII

❧

ADOLPHUS FREDERICK, DUKE OF CAMBRIDGE

THERE is one quality which is almost painfully lacking in the sons of George III who have so far filled the pages of this book. They had various virtues, but it would be difficult to describe any of them, with the possible exception of the Duke of Sussex, as virtuous. This missing quality is supplied by the youngest of the Royal Dukes – Prince Adolphus Frederick. No doubt a virtuous Prince is greatly to be desired: he may well be the pride of the nation. But not everybody will be satisfied with him. He will be a grave disappointment to those sparkling letter-writers, those acid diarists, those resourceful chatterers and the Whig historians who are, in their respective spheres, responsible for the history of England. There could be no room in their pages or their talk for a Prince who was dutiful, sober, moral and honoured his father and mother. From the fact that no scandal ever attached itself to Prince Adolphus and because, taking no part in politics, he was never an object for the inventive genius of his political opponents, he is to-day forgotten – or only remembered to be confused with his son, that fierce and kindly warrior, the second Duke of Cambridge, for many years commander-in-chief of the Army.

Prince Adolphus – George III's seventh son – was born at Kew on 24th February, 1774. During his boyhood he lived in a cottage at Kew with his elder brothers, Prince Ernest and Prince Augustus, with two tutors to instruct them and to keep them out of mischief. In 1786 – when he was twelve – the Prince went with his two brothers to the University of Göttingen. Göttingen is roughly a hundred miles to the south of Hanover, and at the end of the eighteenth century was still a modern university, having been founded in the reign of George II. Soon after the Princes went, George III wrote to a friend: 'My accounts from Göttingen of the little colony I have sent there, is very favourable . . . I think Adolphus seems at present the favourite of all, which from his lively manners is natural.'

The object with which these Princes went to the university was, on the whole, novel. It was not so much that they should draw from the well of knowledge as that they should fill it. They were to impress the Hanoverians with the superior charms of English gentlemen and to encourage them to adopt English manners and customs. Of course, through the accession of a Queen to the English throne in 1837, and the consequent separation of Hanover from England, the problem which faced the Kings of England from 1714 to 1837 of trying to strengthen the ties between Hanover and England, which merely depended on a common sovereign, is one which it is difficult for us to appreciate. One of George III's ideas for strengthening these ties, was that, encouraged by the example of his sons, young Englishmen should flock out to Göttingen and help to anglicise the Hanoverians.

It is doubtful whether Prince Adolphus, at the age of twelve, was old enough to profit by an orthodox university education, even without the additional responsibility of displaying the characteristics of an English gentleman. His fellow-students did their best to encourage him to believe that he was a man, and to put away childish things, by presenting him with a spirited ode on the occasion of his thirteenth birthday:

> In thee, Adolphus, may the world admire
> All that is worthy of thy Royal sire,
> In every action, every virtue shine,
> Honour and truth. Benevolence be thine.
> Proceed, lov'd Prince! Pursue thy chosen plan
> And dare do all that may become a man.

The 'chosen plan' no doubt refers to his university studies which, for a small boy, were fairly rigorous. Classics were learned from the famous Heyne, who was allowed an assistant for the rougher work, and, in addition history, geography, moral philosophy, mathematics and experimental philosophy formed part of the time-table. The Prince gave much pleasure to his father by writing to say how very satisfactory he found the course of theology. He practised the violin and learned to fence.

But the quiet delights of Göttingen were for the piping times of peace. Hanover, the neighbouring state to Prussia, could not be expected to remain unmoved while Prussia and Austria were sharpening their swords in 1790 for what they expected would be a triumphal march to Paris, with nothing to oppose them but a people distracted by Revolution. By 1790 Prince Adolphus had said good-bye to Göttingen, with its philosophers and professors, eternal friendships and deadly feuds, light-hearted students and laborious scholars. He had been appointed an officer in the Hanoverian Army. In the summer of 1793, with his regiment, he joined the English troops in Holland under the command of the Duke of York. During the campaign he was severely wounded in the shoulder, and was for a short time in the hands of the enemy till he was rescued, thanks to a timely sortie on the part of the English Guards. He was obliged to return to England to recover from his wounds, and added greatly to his popularity by saying to the Prince of Wales that he would have resisted and got himself killed rather than be a valuable hostage in the hands of the enemy. Such was the ardour of nineteen.

Prince Adolphus was the favourite son of the King and Queen. Originally this was due to no effort or excellence on his own part, but simply to the fact that George III loved best his youngest children. His youngest child, Princess Amelia, was his favourite daughter. His youngest sons, Prince Octavius and Prince Alfred, were his favourite sons, and when they both died he seemed, quite as a matter of course, to transfer his affections to the next youngest son, Prince Adolphus.

It would, doubtless, be absurd to say that it was a rule of George III's life that the younger the child the more lovable it was. The explanation of his preference is less eccentric. When his elder children were at their most attractive ages,

George III was immersed in politics. It was the manœuvring of placemen in Parliament in order to smash the political power of the Whigs, rather than games with his young children, that occupied the King's time. With the arrival of the seventeen-eighties and the gradual ascendancy of the Tory Party under the younger Pitt, politics ceased to engage the King. He turned to the cultivation of crops and the endearments of family life. It was only natural that he should find his younger children more amusing and entertaining than a fully grown roysterer like the Prince of Wales.

But whatever advantage Prince Adolphus gained in his parents' affections by his youth, he consolidated by his character. People about the Court, who knew how cruelly the King had been used by his elder sons and how bitterly they had disappointed him, were charmed with this Prince, who was quite as lively as his elder brothers but had discovered that the whole object of being young was not simply to bait one's parents. Lady Chatham, who was friendly with the Royal Family, wrote of the Prince just before he returned to Flanders after recovering from his wounds: 'The Dear charming Prince Adolphus took leave of me this night. I shall see him no more, as he's to go in a few days time. I quite pity the King and indeed all the family: he has been so delightfully pleasant with them all that they will be undone without him. You never saw such a picture of a fond father, as the King with him, or indeed anything prettier than the son's constant affectionate attention to his Father.' He served throughout the whole of the spring and summer campaign of 1794, and remained with the Hanoverians during that disastrous winter when they were retreating ever farther into Holland before the onslaughts of the French. He wrote during this retreat to Lady Harcourt: 'Thank God I have borne the campaign very well. The cold was shocking, and the marches we had to make horrid, but I luckily have escaped having any limb frozen.' And he wrote to the King to say that he would not for the world have missed what he had seen and gone through, and to thank him for the experience. But by 1795, after two years of the war, the Dutch showed unmistakable signs that they preferred the

French invaders to their English and Hanoverian allies. The English took to their boats and the Hanoverians marched back to Germany.

Prince Adolphus went with the Hanoverians, and for the next eight years lived in Hanover, being rewarded with regular promotion in the Hanoverian Army. During these years the Prince rose regularly at six, and such time as could be spared from his military duties was devoted to scientific studies and practising the violin, on which he became a very proficient player. Any English visitors to Hanover, or English people who stopped there on the way to Berlin, were sure of a warm welcome from the Prince. An Englishwoman who was in Hanover during the last year of the eighteenth century described him as 'extremely handsome, tall and finely formed with fair complexion and regular features, charming manners and a flow of amusing conversation.' This lady went one evening to call on General Walmoden, who was the son of George II and Lady Yarmouth, and Prince Adolphus, who was there and whom she describes as 'extremely animated,' sang to them with very good taste and a charming voice. She attended a ball in the Prince's house, which was decorated with such splendour – its ceilings, floors, doors and windows painted in the Italian style, a marble saloon and a boudoir lined with looking-glasses – that she was reminded of *The Arabian Nights*.

But sterner business was facing the Prince. In 1801 he was created Duke of Cambridge, Earl of Tipperary and Baron Culloden, and in that year Prussia, egged on by Napoleon and angered by the dislocations to trade resulting from the British control of the sea, occupied Hanover. The Duke seems to have stayed in Hanover during the occupation which was ended in the following year by the Treaty of Amiens. In the spring of 1803, before war had officially broken out again between England and France, the French threatened Hanover with a small force under General Mortier, declaring that any Hanoverians found in the service of the King of England would be regarded as enemies of France. The Duke of Cambridge was put in command of the Hanoverian Army to resist this

French attack, and he made valiant efforts to recruit the civil population in defence of the country. But the Hanoverians, who were a simple, peaceful people, had other ideas of resisting the French. They raised large placards on their borders with the legend, in French, 'Neutral Territory.' Such a defence could have little effect on the soldiers of Napoleon. But their second line of defence was more desperate and more effective. Although they easily outnumbered the enemy, they made it known that they would gladly accede to any terms the French were kind enough to offer.

It was a very galling position for the Duke of Cambridge. He was longing to fight for Hanover, and wrote to a Hanoverian friend: 'Rest assured that I will sacrifice my blood and life for a country to which I am so much attached.' It was only unfortunate that Hanover had no desire that the sacrifice should be made. So zealous was the Duke that General Walmoden complained that he had the greatest difficulty in restraining him from making a reckless assault on the French. It was, unluckily, useless for the Duke to stand up like David of old to do battle with the enemy while the Hanoverians sulked in their tents. There were no giants among the French in those days. He could have expected nothing but death or capture from the grimly efficient troops of France. Reluctantly he slipped away to England.

For the next ten years of his life the Duke lived quietly in England. He had apartments in St James's Palace and also at Windsor Castle, so that much of his time was spent with his parents and sisters. He was perhaps lucky in remaining on good terms with his eldest brother, for it was generally believed that he was responsible for the Prince of Wales's disastrous marriage by bringing back an enthusiastic account of the Princess Caroline and adding – what was the highest possible praise from him – 'She is exactly like my sister Mary.' (From childhood the Duke of Cambridge had been absolutely devoted to the Princess Mary.) It is well known that the Prince of Wales could only get through the marriage ceremony with the support of copious draughts of brandy. The Prince of Wales might well have vented his anger on his youngest brother, like Henry VIII, who beheaded Thomas Cromwell for buoying him up with the belief that Anne of Cleves would be lovely. But it did not impair their friendly relations, and it was, unjustly enough, the Princess of Wales who wrote savagely of the Duke of Cambridge: 'He looked exactly a sergeant and so vulgar with his ears full of powder.' He was, however, rapidly promoted in the English Army, and was put in command of the Home District. When in London he was frequently to be seen at concerts, and was active with his brothers in a variety of charities. In 1809, in company with the Dukes of Cumberland and Sussex, he went to the Great Synagogue in Duke's Place to see a Jewish service. The synagogue was brilliantly illuminated and magnificently decorated for the occasion, and it was remarked that the Royal brethren seemed most impressed by the beautiful singing of the choruses and by the beautiful Jewesses in the gallery. They stayed the night in Finsbury Square with Mr Abraham Goldsmid, who gave a banquet, followed by a concert, in their honour.

In an age when Jews in England were still very much a caste to themselves, and were suspected and feared by the Christian population, this visit of the Royal Dukes showed an agreeable tolerance, which was sharply criticised in the public Press. It is no doubt to this experience of Jewish life and customs that the Duke of Cambridge owed the sympathy and interest which he ever afterwards showed to Jews and Jewish institutions both in Hanover and England. Apart from this episode, the Duke of Cambridge was never attacked by the public or in the newspapers as his brothers were. People who came in contact with him were all impressed by his excellent qualities and handsome bearing. Mr Farington, the artist, who saw him strolling with the Prince of Wales at Weymouth, was struck by his handsome, magnificent appearance and thought that, beside him, the Prince of Wales had 'a shattered look.' But he was too remote from the succession to become a popular figure and had to content himself with the adoration of his parents and sisters, the tolerance of his brothers and the respect and admiration of the public. The respect in which the Duke of Cambridge was held at least showed that his brothers had only to thank their political and amorous activities for the public contempt in which they were then held by practically the whole country.

II

No doubt the fortunes of every European family were altered by the existence of Napoleon. Those who escaped losing their sons, husbands or brothers found that, in addition to a terrible rise in prices, the established laws of commercial life were fast altering, and that the opportunity of earning a living was becoming increasingly perilous. During the last decade of the Napoleonic War the French could not sail on the waters of Europe, and the English, apart from their own country, could not set foot on the soil of Europe. These personal restrictions were more confusing to commerce than any trade barriers.

And even to those fortunate people who, like the English Royal Family, were independent of commerce, these personal barriers were very cramping. Ever since the Elector of Hanover had ascended the English throne in 1715, the English Royal Family had regarded Germany as their marriage-market. For ten years Napoleon cut them off from their promised land, with its lovely, penniless brides and its uncouth, princely bridegrooms. The Princess Royal had married a German Prince in 1797, but, excepting her, neither the King nor the Queen, their sons or daughters, were able to leave England between the years 1803 and 1813.

But in 1813 there was a change. Previously the peoples of Europe had watched, almost supinely, while Napoleon defeated their armies and subjected their countries to his rule. But in 1813 they rose to break his power and to smash down his barriers. English Princes and English soldiers were once more welcomed in Germany.

So it was that at the end of 1813 the Duke of Cambridge was sent over to represent the Regent in Hanover and to organise the national feeling against France. There could be no more vivid illustration of how Napoleon brought about his own downfall than by comparing the departure of the Duke of Cambridge from Hanover in 1803 with his return in 1813. In 1803 the Hanoverians had gladly let him go and submitted to Napoleon; after ten years' experience of Napoleonic rule, and of his disregard for the feelings of nationalities, they gave the Duke an uproarious welcome. People remembered the Duke's affability, good nature and regularity of life: rumour reached them of the protection he had given to such Hanoverians as had gone to England while Hanover was under Napoleon's yoke. An enthusiastic Hanoverian said that everywhere in Hanover was heard the exclamation, 'Our Adolphus is coming.'

The Duke rode towards the city on horseback. At the outskirts he was met with the request that he would mount a triumphal car, lined with white satin and hung with garlands of flowers. Thirty brewers seized the traces and dragged the Duke through the streets to the Herrenhausen Palace. As he swayed through the wildly cheering crowd, bands played 'God save the King,' trumpets blew, bells were rung, cannon thundered and handkerchiefs fluttered from every window. It was only unfortunate that the Duke was so moved by his reception that he was in tears.

It was not by any means an easy or a pleasant task to which the Duke was called. In 1814 he was appointed Governor-General of the kingdom. He wrote to the Prince Regent that the only reason he had undertaken it was 'to be of use to you and the country.' The main difficulty which faced him was one which was then facing all the sovereigns of Germany. The people of Germany had thrown off the tyranny of Napoleon. They were in no mood to tolerate the scarcely less tyrannical government of their own mediæval Constitutions. On the other hand, the sovereigns of the German States, at a time when reactionary views were everywhere triumphant, were not disposed to grant their people a more Liberal Constitution. The rulers of Germany in 1815 were rather like the improvident traveller who stuffs his trunk burstingly full and just manages to fasten it: it serves for the moment, but it has no chance of surviving the journey. They restored the ancient

Constitutions of their country. Superficially all looked well, but trouble was bound to break out within a very few years.

The Duke of Cambridge, partly because he was an Englishman and accustomed to a free Constitution, had considerable sympathy with the aspirations of the Hanoverians. In opening the first Assembly of the Hanoverian Houses of Parliament, he addressed the members as 'Venerable, noble and loyal Friends and Countrymen' and, after stating that the House of Guelph was ever known for its justice and moderation, he assured them that they might expect a new Constitution which would give them power to help in the task of reorganising the country. At the same time he wrote to the Prince Regent saying that it was absolutely essential to give the people a reformed Constitution. But Count Münster, who was the Hanoverian Minister in London and a strong reactionary, had planned to build up a great, powerful Hanoverian kingdom as the centre of anti-Prussian feeling in Germany. He had great influence with the Regent and regarded the Duke of Cambridge as a docile nonentity. Consequently it was not till 1831, when William IV dismissed Count Münster and raised the Duke of Cambridge to the rank of Viceroy, which gave him the political power which as Governor-General he had lacked, that a Liberal Constitution was granted to Hanover.

The Duke had only been in Hanover three years when Princess Charlotte died, which completely altered the circumstances of his life. He was forty-three and, judging from the fact that he had only once made an effort to change his condition by lawful marriage and never by an unlawful establishment, it may be assumed that he was well content with a bachelor's life. But the necessity of providing an heir to the throne made marriage essential for him.

Of all the unmarried sons of George III, it was most important that he should marry. (The Regent and the Duke of York were childless.) The Duke of Clarence and the Duke of Kent, both over fifty, one with an enormous family of natural children and the other with a mistress of nearly thirty years' standing, were hardly eligible bachelors even to the eager Princesses of Germany. The Duke of Cumberland had married an elderly wife who, it was thought, would not bear him another child after the death of her daughter in 1817. The Duke of Sussex, by his 'marriage' to Lady Augusta Murray, was prevented from seeking another bride. The Duke of Cambridge, still comparatively young and untouched by scandal, was the most eligible suitor and, in the eyes of the country, the most likely to satisfy its desire for an heir. No time was lost. A fortnight after the Princess Charlotte's death, the Duke of Cambridge wrote to the Regent: 'I have sent my proposals to the Princess Augusta and have received a favourable reply.' Such haste certainly seemed to justify Peter Pindar's description of the state of the Royal Dukes after Princess Charlotte's death:

> *Agog are all, both old and young*
> *Warm'd with desire to be prolific*
> *And prompt with resolution strong*
> *To fight in Hymen's war terrific.*

The Princess Augusta to whom the Duke had sent his proposals was the youngest daughter of the Landgrave of Hesse-Cassel and was the great grand-daughter of King George II of England. She was only twenty, beautiful and, according to the newspapers, 'amiable.' The Duke was charmed with her and enthusiastically wrote to the Regent: 'I am the happiest of men.' They were married at Cassel in the middle of May and set out from there for England, accompanied by the bride's father, the Landgrave, 'a venerable old gentleman of seventy.'

They arrived off Dover one lovely evening at the end of May, and thousands of people, their work finished, stood along the shore to watch the Royal party land. At six o'clock the *Royal Sovereign* anchored in the roads and the Royal Standard was transferred to the barge in which they were to be rowed ashore. The crowd cheered lustily when they saw the Duke, with the Duchess in his arms, boarding the barge. They cheered even louder as the Duke landed, still supporting the Duchess, who was far too ill to stand and could only contrive a faint nod to show that she appreciated the welcome. The Duke wrote to the Regent from the inn at Dover: 'The Duchess has been dreadfully sick.' But the following morning all was well, and at eight o'clock the Duke and Duchess were seen strolling arm in arm along the pier. The Duchess was dressed in white; with a purple pelisse and scarf, and a small straw bonnet decorated with white ostrich feathers. It was reported that the *tout ensemble* was highly interesting. They arrived in London that evening and were re-married before Queen Charlotte on June 1st at Buckingham Palace.

This was the first of the three Royal marriages since Princess Charlotte married Prince Leopold that roused the romantic enthusiasm of the British public. They could hardly be expected to feel very strongly about the marriage of the Princess Mary, over forty, to her almost imbecile cousin the Duke of Gloucester, more generally known as 'Silly Billy.' There was not even anything to rouse their interest in the marriage of the Princess Elizabeth, who was older and stouter than the Princess Mary, to the Landgrave of Hesse-Homburg — except the fact that the Landgrave was sick in the carriage driving off for the honeymoon and was very sensibly made to travel the rest of the way on the box. So when the Duke of Cambridge brought back this rather lovely girl of twenty, the public gave expression to their pent-up feelings. The Duke and Duchess had only to show themselves to be loudly cheered. The first Sunday after their arrival in England they were recognised strolling together in Hyde Park, and were at once surrounded and jostled by a large crowd, cheering and yelling. The Duchess, who had never experienced anything of the kind from the quiet, sober citizens of Cassel was not only astounded but absolutely terrified. On another occasion they were recognised in their carriage outside the famous City jewellers, Rundle and Bridge, and a great crowd came yelling round them, so that it was twenty minutes before their coachman dared move. The Duchess was also very popular with the English Royal Family, although she narrowly escaped causing Queen Charlotte's death. The Duchess of Cambridge could not speak a sentence of English, and seeing the Duchess of Cumberland in Kew Gardens, who was German by birth and had lived in Germany all her life but was not received at the English Court, she went up to enjoy a little conversation. News of this encounter reached the Queen; she at once had such a severe heart-attack, brought on by rage, that it was thought she would have died.

That autumn the Duke and Duchess returned to Hanover. So far as the English public was concerned, the marriage was everything they could have expected. At the beginning of 1819 it was known that the Duchess was expecting a child. When, towards the end of March, the birth was imminent, the Duke of Clarence, who was then living in Hanover, with two other gentlemen, sealed all the doors of the bedroom in which the Duchess was lying and posted themselves in an adjoining dressing-room from where they could watch the proceedings. As soon as the child was born they hurried in 'to determine its sex by actual inspection.' Immediately afterwards couriers dashed off to England to announce that at long last a grandson had been born to the King of England. The boy was christened George after his uncle, the Regent, and was in the direct succession to the thrones of England and Hanover. But it was only for two months, because the birth of Princess Victoria on 24th May, 1819, destroyed his chance of the English throne, and the birth of Prince George of Cumberland on 27th May, 1819, destroyed his chance of the Hanoverian throne.

In 1822 the Duchess had a daughter, Princess Augusta, and eleven years later, in 1833, a second daughter, Princess Mary, mother of Queen Mary.

And if the English public had good reason to be satisfied with the marriage, so had the Duke of Cambridge. He wrote of himself when he was first married: 'I really believe that on the surface of the globe there does not exist so happy a Being as myself . . . Truly, truly grateful do I feel to Providence for having reserved this blessing in store for me, and Heaven grant that I may be deserving of it and not forfeit my happiness by any misconduct.' It was a happiness that lasted, and many years later the Duke's sister, the Landgravine of Hess-Homburg, writing of the Duchess of Cambridge, said 'my brother's amiable and devoted attachment and affection for her.' Fifteen years after they had been married, at the time of

THE CAMBRIDGE BRANCH OF THE ROYAL FAMILY

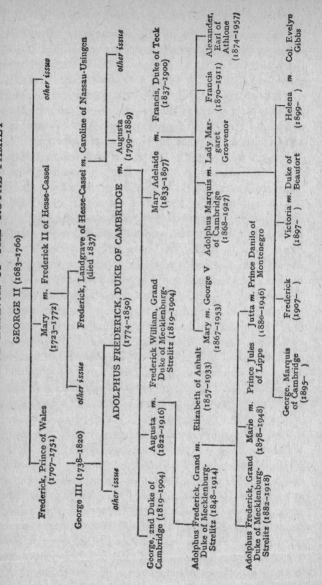

Princess Mary's birth, the Duchess was seriously ill. The Duke was so excited and alarmed that it was feared that he would die. The doctors announced that they could do nothing more for the Duchess, and it was left to the Chief Rabbi of Hanover, Dr Adler, to summon his flock with all speed and to offer up fervent prayers for the recovery of the Duchess. She recovered. The Duke could not so easily throw off the effects of his anxiety and the doctors, with some felicity of phrasing, declared that he was suffering from 'confined gout.' But by the time of the baby's christening all was well and the Duke was fondly gazing on his wife who was wearing a beautiful dress of white crape and blonde over pink which he had ordered for her from Paris. (The Duke never forgot Dr Adler's share in this happy result and was partly responsible for his appointment as Chief Rabbi in London in 1844.)

The Duke of Cambridge was no sportsman although he occasionally went shooting in Hanover. He preferred, by showing his interest in music and exhibitions of paintings, to encourage the Hanoverians to develop their artistic taste. He was far more of the cultured, cosmopolitan, eighteenth-century ruler than the sporting prince of the nineteenth century — there was far more of Versailles about him than Balmoral.

For nearly a quarter of a century, from 1813 to 1837, he was absorbed by the interests of his family and the concerns of Hanover. He was in England for a short time in 1816 for the wedding of 'dearest Minny' — his favourite sister, the Duchess of Gloucester. He was ordered to England in 1822 to take sea-bathing at Brighton for his gout, and he came over once or twice again to bring his son, Prince George, who spent most of his boyhood at Windsor with King William and Queen Adelaide. He was colonel of the Coldstream Guards and his letters to Sir Alexander Woodford, who was in command of the regiment, show that he took an interest not only in the standard of efficiency and recruiting but in the minute details of the soldiers' dress. But, inevitably, he was very much out of touch with English opinion. Lord Grey wrote in 1831 to press him to come to England to vote in the House of Lords in favour of the Reform Bill, but he refused, not for political reasons but on account of leaving Hanover and of the Duchess, who dreaded another channel-crossing.

But the death of William IV in 1837 and the accession of the Duke of Cumberland to the throne of Hanover, broke up his home and revolutionised his life. He set out for England at the beginning of July, and issued a public farewell to his beloved Hanoverians:

> At the moment of separation, I cannot leave this country without addressing to its beloved inhabitants a word of *adieu*. In my early youth I often resided in this native land of my forefathers and many delightful recollections are connected with that long by-gone period . . . Painful to me is the separation from this city, where my children first beheld the light of Heaven, where I have spent so many happy hours, and where I have maintained friendly relations with so many whom I love and esteem . . . And now, dearly beloved people of this Kingdom, I wish you all an affectionate adieu and leave you in the hope that you also will hereafter think with affection of me — ADOLPHUS.

III

When King William the Fourth died, Prince George of Cambridge, who was eighteen, wrote in his diary: 'My Uncle, the Duke of Cumberland, has now become King of that Country [Hanover], and my cousin Princess Victoria is Queen of England. I am thus nearly allied in blood to two great and happy families that are governing two happy and prosperous countries . . . Our position in the world is entirely changed.'

It was indeed. The Duke of Cambridge, from being a King in all but name, and meeting the Sovereigns of Germany as one of themselves, was returning to England to become, with the Duke of Sussex, the Duchess of Gloucester, the Princess Augusta and the Princess Sophia, merely one of the children of George III, or, which was not much more distinguished, one of the uncles and aunts of Queen Victoria.

And it was not only a changed position in the sense that he was stepping down from a place of eminence to one of ornamental obscurity, but he was returning to a changed world. The England of 1837 which he found was completely different from the England of 1813 which he had left. In 1813 his father was alive, his mother was Queen: in 1837 his parents, and most of his brothers, were dead, his niece was Queen. In 1813 Carlton House was still the scene of the Regent's splendid parties: in 1837 it had disappeared and Carlton House Terrace, with the memorial column to his second brother, stood in its place. In 1813 Lord Byron was the lion of London Society and *Sense and Sensibility* was the novel that everyone was reading: in 1837 Tennyson was an established poet and *The Pickwick Papers* were appearing in monthly parts. In 1813 William Windham, a devoted colleague of Pitt and a close friend of Dr Johnson, had only been dead three years: in 1837 Mr Gladstone had been a member of the House of Commons for five years. In 1813 an Englishman, with a great display of horse-energy, whirled along at ten miles an hour: in 1837 he was enjoying the exhilarating speed of forty miles an hour behind a steam engine.

It is true that all people of the Duke's generation had to accustom themselves to these marked changes, but the majority of them at least had the advantage of being in England and watching the changes from day to day. The Duke had been cut off from it all. In 1813 he left England quiet, Georgian and on the whole agricultural; he returned in 1837 to find the stage being set for a clanging, Victorian, industrial England. There was no part for him to play on such a stage and, as he flitted backwards and forwards before the people of England for the last thirteen years of his life, they thought him a very curious old gentleman. Perhaps, too, nature had made him up a good deal funnier than was necessary. In middle life he had always affected a very blonde and very obvious wig, but he looked nearly as odd when he left it off, displaying a bald head with the compensation of a Newgate frill below his chin. His conversational powers were almost terrifying: he had a prodigious flow of chatter which he always delivered at the top of his voice.

He continued his interest in music. But even this was apt to be embarrassing. He once went out to a musical party and startled the guests by joining vociferously in the performance as *primo basso assoluto*, and then applauding no less loudly. It is impossible not to feel sympathy for his son, Prince George, when he wrote after one of his father's musical evenings: 'This evening my father played with three musicians' quartets. I had not heard him for a long time, and must confess that though he made notes well, yet from want of practice, his execution is very imperfect and we heard unfortunately many false notes.'

But perhaps his finest and most eccentric efforts were reserved for church. He became very deaf and always sat right in the front of the church, where he was seen by the whole congregation. This might not have been so serious if he had not made a practice of being heard all over the church as well, in a running commentary on the service. No doubt many of his funnier remarks are apocryphal as, for example, the story that when the clergyman came to the commandment 'Thou shalt do no murder,' a loud voice was heard in reply: 'I don't: I leave that to my brother Ernest.' But it was a common occurrence to hear in reply to the clergyman's 'Let us pray,' an agreeable 'By all means' from the Duke, or, in answer to a prayer for rain, 'Amen but you won't get it till the wind changes,' or, in answer to the sentence, 'For we brought nothing into the world, neither may we carry anything out,' the reply, 'True, true – too many calls upon us for that.' And a curate at Kew was so embarrassed by the Royal devotions, and so uncertain whether to drown them, that he resigned his curacy. Another clergyman, who was in the congregation taking no part in the service, has given a graphic description of the Duke at prayer: 'The Duke of Cambridge was there to hear the Bishop preach and sat in the pew before me. Such a noise he made in responses, Psalm-reading and singing, a sort of old Walpole with eyes. I had not caught what Psalm the clerk had given out and turning to look on my neighbour's page, fidgety restless H.R.H. turns round and bawls loud enough to drown the organ, "It begins at the third verse, the third verse." All eyes turned on Royalty speaking to inferior clergy. Royalty went on singing like a bull.'

It was, no doubt, a wise decision of his to keep aloof from party politics. He only spoke once on an important political question in the House of Lords and his argument was most difficult to follow. It was in 1846, on the Bill repealing the Corn Laws, which had been introduced by Sir Robert Peel's Conservative Government. The Duke began by stating that he was no politician, and indeed no speaker, and that he had always made it a rule never to vote with the Opposition but, if he could not vote with the Government, to abstain. His fellow-Peers may have been slightly startled when they heard him saying that on this question of the Corn Laws his character was at stake. Having followed this reasoning with some difficulty, they were treated to the familiar arguments against the Repeal of the Corn Laws. Having, as he said, stated his arguments 'fairly and frankly and honestly,' he announced that he would abstain from voting. The supporters of the Repeal found it difficult to distinguish between speaking against the Government and voting against it, and as a result the speech was very sarcastically handled by the Press, particularly by *Punch*. But the Duke of Cambridge was more at home entertaining his friends in Cambridge House in Piccadilly,[1] playing in the garden with his younger daughter at Cambridge Cottage down at Kew, or even sitting in his own carriage on the express to Stockton drawn by an engine decorated with the Union Jack, than in talking politics in the House of Lords.

He was most energetic and most tactful in working for a variety of charitable causes and, if it was whispered that the guineas which he so loudly subscribed bore much the same relation to real money as the china egg that is put in a hen's nest to encourage her to lay, such whispers must be attributed to the cynical mind of the eighteen-forties. The Duke of Cambridge was the only son of George III who contrived to live within his income. He was given £12,000 a year in 1801,

[1] Now the Naval and Military Club.

which was raised to £18,000 in 1806 and was further increased
by a few thousands from his position as commander of the
home forces. When he became Viceroy of Hanover in 1831,
William IV allowed him £25,000 a year from the Hanoverian
revenue. He invested part of this in the purchase of a large area
of land between Wimbledon and Surbiton. He was certainly
most generous with his time, and equally generous with his
money to an almost incredible number of charitable causes. He
even lent money to the Duke of Kent.

It was only unfortunate that this generosity roused no
gratitude in the heart of the Duke of Kent's daughter. On
coming to the throne, she wrote to the Duke of Cambridge
cordially enough to thank him for his letter of congratulations
on her accession, and ended:

> . . . I trust you will always find me an affectionate niece to
> an Uncle who has always been so kind to me. I rejoice to see
> you soon, as also I hope, my Aunt and dear cousins. Pray,
> dear Uncle, give them my best love, and believe me always
>   Your affectionate niece
>   VICTORIA R.

But in 1837, when the Duke had not been six months in
England, the Queen was writing angrily to Lord Melbourne:
'The Duke and Duchess of Cambridge are here, and the
Queen is very sorry to say, that from what she *sees* and *hears*,
she has reason to fear all is *not* as it *should* be: *her* mother is
most *markedly* civil and affectionate towards both the Duke and
the Duchess and spoke Politics with the former. The Queen
will tell Lord Melbourne more about this when she sees him.'
This letter refers to an incident which was well known at the
time and which has since stirred the spleen of certain imaginative writers. The reason why King William and Queen
Adelaide had brought up Prince George of Cambridge at
Windsor was in the hope that he would see much of the
Princess Victoria, that they would become attached to each
other and marry. The Duke and Duchess of Cambridge both
favoured the marriage though Prince George, almost certainly,
did not. There was no question of any intrigue, still less of any

compulsion. It is only equally absurd to suggest that the marriage would have been unpopular because the country was sick of the Hanoverians. The Cambridge branch of the House of Hanover, so far as it was known in England, was popular. Certainly Prince George was quite as popular a candidate as the slightly obscure first cousin from Saxe-Coburg-Gotha whom Queen Victoria subsequently married.

There were two reasons why Queen Victoria did not marry Prince George. The first was the influence of that rather troublesome Coburg, her uncle Leopold, who disliked his dead wife's family and was anxious that so great a matrimonial prize as the Queen of England should not escape his own family who, for half a century, had compensated themselves for the smallness of their territory by the importance of their marriages. The second reason, which was more effective, was that neither the Queen nor Prince George had any particular desire to marry each other. The Queen, who as a young girl was not that repository of all wisdom which she became at the end of her life, seemed to regard it as almost an insult that the Duke of Cambridge should have ever thought of marrying his son to her. She wrote rather maliciously to Prince Albert just after they were engaged at the end of 1839: 'I saw to-day the Duke of Cambridge, who has shewn me your letter [in answer to one from the Duke congratulating the Prince on his engagement], with which he is quite delighted – and, indeed it is a very nice one. The Duke told Lord Melbourne he had always greatly desired our marriage, and never thought of George: but that *I* don't believe.'

The result of all this was that the Queen and the Duke of Cambridge were not on the best of terms. No doubt there were faults on both sides. The Duke of Cambridge, perhaps naturally from his experience of sovereignty and his position as uncle to a fatherless girl, was too prompt with advice. The Queen was truculent and plainly showed that she preferred Lord Melbourne's advice to that of her uncle. But when Prince Albert arrived in England, the disagreement between the Queen and the Duke and Duchess of Cambridge almost amounted to a scandal.

In 1840, the Duke of Cambridge consented that Prince Albert should take precedence before him. The Duke and Duchess probably did not attach great importance to 'the precedence question' but they were very much hurt at the ungenerous way this concession was received, the Queen taking it as a matter of course. The Duchess of Cambridge was particularly annoyed and showed her feelings at a party given by the Queen Dowager, who was then living at Marlborough House. When Prince Albert's health was given, the Duchess remained seated. A few days later the Queen retaliated. She gave a ball at Buckingham Palace in honour of a foreign Prince. No member of the Cambridge family was invited. This was a marked and public insult.

But worse was to follow. In August 1840, Prince Albert was to go to the City of London to receive the Freedom of the City. This ceremony was to be followed by a banquet, of which the Lord Mayor had said that 'the Venison and turtle soup would be such as to astonish the company.' The Duke of Cambridge was to accompany the Prince. When the Prince arrived, he told the Duke that he was very sorry that he would not be able to stay for the banquet as he must get back to Windsor owing to the serious news of the Queen's aunt, the Princess Augusta. The Duke of Cambridge replied, with some force, that the latest accounts of the Princess were much more favourable and that if he, the Princess's brother, could attend the banquet there was no reason why Prince Albert should not. But nothing would dissuade Prince Albert, and the Duke of Cambridge was left to reply to the Prince's health at the banquet. The Duke afterwards said that the company were so disappointed at Prince Albert's absence that they might have turned down their glasses. And in his reply he accounted for the Prince's absence in the only way that could mollify the company. He said: 'The illustrious Prince was not present at the Banquet, and his absence was a disappointment to many, but he [the Duke of Cambridge] could account for it, and he thought that every one of the company would admit the validity of the excuse. In fact Prince Albert had lately married a very fine girl, and they were somehow or other very fond of each other's society. (Laughter and immense cheering.) He perceived that the Prince was readily excused. Indeed, there was not a lady or gentleman present who would not at once give him credit for the performances. (A laugh and cheering.)'

The whole speech was perhaps a trifle broad. It was the voice of the eighteenth century calling from the background to the decorous Victorians. It may be imagined that when Queen Victoria read this description of herself in the papers the following day, she was horrified and shocked. She wrote to her aunt, the Duchess of Gloucester, bitterly complaining of the Duke's behaviour and asking her to rebuke him. It is fair to add that Melbourne said that the Duke was 'the foolishest man I ever saw.'

This did not end a squabble which was worthy of the Hanoverians of an earlier generation. At the end of 1842 there had been a quite unfounded scandal that the Duke of Beaufort's daughter, Lady Augusta Somerset, was with child by Prince George of Cambridge. It was publicly denied in *The Times* by the 7th Duke of Beaufort and by Lord Adolphus FitzClarence, on behalf of Prince George. A few months later, the Duchess of Cambridge was invited to stay at Windsor and brought Lady Augusta Somerset with her, with the object of silencing scandal. The Queen was furious and gave orders that her ladies-in-waiting should not speak to Lady Augusta. After the Duchess of Cambridge had left, the Queen sent for the Duchess of Gloucester, and burst out to her: 'I know that the stories are all true,' and asked her to tell the Duchess of Cambridge how very angry she was. The Duchess of Gloucester was so astonished that she asked the Queen to put it in writing. The Duke of Cambridge was naturally very angry when he heard what the Queen had written, and wrote bitterly complaining to Prince Albert, who simply replied: 'As Prince George has given his word of honour that the story is untrue, I suppose that we *must* believe *it is so*.' It is difficult not to agree with Mr Greville's comment that the whole affair rose 'between the prudery of Albert and her [Victoria's] own love of gossip and exceeding arrogance and heartlessness.'

A further example of the Coburg attitude towards the

English Royal family is shown by a remark of Prince Albert's about the Prince of Wales's education which was made in the hearing of Mr Greville: '. . . the great object must be to make him as unlike as possible to any of his great-uncles.' Mr Greville describes this as 'impudent and ungracious,' and pertinently added: 'his [i.e. The Prince of Wales's] own grandfather was by far the worst of the family, and it will be fortunate if no portion of that blood is eventually found flowing in his veins and tainting his disposition.'

The Duke of Cambridge behaved with great dignity throughout all these unpleasant squabbles and acquitted himself well in the difficult rôle of uncle and subject. At the end of his life both the Queen and Prince Albert had learned to love and respect him. He died on 8th July, 1850, after a short illness. It was not possible – nor would it have been accurate – for the newspapers to say that 'the country was plunged in grief,' or that, 'that day a great man fell in Israel.' It would have been rather true to say that the country mourned a Prince who had inherited all the good looks of his family and none of its grossness, all its good taste and none of its prodigality, all its kindliness and few of its oddities, and added to these a modesty and decency all his own.

SHORT BIBLIOGRAPHY

GENERALLY

The Cambridge Modern History, Volumes VI, VII, VIII, IX and X.
The Encyclopædia Britannica.
The Dictionary of National Biography.
The Times.
The Gentleman's Magazine.
Hansard's Parliamentary Debates.
The Annual Register.
Papers from the Lord Chamberlain's Office at the Public Record Office.
The Harcourt Papers. Privately Printed. 1880–1905.
The Greville Memoirs. Edited by Henry Reeve. 1874.
The Greville Memoirs. Edited by P. Wilson. 1927.
The MSS. of the Greville Diary in the British Museum.
The Creevey Papers. Edited by Sir H. Maxwell. 1904.
Madame d'Arblay's Diary. Edited by Austin Dobson. 1904–6.
The Letters of Queen Victoria. Edited by A. C. Benson and Viscount Esher. 1907.
The Girlhood of Queen Victoria. Viscount Esher. 1912.
Peter Pindar's Poems.
The Letters of George III. Edited by Sir John Fortescue. 1927 *et seq.*
George III: His Court and Family. Anonymous. 1820.
Royal Dukes and Princesses of the Family of George III. Percy Fitzgerald. 1882.
Mrs Delany's Correspondence. Edited by Lady Llanover. 1861.
Journal of Kew Guild. 1896 *et seq.*
Buckingham Palace. H. Clifford Smith. 1931.
Queen Victoria. Lytton Strachey. 1920.

THE DUKE OF YORK

GENERALLY

The Duke of York: a Biographical Memoir. J. Watkins. 1827.
The Farington Diary. 1922 *et seq.*
Victoria County History of Surrey.
Philippart's Royal Military Calendar. 3rd Edition. 1820.
Memoirs of George III. J. H. Jesse. 1867.
Life of George IV. Huish. 1831.
Personal History of George IV. Croly. 1846.
Autobiography. Miss Cornelia Knight. 1861.

The Paget Brothers. Lord Hylton. 1918.
Manuscript letters in the British Museum.

I. Pages 52–56
Horace Walpole's Letters. Edited by Mrs Toynbee. 1903–5.
Secret History of the Court of Berlin. Mirabeau. 1788.
Correspondence of Lord Cornwallis. Edited by C. Ross. 1859.
Mrs Papendieck's Journals. Edited by Mrs Broughton. 1887.
Memoirs of Reign of George III. Horace Walpole. 1845.

II. Pages 56–63
Horace Walpole's Letters. Edited by Mrs Toynbee. 1903–5.
Correspondence and Memoirs of C. J. Fox. Edited by Lord J. Russell. 1853–7.
Memoirs of Reign of George III. Horace Walpole. 1845.
Ancient Royal Palaces In and Near London. Way. 1902.
History of Surrey. Brayley. 1850.

III. Pages 63–73
Narrative of the Campaign in Holland. Bunbury. 1849.
History of British Army. Volumes III, IV, V, VI and VII. Fortescue 1899–1930.
The Diaries of the Earl of Malmesbury. 1844.
Lord G. Leveson-Gower Correspondence. Edited by Lady Granville. 1916.

IV. Pages 73–85
A letter to His Royal Highness or a delicate inquiry into the doubt whether he is more favoured by Mars or Venus with hints. By an Englishman. 1806.
Investigation of the charges brought against the Duke of York. 1809.
Authentic Life of Mrs M. A. Clarke. W. Clarke. 1809.
The Royal Criterion. 1814.
Authentic Memoirs of Mrs Clarke. Miss Elizabeth Taylor. 1809.
The Rival Princes. Mrs Clarke. 1809.
The Rival Dukes: An Answer to Mrs Clarke's Pamphlet 1810.

V. Pages 85–101
Life of Lord Eldon. Twiss. 1844.
The Croker Papers. Edited by L. J. Jennings. 1884.
Moore's Memoirs. Edited by Lord John Russell. 1853–6.
Memoirs of the Court of England, 1811–1820. The Duke of Buckingham and Chandos. 1856.

Memoirs of the Court of George IV, 1820–1830. The Duke of Buckingham and Chandos. 1859.

Memoirs of Sir William Knighton. 1838.

Diary Illustrative of the Times of George IV. Lady Charlotte Bury. 1838–9.

Diary of Lord Colchester. 1861.

Coke of Norfolk. Stirling. 1908.

Memoirs. Baron Stockmar. 1872.

An Account of the Death and Funeral Procession of His Royal Highness the Duke of York. Printed in Newcastle. 1827.

Last Moments of the Duke of York with Some Account of his Early Life and Exploits. 1827.

The Duke of York's Posthumous letter. 1827.

Debts of H.R.H. the Duke of York. Extracts from the London daily and weekly Press. 1832.

Life of George Brummell. Captain Jesse. 1886.

WILLIAM IV

GENERALLY

Life and Times of William IV. P. FitzGerald. 1884.

The Sailor King. J. F. Molloy. 1903.

William IV. Wright. 1837.

Manuscript letters in the British Museum.

Journal of Miss Berry. Edited by Theresa Lady Lewis. 1865.

The Jerningham Letters. 1896.

Memoirs of the Court of England, 1811–1820. The Duke of Buckingham and Chandos. 1856.

Correspondence of Lord G. Leveson-Gower. Edited by Lady Granville. 1916.

Farington's Diary. 1922 et seq.

Diary. Philip von Neumann. 1928.

I. Pages 102–112

Memoirs of Mrs Chapone. Edited by J. Cole. 1839.

Journal and Letters of Sir T. Byam Martin. The Navy Records Society. 1902.

Posthumous Memoirs. Sir N. W. Wraxall. 1884.

Naval Administration. Sir J. H. Briggs. 1897.

Horace Walpole's Letters. Edited by Mrs Toynbee. 1903–5.

II. Pages 112–116

Posthumous Memoirs. Sir N. W. Wraxall. 1884.

Horace Walpole's Letters. Edited by Mrs Toynbee. 1903–5.
The Story of Dorothy Jordan. Clare Jerrold. 1914.
Mrs Jordan. P. W. Sergeant. 1913.

III. *Pages* 116–125

Nelson's Dispatches and Letters. Nicolas. 1844–6.
Mrs Jordan. Clare Jerrold. 1914.
Mrs Jordan. P. W. Sergeant. 1913.

IV. *Pages* 126–137

Unpublished Diary of Princess Lieven. Edited by Harold Temperley. 1925.
Lord Ellenborough's Diary. 1881.
Wellington's Dispatches. 1867–80.
The Croker Papers. Edited by L. J. Jennings. 1884.
Lord Colchester's Diary. 1861.

V. *Pages* 137–160

Broughton's Recollections of a Long Life. Lady Dorchester. 1909–11.
Some Recollections of the Last Days of William IV. J. R. Wood. 1837.
Early Court of Queen Victoria. Jerrold. 1912.
Lives of the Lord Chancellors. Campbell. 1845–69.
Memoirs. Baron Stockmar. 1872.
Lord Grey of the Reform Bill. G. M. Trevelyan. 1920.
The Passing of the Great Reform Bill. J. R. M. Butler. 1914.
Wellington's Dispatches. 1867–80.
Correspondence of William IV and Lord Grey. 1867.
Life and Times of Lord Brougham. By himself. 1871.
Lord Melbourne's Papers. Edited by L. C. Sanders. 1889.
Sir Robert Peel. R. Parker. 1891.
Life and Letters of Lord Macaulay. G. O. Trevelyan. 1877.

THE DUKE OF KENT

GENERALLY AND I. *Pages* 161–165

Life. The Rev. Erskine Neale. 1850.
Life of the Duke of Kent and his Correspondence with the Salaberry Family. Anderson. 1870.
Manuscript letters in the British Museum.
Winslow Papers, 1776–1826. Edited by W. O. Raymond. 1901.
Farington's Diary. 1922 *et seq.*
William IV. Wright. 1837.

Memoirs of the Court of England, 1811–1820. The Duke of Buckingham and Chandos. 1856.
A biographical memoir by a clergyman, late of Oxford. 1820.

II. *Pages 165–176*

Nova Scotia Historical Society. 1879.
Royal Military Calendar. Philippart. 3rd Edition. 1820.
Memoirs of George III. J. H. Jesse. 1867.
Barnard Letters, 1778–1884. Edited by Anthony Powell. 1928.
Journal of the late Campaign in Egypt. Thomas Walsh. 1803.
Life and Times of the Hon'ble. Joseph Howe. G. E. Fenety. 1896.
King Edward VII. Sir Sidney Lee. 1925.

III. *Pages 176–187*

Miscellaneous Works. G. Hardinge. 1818.
Autobiography. Miss Cornelia Knight. 1861.
Depositions on the investigation of the conduct of the Princess of Wales before the Commissioners. 1806.
Robert Owen's Life. By himself. 1857.
The Rational Quarterly Review. 1853.
Annals of Ealing. Edith Jackson. 1898.
Personal Memoirs. Pryse Lockhart Gordon. 1830.
Observations of the Duke of Kent's Shameful Persecution. P. F. MacCallum. 1808.
A letter on the income and services of the Royal Dukes . . . Sketch of the Duke of Kent's life and losses. By an Englishman. 1808.

IV. *Pages 187–195*

Memoirs. Baron Stockmar. 1871.
Miscellaneous Works of George Harding. 1816.
Notes of Conversations with the Duke of Wellington 1831–1851. 5th Earl Stanhope.

THE DUKE OF CUMBERLAND

GENERALLY AND I. *Pages 204–210*

Manuscript Letters in the British Museum.
Memoirs of George III. J. H. Jesse. 1867.
Correspondence of Lord G. Leveson-Gower. Edited by Lady Granville. 1916.
Sir Francis Burdett. Patterson. 1931.
Diary Illustrative of the Times of George IV. Lady Charlotte Bury. 1838–9.

Since the original edition of this book, two helpful lives of the Duke have
been published:

Ernest Augustus, Duke of Cumberland by Herbert Van Thal, 1936, and
Ernest Augustus Duke of Cumberland and King of Hanover by G. M.
Willis, 1954.

II. *Pages 210–222*

A minute Detail of the Attempt to Assassinate the Duke of Cumberland.
J. J. Stockdale. 1810.

III. *Pages 222–237*

Memoirs. Baron Stockmar. 1871.
Diary of Lord Ellenborough. 1881.
Diary of Lord Colchester. 1861.
Princess Lieven's Letters. Edited by L. G. Robinson. 1902.
Wellington's Dispatches. 1867–80.

IV. *Pages 237–243*

Sir Robert Peel. C. S. Parker. 1891.
Trial of Joseph Phillips for a Libel on the Duke of Cumberland. 1833.
Letters of Princess Elizabeth of England. Edited by P. Yorke. 1898.
Lives of Lord Lyndhurst and Lord Brougham. Lord Campbell.
Memoirs of the Courts and Cabinets of William IV and Victoria. The Duke
of Buckingham and Chandos. 1861.

V. *Pages 243–251*

Reminiscences of the Court and Times of Ernest, King of Hanover.
Rev. C. A. Wilkinson. 1886.
Letters of the King of Hanover to Lord Strangford. C. Whibley. 1925.
Early Court Life of Queen Victoria. Jerrold. 1912.

THE DUKE OF SUSSEX

GENERALLY

Manuscript letters in the British Museum.
Private information.

I. *Pages 252–258*

Remains of Mrs Trench. Edited by the Dean of Westminster. 1862.
The D'Este Peerage Case.
The Journal of Elizabeth, Lady Holland, 2 Vols. Edited by Lord Ilchester.
1908.

II. *Pages 258–268*

Masonic offering to His Royal Highness in commemoration of his completing 25 years Grand Master of English Freemasons. 1838.
Journal of Honble. H. E. Fox. 1923.
William Allen's Life. 1847.
Manuscript letters to 'Coke of Norfolk.'
Reminiscences of Henry Angelo. 1830.
Moore's Diary. Edited by Lord John Russell. 1853–6.
Robert Owen's Life. By himself. 1857.

III. *Pages 268–280*

Lord Broughton's Recollections of a Long Life. Edited by Lady Dorchester. 1909–11.
Catalogue of Plate, etc., belonging to his late Royal Highness the Duke of Sussex, to be sold by auction. 1843.
Life of Brougham. By himself. 1871.
Recollections of English and French Courts. Rush. 1873.
Reminiscences of Solomon Hart. Edited by A. Brodie. 1882.
Recollections of Adolphus. Edited by Mrs Henderson. 1871.
The Jerningham Letters. 1896.
The Norwich Mercury. 13th April, 1833.
A Political Diary. Lord Ellenborough. 1881.
Sir Francis Burdett. Patterson. 1931.
Letters and Remains. Andrew Robertson. 1895.
Life of Lord Eldon. Twiss. 1844.
Bibliotheca Sussexiana. T. J. Pettigrew. 1827 and 1839.

THE DUKE OF CAMBRIDGE

GENERALLY

H.R.H. Princess Mary Adelaide, Duchess of Teck. Sir C. Kinloch-Cooke. 1900.
George Duke Of Cambridge. Edited by Edgar Sheppard. 1906.
Private information.
Memoirs of George III. J. H. Jesse. 1867.
Memoir of H.R.H. the Duke of Cambridge. Lt.-Gen. Sir J. H. Reynett. 1858.

I. *Pages 281–288*

The depositions on the investigations of the conduct of the Princess of Wales before the Commissioners. 1806.
Remains of Mrs Trench. Edited by the Dean of Westminster. 1862.
Farington's Diary. 1922 *et seq.*

II. *Pages* 288–296

Gesch. d. Königreichs Hannover. Von Hassall. 1898–1901.
Memoirs of Lord Combermere. 1866.
Wellington's Dispatches. 1867–80.
England and Hanover. A. W. Ward. 1899.
Arrival and Reception of Adolphus Frederick, Duke of Cambridge, at Hanover. F. Rechberg. 1814.
Princess Elizabeth of England. Letters edited by P. Yorke. 1898.

III. *Pages* 296–304

Memoirs. Baron Stockmar. 1871.
Diaries of Sir George Jackson. 1872.
Early Court Life of Queen Victoria. Jerrold. 1912.
Broughton's Recollections of a Long Life. Edited by Lady Dorchester. 1909–11.

INDEX

The British Monarchy

This series describes the evolution of the British monarchy from the Saxon and Norman kings to George V—their personalities and lives, their influence on their ages. Six volumes, each with twelve pages of photographs.

The Saxon and Norman Kings Christopher Brooke **45p**
'An illuminating and imaginative reconstruction of what it really meant to be a king in Saxon and Norman times. The essential merits of this book are its lightness of touch and its firm grounding in scholarship.' *The Economist*

The Plantagenets John Harvey **45p**
'A portrait gallery of medieval English sovereigns, illustrated with many splendid photographs. Learned, informative and entertaining.' *Daily Mail*

The Tudors Christopher Morris **45p**
'Brilliant . . . Mr. Morris's flair for the apt point or quotation is remarkable.' *History*

The Stuarts J. P. Kenyon **45p**
'A sardonic, witty, yet scholarly book, written with splendid gusto.' *Sunday Times*

The First Four Georges J. H. Plumb **45p**
'The vitality and frankness of a literary Hogarth. He is never dull or merely derivative.' *The Economist*

Hanover to Windsor Roger Fulford **45p**
'As accurate as it is amusing, and conspicuously fair in its judgments.' *The Times Literary Supplement*

Fontana Books

Fontana is at present best known (outside the field of popular fiction) for its extensive list of books on history, philosophy and theology. Now, however, the list is expanding rapidly to include most main subjects, such as literature, politics, economics and sociology. At the same time, the number of paperback reprints of books already published in hardcover editions is being increased. Further information on Fontana's present list and future plans can be obtained from: The Non-Fiction Editor, Fontana Books, 14 St James's Place, London S.W.1.

All Fontana books are available at your bookshop or newsagent; or can be ordered direct. Just fill in the form below and list the titles you want.

....

FONTANA BOOKS, Cash Sales Department, P.O. Box 4, Godalming, Surrey. Please send purchase price plus 5p postage per book by cheque, postal or money order. No currency.

NAME (Block Letters)
_____

ADDRESS
_____

_____

_____